Rethinking God As Gift

Perspectives in Continental Philosophy
John D. Caputo, Series Editor

1. John D. Caputo, ed., *Deconstruction in a Nutshell: A Conversation with Jacques Derrida.*
2. Michael Strawser, *Both/And: Reading Kierkegaard—From Irony to Edification.*
3. Michael Barber, *Ethical Hermeneutics: Rationality in Enrique Dussel's Philosophy of Liberation.*
4. James H. Olthuis, ed., *Knowing* Other-*wise: Philosophy at the Threshold of Spirituality.*
5. James Swindal, *Reflection Revisited: Jürgen Habermas's Discursive Theory of Truth.*
6. Richard Kearney, *Poetics of Imagining: Modern and Postmodern.* Second edition.
7. Thomas W. Busch, *Circulating Being: From Embodiment to Incorporation—Essays on Late Existentialism.*
8. Edith Wyschogrod, *Emmanuel Levinas: The Problem of Ethical Metaphysics.* Second edition.
9. Francis J. Ambrosio, ed., *The Question of Christian Philosophy Today.*
10. Jeffrey Bloechl, ed., *The Face of the Other and the Trace of God: Essays on the Philosophy of Emmanuel Levinas.*
11. Ilse N. Bulhof and Laurens ten Kate, eds, *Flight of the Gods: Philosophical Perspectives on Negative Theology.*
12. Trish Glazebrook, *Heidegger's Philosophy of Science.*
13. Kevin Hart, *The Trespass of the Sign. Second edition.*
14. Mark C. Taylor, *Journeys to Selfhood: Hegel and Kierkegaard. Second edition.*
15. Dominique Janicaud, Jean-François Courtine, Jean-Louis Chrétien, Michel Henry, Jean-Luc Marion, and Paul Ricoeur, *Phenemenology and the "Theological Turn": The French Debate.*
16. Karl Jaspers, *The Question of German Guilt. Introduction by Joseph W. Koterski, S.J.*
17. Jean-Luc Marion, *The Idol and Distance: Five Studies.* Translated with an introduction by Thomas A. Carlson.
18. Jeffrey Dudiak, *The Intrigue of Ethics: A Reading of the Idea of Discourse in the Thought of Emmanuel Levinas.*

Rethinking God As Gift

MARION, DERRIDA, AND THE LIMITS OF PHENOMENOLOGY

ROBYN HORNER

Fordham University Press
New York
2001

Perspectives in Continental Philosophy No. 19
ISSN 1089-3938

Library of Congress Cataloging-in-Publication Data

Horner, Robyn.
Rethinking God as gift : Marion, Derrida, and the limits of phenomenology / Robyn Horner.
p. cm. — (Perspectives in continental philosophy, ISSN 1089-3938 ; no. 19)
Includes bibliographical references and index.
ISBN 0-8232-2121-0 — ISBN 0-8232-2122-9 (pbk.)
1. God. 2. Gifts—Religious aspects—Christianity. 3. Marion, Jean-Luc, 1946—Contributions in religious aspects of gifts. 4. Derrida, Jacques—Contributions in religious aspects of gifts. 5. Phenomenological theology. I. Title. II. Series.
BT55.H67 2001
231.7—dc21 2001018931

Printed in the United States of America
01 02 03 04 05 5 4 3 2 1
First Edition

CONTENTS

ACKNOWLEDGMENTS

A volume such as this is never the result of just one person's labor. It is made possible in the first place by the hard work of many who have already risked themselves in print, those who have entered into long and serious discussions, and others who might have simply prompted moments of insight in conversation over a meal. But it is also enabled by the belief and commitment of those who offer encouragement and support, and the preparedness of family and friends to tolerate, on the part of the author, preoccupation, anxiety, doubt, dreams, and domestic disorganization in order to make it happen. This book bears the traces of many people: colleagues, advisers, mentors, family, and friends, a few of whom I name here, in the knowledge that there are many others who go unnamed, and others still whom I do not even know: Kevin Hart; John D. Caputo; Michael Fagenblat; Thomas A. Carlson; Jean-Luc Marion; Tony Kelly; Joseph S. O'Leary; Anthony Chiffolo; Jonathan Lawrence; Thomas Doyle; Mark Reynolds; my colleagues and students at Monash University in Melbourne, including Mark Manolopoulos; Peter Howard, Damian Whelan, and Meg Gilfedder; my family, especially my parents, Les and June Horner; Julie Morgan; and Bosco Rowland.

Earlier versions of some sections of this book appeared in: "Derrida and God: Opening a Conversation," *Pacifica: Journal of the Melbourne College of Divinity* 12, no. 1 (February 1999): 12–26; and "Emmanuel Levinas: God and Philosophy—Practical Implications for Christian Theology," *Philosophy in the Contemporary World* 7, no. 1 (Spring 2000): 41–46.

INTRODUCTION

> But God, who is rich in mercy, out of the great love with which he loved us even when we were dead through our trespasses, made us alive together with Christ—by grace you have been saved—and raised us up with him and seated us with him in the heavenly places in Christ Jesus, so that in the ages to come he might show the immeasurable riches of his grace in kindness toward us in Christ Jesus. For by grace you have been saved through faith, and this is not your own doing; it is the gift of God—not the result of works, so that no one may boast (Eph. 2:4–9).

IN CHRISTIAN THEOLOGY, the way in which the relationship between God and human beings is accomplished is frequently described as gift. It is God's self-gift that initiates this relationship, facilitates it, and enables it to be sustained. This is the meaning of grace: that God is for the world giver, gift, and giving, a trinity of self-emptying love who is beyond all imagining, and that in this gift what seems like an impossible relationship is made possible. So it is suggested in the letter to the Ephesians, that relationship with God—which is the very meaning of salvation—is made possible only because of God's mercifulness and love ("God, who is rich in mercy, out of the great love with which he loved us . . . made us alive . . ."). The initiative and the capacity to achieve relationship lie totally with God ("this is not your own doing"), and the movement toward relationship is seen to be motivated not by justice (which is essentially a moment of recuperation—justice tries to restore a certain balance to the scales) but by a merciful love that is pure expenditure ("so that in the ages to come he might show the immeasurable riches of his grace in kindness toward us in Christ Jesus"). The movement toward relationship is made without the motivation of return. In other words, relationship with God (salvation) occurs in the self-offering of God, which does not hinge on any condition. The gift of God is pure as it is perfect and absolute. To speak of God as gift is theologically compelling, not least because it appeals to a particular aspect of Christian experience: if it is possible at all to describe an "encounter" with God, it will be one that is utterly gracious, impossible to predict, manipulate, or objectify—sheer gift. And yet here we begin to glimpse the problem that motivates the writing of this book. For how might such a gift—pure, absolute, unable to be objectified—be received?

The problem of God's self-giving has a number of faces. We are immediately referred to the whole question of human experience, which resonates in many registers and will of necessity be treated here within particular limits. The more strictly theological angle on this question is well worn but no less pressing for being repeated: if God is utterly greater than that which human experience can contain, how is God to enter into that experience at all? But in this context a further question arises that will serve as the prism through which the previous questions will be examined: the question of the gift itself. Significant in the passage from Ephesians noted above is the unconditionality of the gift, and even momentary reflection on a common understanding of the word "gift" reveals that unconditionality is one of its most important conditions. If I give expecting something in return, I have not really given in the right spirit. But unconditionality extends further than not intending that the gift be returned; it extends to the fact of its not being returned or even returnable. Few theologians would contest that God's gift is too great to be returned, and therefore the difficulty does not seem to apply in this instance. Yet there is an argument emerging from the work of Jacques Derrida, and yet to be fully articulated or tested here, to suggest that no gift that is recognized as such in the present is ever given unconditionally because such a gift is always and inevitably returned. In my receiving the gift as a gift, the gift is undone, it turns to ashes in my hands, it is no longer a gift. The question of the gift here closely resembles the question of how God is to enter into human experience. "If you meet the Buddha on the road, kill him." If you have seen God, what you have seen is not God.

The question of the gift as it is analyzed by Derrida arises in a very specific context, one that assumes a heritage of that type of philosophy known as phenomenology while pushing that heritage to the limits. Given the extent to which the phenomenological and post-phenomenological debate dominated European philosophy in the twentieth century, as well as the intersection of this debate with Christian thought at various points and in differing ways, it seems appropriate to question the relationship between philosophy and theology anew with phenomenology in mind. It is all the more pertinent in the light of the work of another contemporary Frenchman, Jean-Luc Marion, whose phenomenological investigations of the possibility of revelation focus the difficulties with precision. For our purposes, Marion's response to Derrida on the question of the gift serves to gather together all these faces of the problem of God's self-giving. The question of whether or not there can be a phenomenon of gift frames a discussion of the successes and failures of phenomenology as well as its theological possibilities. What follows proceeds by way of phenomenology, as it is read by each of the two main protagonists, in an examination of the gift and a consideration of some of the theological implications that emerge as a result.

Rethinking God As Gift

1
The Problem of the Gift

The Question of the Gift

A GIFT IS ANY OBJECT given by one person to another, gratuitously (in the *OED* we read that it is the "voluntary transference of property without consideration," where "consideration" is taken to mean "reward" or "compensation"). This gratuitousness is emphasized as an essential part of the gift: a gift has to be given in a certain spirit if it is to be a gift at all, and that spirit is sheer generosity. The purest of gifts is the one that is given without motive, without reason, without any foundation other than the desire to give. A gift is, in the best sense, something that emerges from a preparedness to expect nothing in return, to be dispossessed unconditionally. The attitude of the giver of the true gift must be to expect nothing in return. And the recipient, in like spirit, must accept in complete surprise and genuine appreciation. For a gift cannot be something earned, something automatically due, any more than it can be something passed on merely out of obligation. When I receive a gift that is not given in a spirit of generosity, I am instantly suspicious. Once there are "strings attached," what is given is no longer a gift, but a sign of something else. Perhaps it is a bribe. Perhaps it is like a contract, binding me in debt once accepted. Perhaps it befalls me as a blow, something intended to embarrass me, a sign of an unequal relationship between myself and the giver. And I may sometimes give a gift simply because it is expected or necessary. There may be a situation where a gift is appropriate but where my intention is begrudging rather than generous. In each of these cases, the gift becomes something burdensome, and the title "gift" is used only tentatively. There is no other word, but we recognize a certain lack that undermines the very gift itself.

Of what, then, does the gift consist? It would seem that the gift is the object that passes from one to another. Or does the true gift consist in the givenness? Does the gift-object serve only as a conduit for a certain excess: an excess of generous intention on the part of the one who gives, and a recognition and acceptance of that excess on the part of the one who receives? This focus on the excessiveness of the intention forms part of the work of Russell Belk, who tries to define the characteristics of the "perfect gift."[1] Belk interprets the expression of the perfect gift as agapic love, where the gift "is not selected and given to communicate a message . . . but rather to express and celebrate our love for the other. It is spontaneous, affective and celebratory rather than premeditated, cognitive, and calculated to achieve certain ends."[2] Such a gift, he suggests, would have the following properties: the giver makes an extraordinary sacrifice; the giver wishes solely to please the recipient; the gift is a luxury; the gift is something uniquely appropriate to the recipient; the recipient is surprised by the gift; and the recipient desires the gift and is delighted by it.[3] Belk's list does not reduce the gift solely to the intentions with which it is given and received, but the determinative value of the gift clearly resides in the intentional realm. Nevertheless, there can be no gift-intention without a gift-object, whether that object itself be real or ideal. Yet is there such a thing as an ideal gift-object? It is common to speak of gifts such as friendship, although there may be a degree of imprecision in their definition. If a gift-object were ideal, would it be possible to separate this object from its givenness? Imagining such gifts as forgiveness, friendship, love, or inclusion, it is interesting to note that the same measure of freedom and generosity that would characterize what has been called "the excess" also necessarily characterizes each of these particular gifts. So at least in some cases, there may be ideal gift-objects that also embody the quality of givenness, although they are not inevitably identical with it.

Perhaps there is still something else to learn regarding the definition of the gift from the way in which it can also be known as a present. The use of the word "present" to mean a gift appar-

[1] Russell W. Belk, "The Perfect Gift," *Gift-Giving: A Research Anthology*, ed. Cele Otnes and Richard F. Beltramini (Bowling Green, Ohio: Bowling Green State University Popular Press, 1996), 59–84 [hereafter Belk, *TPG*].

[2] Belk, *TPG*, 61.

[3] Belk, *TPG*, 61.

ently originates in the Old French locution *mettre une chose en présence à quelqu'un,* to put a thing into the presence of someone (*OED*). We also speak of presenting someone with something, making a presentation, or making a present of something. So a gift seems to have something to do with presence in the present. A gift is made present, it is brought before its intended recipient, it enters into the presence of the one who is to receive. Does this mean that there can be no giving in secret? If I am present to a present do I have to be completely aware of it, or aware of its value as a gift? On the basis of the definition suggested earlier (that a gift is something given to someone, gratuitously), possibly not. A gift may be present, but it need not necessarily be present as a gift. This introduces a distinction between receiving and accepting. To receive is to take something into one's possession, which does not focus the attention so much on its origins. To accept, on the other hand, means to "consent to receive" (*OED*), to agree to take something, which implies a greater scrutiny of its importance or its impact. But can someone give without knowing that he or she gives? At first glance this would not appear to fulfill the conditions of gift-hood, because it would alter the necessary factor of gratuity. One cannot give freely without some intention of the will. At the same time, a puzzling passage in the Christian scriptures suggests that in giving alms, the left hand should not know what the right is doing.[4] And if it is possible for a gift to be received without being identified as such by the recipient, why should it be impossible for a gift to be given without a similar identification? If I accept as a gift what I understand to be freely given, it effectively operates for me as a gift. In other words, to the extent that I perceive a gift to be gift, on one side or the other, it functions as a gift, and this may well be sufficient to define it as a gift. On the other hand, the risk of self-deception seems large.

This leads us to the consideration of another, related word that emerges in this context, the given. If something is a given, then it is assumed, it is already there, or it is simply what presents itself.

[4] Matt. 6:3–4: "But when you give alms, do not let your left hand know what your right hand is doing, so that your alms may be done in secret; and your Father who sees in secret will reward you." All quotations from the Bible will be from the New Revised Standard Version with Apocrypha (New York: Oxford University Press, 1989).

In this last sense, the given is that to which the philosophical discipline of phenomenology is oriented. The origin of a given may well be unknown. So the given may also be a gift, or it might not be. At times it will be impossible to say, or the affirmation that the given is a gift will rest on criteria other than demonstrable proofs.

At the most fundamental level, then, giving takes place where a gift-object is transferred freely from one person to another. But additional specifications have emerged that inevitably amplify this definition. It is clear that for a pure gift to occur, there should be no motive of return on the part of the donor and no anticipation of reward on the part of the recipient. Further, according to Belk's analysis, a gift should involve some sacrifice by the donor, and it should have luxurious and particularly personal qualities that place it out of the realm of the ordinary for the recipient. It has also been noted that it is givenness on the one hand and/or acceptance on the other that modify a real or an ideal object into a gift-object. Further, a gift is a present, that is, something brought into the presence of its recipient. Finally, a gift is a given, although a given may bear some or even no relation to a gift. With regard to the phenomenon or concept we call gift, these appear to be its conditions of possibility. Summing up, it seems to me that these conditions are reducible to two. One is that the gift is free. That is expressed in the demand for no motive of return, the requirement of sacrifice, and the need for placing the gift beyond the necessities of the everyday. The other condition is that the gift is present. This relates to the recognizability of the gift as a gift and draws in the corollaries of giving and receiving (or accepting). Freedom and presence are the conditions of the gift as we know it.

The Impossibility of the Gift

In the preceding analysis of the gift, I described those conditions that seem to determine what can be known as a gift. But has a gift ever met these conditions? There is a kind of purity about giving reflected in the desire that such conditions be met, but this is almost inevitably lost in the fact. The name of gift seems to preserve the hope of its integrity, but it leaves unspoken the constant compromise of that integrity. The gift is never as we would like it to be. For is any gift given in complete freedom, where nothing returns to the giver, even gratitude on the part of the recipient? When I acknowledge the birthday of a friend, do I really relinquish the expectation that I will be similarly acknowledged in due course? Do I ever give when there is no reason to give, or if I give spontaneously and not in relation to any occasion or act, do I not enjoy the excitement and surprise of the one to whom I give? And if I give anonymously, do I not still receive my reward in the subtle self-congratulation that frequently attaches itself to acts of altruism? In short, does not the whole enterprise of giving essentially depend on conditions to which it cannot adhere? The pure gift must not return to the one who gives, but as soon as we recognize a gift, the gift gives back, contradicts itself, stubbornly resists being truly given. Our gifts are tainted with the stain of self-interest. Why is this the case? Why is it so difficult to give without getting, to avoid what in effect becomes a series of exchanges? Why does my gift always end up having a purpose, or being a response to someone or something? Why does your gift to me never say everything? Why are gifts always set in the context of other gifts, of lesser or greater gifts, of gifts that measure each new gift within an inch of its life? Perhaps it is because our gifts always take place according to a particular horizon, and therefore within a restricted economy, whose measure cannot be escaped.[5]

In nuce, there are two dimensions of gift-giving that make it problematic. The giving of a gift depends on freedom: the freedom of the giver to give and the freedom of the recipient to receive. Any compulsion on either side fundamentally alters the gift-character of what is given. The first part of the problem therefore resides in the relation between freedom and the economy. If the gift forms part of an economy, it is implicated in a process of exchange, and the gift is no longer gift but obligation, payback, return, tradition, reason, sweetener, peace offering, or a thousand other things. The giving of a gift also depends in varying degrees on its presence, that is, on our ability to identify it as

[5] Regarding the association between gifts, relationships, and economies, see the introduction by Aafke E. Komter, editor of *The Gift: An Interdisciplinary Perspective* (Amsterdam: Amsterdam University Press, 1996), 3–14.

something that is a present, that is transferred between one person and another. It depends, in other words, on our knowing that it *is* a gift, our perceiving its dimensions or borders. The second part of the problem therefore resides in the relation between presence and the economy. If the gift is present—that is, if it can be identified as such—then the gift is no longer gift but commodity, value, measure, or status symbol. The basic definition of the gift (someone freely gives something to someone) never seems to accord with its practical reality. A gift is ideally something for which we do not try to take account, and yet our gifts seem to suffer the malaise of being measured. This difficulty relates especially to two factors that are central to the whole idea of the gift, the features of freedom and presence. The significance of these features, and the way in which they become problematic, is brought out in the analysis of giving offered by Jacques Derrida in *Given Time: 1. Counterfeit Money,* which I shall now follow in some detail.[6]

In his discussion of the gift, Derrida locates one of many points of resistance to economic thought, that is, to thought that tries to take account of everything. That there can be such points of resistance does not mean it is possible for us through them to escape an economy altogether, for we always and already find ourselves within at least one, but instead indicates that it is impossible to reduce everything to economic terms.[7] There are some ideas,

[6] Jacques Derrida, *Given Time: 1. Counterfeit Money,* trans. Peggy Kamuf (Chicago: University of Chicago Press, 1992) [hereafter Derrida, *GT1*]. *Donner le temps: 1. La fausse monnaie* (Paris: Galilée, 1991) [hereafter Derrida, *DT1*].

[7] This is where a distinction drawn by Georges Bataille and others becomes highly relevant. Bataille compares "restricted economies" to "general economies": the former term refers to systems where the capital that is invested eventually returns to the investor; the latter refers to the situation where expenditure occurs without return, or apparently goes to waste. Bataille argues that economic growth cannot be separated from loss, that unconditional expenditure, which has no end in itself, is inevitable. No system can escape this loss; all organisms are structured in such a way that there is an excess of energy for which we cannot take account. The idea of a totality is in fact impossible. Economies bear an excess, or better, economies are interrupted by an excess, which means that there is ultimately no bottom line. The books are never complete. We may always and already find ourselves within a general economy, but that does not mean we can comprehend it as though it were completely restricted. See Georges Bataille, *The Accursed Share: An Essay on General Economy,* trans. Robert Hurley (New York: Zone Books, 1988). See especially vol. 1, *Consumption.* Derrida puts

for example, that exceed the capacity of economic thinking, and hence that exceed the human capacity to achieve their reality. Such an idea would be that of the gift. Economically speaking, the gift simply does not work. It is resistant to calculation, unable to be fully thought, impossible, a black hole. In Derrida's words, the gift is structured as an aporia.[8]

An aporia is, in the Aristotelian sense, a problem. Derrida suggests it is "the difficult or the impracticable, here the impossible, passage, the refused, denied, or prohibited passage, indeed the nonpassage, which can in fact be something else, the event of a coming or of a future advent, which no longer has the form of the movement that consists in passing, traversing, or transiting."[9] In other words, an aporia is a problem that resists being solved because it defies any usual frame of reference. An aporia is a problem that exceeds our capacity even to hold onto it as a problem.[10] It is resolved, not by reasoning or by proof, but only by decision.[11]

Derrida is not the first to write on the question of the gift, but it is he who powerfully highlights the contradictory tension in its very definition, who points out its aporetic qualities. "These

---

forward the idea that it is not possible to attain to a position of complete exteriority with regard to textuality, and we can apply this very widely as an example of the functioning of the economic. Jacques Derrida, *Of Grammatology,* trans. Gayatri Chakravorty Spivak, rev. ed. (Baltimore: Johns Hopkins University Press, 1998), 158. On economy generally, see *GT1,* and also Derrida, "From Restricted to General Economy: A Hegelianism without Reserve," *Writing and Difference,* trans. Alan Bass (London: Routledge, 1978), 251–77, 270 [hereafter Derrida, *WD*].

[8] Derrida, *GT1,* 27–28.

[9] Jacques Derrida, *Aporias,* trans. Thomas Dutoit (Stanford: Stanford University Press, 1993), 8 [hereafter Derrida, *Ap*].

[10] Derrida, *Ap,* 12: "I knew what was going to be at stake in this word was the 'not knowing where to go.' It had to be a matter of the nonpassage, or rather from the experience of what happens and is fascinating in this nonpassage, paralyzing us in this separation in a way that is not necessarily negative: before a door, a threshold, a border, a line, or simply the edge or the approach of the other as such. It should be a matter of what, in sum, appears to block our way or to separate us in the very place where *it would no longer be possible to constitute a problem,* a project, or a projection."

[11] On the decision that resolves the aporia, see Derrida's essay "Sauf le nom," trans. John P. Leavey, Jr., in *On the Name,* ed. Thomas Dutoit (Stanford: Stanford University Press, 1995), 35–85, 54 [hereafter Derrida, *SLN*]. On undecidability generally, see his *Dissemination,* trans. and ed. Barbara Johnson (Chicago: University of Chicago Press, 1981) [hereafter Derrida, *D*].

conditions of possibility of the gift (that some 'one' gives some 'thing' to some 'one other') designate simultaneously the conditions of impossibility of the gift. And already we could translate this into other terms: these conditions of possibility define or produce the annulment, the annihilation, the destruction of the gift."[12] In Derrida's analysis, the gift cancels itself by being elemental in an economy, a cycle of return. The gift cancels itself because as a present, it is never completely free. Derrida analyzes these conditions rigorously with reference to each element of the gift formula: donor, recipient and gift-object.

On the part of the donor, any recognition of the gift as gift anticipates some kind of return. For according to Derrida, whenever I intentionally give, I invariably receive. I may receive another tangible gift, or I may simply receive gratitude. Even if the worst happened, and my giving were greeted with displeasure or rejection, there would still be some return, if nothing more than the reinforcement of my own identity as a subject.[13] From the point of view of the recipient, any awareness of the intentional meaning of a gift places that person, too, in the cycle of exchange. When I receive something I perceive to be a gift, I have already responded with recognition. Even if my response to the giver is one of indifference, it would be in my recognizing the gift as gift, in recognizing that I am indebted, that I would have unwittingly entered the gift economy.[14] The goodness of the gift is transformed into a burden as soon as I recognize it and therefore contract it as a debt.[15] Considering the gift-object itself, we are faced with further difficulties. The gift-object may be a real thing or it may be simply a value, a symbol, or an intention.[16] Again, the problem is one of recognition, which always has a reference to perceiving subjects in the present. So the problem is not whether

---

[12] Derrida, *GT1,* 12

[13] "If he recognizes it *as* gift, if the gift *appears to him as such,* if the present is present to him *as present,* this simple recognition suffices to annul the gift. Why? Because it gives back, in the place, let us say, of the thing itself, a symbolic equivalent." Derrida, *GT1,* 13.

[14] "It cannot be gift as gift except by not being present as gift. . . . There is no more gift as soon as the other *receives*—and even if she refuses the gift that she has perceived or recognised as gift." Derrida, *GT1,* 14.

[15] Derrida, *GT1,* 12.

[16] Derrida, *GT1,* 12–13.

or not the gift is phenomenal, but the fact that as soon as it appears *as* a gift, its gift-aspect disappears. As Derrida notes, "its very appearance, the simple phenomenon of the gift annuls it as gift, transforming the apparition into a phantom and the operation into a simulacrum."[17]

The conditions of possibility of the gift are also its conditions of impossibility. Those conditions that make the gift what it is are also the very conditions that annul it. If to give a gift means to give something freely, without return, then in its identification as a gift in the present, no gift is ever accomplished. Derrida insists: "If the gift appears or signifies itself, if it exists or is presently *as gift*, as what it is, then it is not, it annuls itself. . . . The truth of the gift (its being or its appearing such, its *as such* insofar as it guides the intentional signification of the meaning-to-say) suffices to annul the gift. The truth of the gift is equivalent to the non-gift or to the non-truth of the gift."[18] One of the critical points in this analysis is that the investiture of a gift-object with an excess of givenness on its own does not suffice to make the gift possible as such. The question has not only to do with givenness or generosity but with whether or not the gift becomes part of a circle, or is reduced to the terms of a restricted economy. At the same time, it is impossible to imagine the gift in terms other than these, since it seems that they are all we have. The difficulty that Derrida isolates is borne out by his reading of the linguistic, sociological, and anthropological material available, where it seems that the word "gift" is frequently used in a highly ambivalent way.

From the linguistic side, a tension emerges within "gift" (and related words) between good and bad. A gift is most often taken to be a positive thing, but the word nevertheless demonstrates some instability. For example, the Latin (and Greek) *dosis,* which enters English as "dose," bears the meanings of both "gift" and "poison."[19] Or again, "gift" in English can translate as either "poison" or "married" in languages based on German.[20] Derrida also makes reference to Gloria Goodwin Raheja's study *The Poison*

---

[17] Derrida, *GT1,* 14.
[18] Derrida, *GT1,* 26–27.
[19] Derrida, *GT1,* 36 n. See also Derrida, *D,* 131–32 n.
[20] See Derrida, *D,* 131, in a note by the translator.

in the Gift.[21] This study explores how, in a society in northern India, a gift (*dan*) involves the transfer of "inauspiciousness" from giver to recipient.[22] In other words, the gift works for the good of the donor, but the recipient obviously fares less well. What these instances collectively seem to suggest is that a gift need not be a good thing. Referring to the work of Émile Benveniste, Derrida observes the tension between giving and taking within the family of gift-related words.[23] Benveniste traces the verb "to give" (in French *donner*) back to the Hittite *dô,* suggesting that it lies at the origin of most Indo-European versions of giving. Yet he notes the similarity of this root to the Hittite *dâ,* which refers not to giving but to taking. He then concludes that giving and taking actually have the same origin, or at least that it is impossible to derive one from the other. To solve the linguistic problem that thus arises, Benveniste proposes a syntactic rather than semantic solution. The meaning would thus depend on the way the word was used.[24] Yet as Derrida observes: "This syntactic decidability can function only against a background of 'semantic ambivalence,' which leaves the problem intact. Benveniste seems to recognise this."[25] Then there is the tension in the word "gift" between something that returns and something that does not return. In his analysis of five Greek words that can be rendered "gift," Benveniste observes that at least one includes the recognition of necessary return, the word δωτινη (*dotine*): "One would not know how to underline more clearly the functional value of the *dotine,* of this gift that obliges a counter-gift. This is the constant sense it has in Heroditus; that the *dotine* is designed to prompt a gift in return or that it serves to compensate for an anterior gift, it always includes the idea of reciprocity."[26] Benven-

---

[21] Gloria Goodwin Raheja, *The Poison in the Gift: Ritual, Prestation, and the Dominant Caste in a North Indian Village* (Chicago: University of Chicago Press, 1988) [hereafter Raheja, *PG*].

[22] Raheja, *PG,* 31ff.

[23] Derrida, *GT1,* 78–82. Émile Benveniste, *Problèmes de linguistique générale* (Paris: Gallimard, 1966) [hereafter Benveniste, *PLG*], especially the chapter entitled "Don et échange dans le vocabulaire indo-européen," 315–26.

[24] Benveniste, *PLG,* 316: "Nous considérons que **do-* ne signifiait proprement ni 'prendre' ni 'donner' mais l'un ou l'autre selon la construction."

[25] Derrida, *GT1,* 79.

[26] Benveniste, *PLG,* 319: "On ne saurait souligner plus clairement la valeur fonctionnelle de la δωτινη, de ce don qui oblige à un contre-don. C'est là le sens constant du mot chez Hérodote; que la δωτινη soit destinée à provoquer

iste further makes a connection between gift and hospitality.[27] Studying the Latin *hostia,* Benveniste relates it to a kind of compensatory offering to the gods. In turn, this is related to *hostis.* "Through *hostis* and allied terms in old Latin we can grasp a type of *compensatory prestation* that is at the foundation of the notion of hospitality in Latin, Germanic and Slavic societies: equal conditions assert themselves in the right to parity between persons that is guaranteed by reciprocal gifts."[28] This adds to the sense of ambiguity in the gift—how can a gift be obligatory, or reciprocal? How can hospitality be something that is owed?

Some associated observations can be made on this point. Responsibility, or the ordering or obligation to hospitality, is an important part of the work of Emmanuel Levinas.[29] He suggests that the order to hospitality is an order to an excess: I am called upon to welcome the Other out of my own very substance, and ultimately beyond my capacity. In another context, but expressing this very idea, Levinas writes: "The immediacy of the sensible is the immediacy of enjoyment and its frustration. It is the gift painfully torn up, and in the tearing up, immediately spoiling this very enjoyment. It is not a gift of the heart, but of the bread from one's mouth, of one's own mouthful of bread. It is the openness, not only of one's pocket-book, but of the doors of one's home, a 'sharing of one's bread with the famished,' a 'welcoming of the wretched into your house' (Isaiah 58)."[30] Crucial to Levinas's un-

---

un don en retour ou qu'elle serve à compenser un don antérieur, elle inclut toujours l'idée d'une réciprocité."

[27] Benveniste, *PLG,* 320: "Un rapport évident unit à la notion de don celle de l'hospitalité."

[28] Benveniste, *PLG,* 320–21: "A travers *hostis* et les termes apparentés en vieux latin nous pouvons saisir un certain type de *prestation compensatoire* qui est le fondement de la notion d''hospitalité' dans les sociétés latine, germanique et slave: l'égalité de condition transpose dans le droit la parité assurée entre les personnes par des dons réciproques."

[29] Derrida does not refer to this part of the Benveniste text in *Given Time,* but he deals extensively with Levinas's treatment of hospitality in two more recent books, *Adieu: à Emmanuel Levinas* (Paris: Galilée, 1997) [hereafter Derrida, *Ad*], now in translation as *Adieu: to Emmanuel Levinas,* trans. Pascale-Anne Brault and Michael Naas (Stanford: Stanford University Press, 1999), and Anne Dufourmantelle and Jacques Derrida, *De L'hospitalité* (Paris: Calmann-Lévy, 1997) [hereafter Dufourmantelle and Derrida, *DL'H*], now available as *Of Hospitality,* trans. Rachel Bowlby (Stanford: Stanford University Press, 2000).

[30] Emmanuel Levinas, *Otherwise Than Being or Beyond Essence,* trans. Alphonso Lingis (The Hague: Martinus Nijhoff, 1981), 74 [hereafter Levinas, *OBBE*]. For

derstanding is that my being called to excess involves no reciprocity. This lack of symmetry is reflected in the saying from Dostoyevsky's *The Brothers Karamazov,* which Levinas regularly quotes: "Each of us is guilty before everyone, for everyone and for each one, *and I more than others.*" [31]

What are the limits of hospitality? This question is picked up by Derrida in the "Villanova Roundtable" and is also explored by John D. Caputo in his discussion of that text. Derrida's point, as it is explained by Caputo, is that essential to any understanding of hospitality is its being a generous welcoming of another into one's home. But at the same time, "[a] host is a host only if he owns the place, and only if he holds onto his ownership, if one *limits* the gift."[32] Caputo describes the necessary tension built into hospitality, and asks: "How can I graciously welcome the other while still retaining my sovereignty, my mastery of the house?"[33] As with the gift, the conditions of possibility for hospitality are its conditions of impossibility. The gift of hospitality has to do with unconditioned generosity, but it inevitably confronts us with the limits of ownership—limits that exclude the stranger but make hospitality possible. The question of hospitality, of the gift of hospitality, is confounded not only by its obligatory aspect but by the fact that it must be limited if it is to be what it is, and therefore what it is not.

Turning to the anthropological material, there is only one point to be made, although several illustrations will serve as useful reinforcements of this idea. The question Derrida raises concerns that to which social scientists refer when they use the word "gift." Standing almost at the head of a long line of sociologists and anthropologists whose work focuses on the phenomenon of the gift is Marcel Mauss.[34] Mauss's professed interest in the gift relates

---

the original French, see Emmanuel Levinas, *Autrement qu'être ou au-delà de l'essence* (1974; Paris: Livre de Poche, 1990), 119–20.

[31] Quoted, for example, in "God and Philosophy" [hereafter Levinas, *GP*], trans. Richard A. Cohen and Alphonso Lingis, *The Levinas Reader,* ed. Seán Hand (Oxford: Blackwell, 1989), 166–89, 182; emphasis added. See Fyodor Dostoyevsky, *The Brothers Karamazov,* trans. Constance Garnett (New York: New American Library, 1957), 264.

[32] John D. Caputo, in Caputo, ed., *Deconstruction in a Nutshell: A Conversation with Jacques Derrida* (New York: Fordham University Press, 1997), 111 [hereafter Caputo, *DN*].

[33] Caputo, *DN,* 111.

[34] Marcel Mauss, *The Gift: The Form and Reason for Exchange in Archaic Societies,* trans. W. D. Halls (London: Routledge, 1990) [hereafter Mauss, *GFREAS*].

to that which prompts its inevitable repayment.[35] He observes in particular cultures the superimposition of the form of gift onto what is in fact an obligatory exchange. "We intend in this book to isolate one important set of phenomena: namely, prestations which are in theory voluntary, disinterested and spontaneous, but are in fact obligatory and interested. The form usually taken is that of the gift generously offered; but the accompanying behaviour is formal pretence and social deception, while the transaction itself is based on economic self-interest."[36] However, while Mauss exposes the "social deception" of gift-giving in some societies, he explores how the system of exchange operates to create and preserve relations between people in these societies. To do this, he must reconsider the gift itself. His explanation of why the gift must return is a spiritual one: the gift is an inalienable part of the giver, given to create a bond with others, and is necessarily returned as part of that bond. Mauss positively evaluates gift-based economies, finding them superior to barter or cash economies because of their emphasis on the well-being of the whole group. Giving occurs as part of a circle of reciprocation that maintains social cohesion through the redistribution of wealth.[37] In some cultures, Mauss asserts, the gift-object itself is understood to hold a spirit (*hau*) which determines that it cannot rest as the possession of any one owner. It must therefore be kept on the move as a perpetual gift, passing through the social group via many temporary holders.[38] In other cultures, the cycle relies on each gift's prompting not only the return of an equivalent outlay, but an increased expenditure that goes to express the givenness of the gift.[39] Overall, Mauss suggests that there is an attribute of surplus about the gift in a gift economy which, in spite of the circular movement in which it is involved, expresses relationship and is therefore non-economic. This quality distinguishes the gift economy from the barter or cash economy, assures distribution, and

---

[35] "We shall confine our detailed study to the enquiry: *In primitive or archaic types of society what is the principle whereby the gift received has to be repaid? What force is there in the thing given which compels the recipient to make a return?*" Mauss, *GFREAS*, 1.

[36] Mauss, *GFREAS*, 1.

[37] Mauss, *GFREAS*, 31.

[38] Mauss, *GFREAS*, 22.

[39] As well as the social superiority of the giver. See Mauss, *GFREAS*, 35.

maintains a kind of spiritual health in the society. Later anthropologists, such as Raymond Firth, Claude Lévi-Strauss, and Marshall Sahlins, argue extensively about Mauss's interpretation of the gift in terms of its spirit.[40] Instead of emphasizing the spirit of the gift, these researchers focus on the factor of reciprocity underlying social cohesion. Ironically, contemporary research has returned to a consideration of the inalienability, and hence of the spiritual quality, of the gift.[41] Yet at stake in Mauss and in what follows from Mauss, for our purposes, is ultimately not the question of reciprocity, but whether reciprocity is all there is, and whether reciprocity nullifies any surplus.

An almost romantic attempt to locate in gift exchange something more than simple exchange is exemplified in the work of Lewis Hyde.[42] Hyde attempts to underline the property of being uncalculated as the central feature of the gift, especially in the sense of the sharing of artistic gifts: "The moral is this: the gift is lost in self-consciousness. To count, measure, reckon value, or seek the cause of a thing, is to step outside the circle, to cease being 'all of a piece' with the flow of gifts and become, instead, one part of the whole reflecting on another. We participate in the esemplastic power of the gift by way of a particular kind of unconsciousness, then: unanalytic, undialectical consciousness."[43] Hyde raises the issue of "unconsciousness," and Derrida anticipates this possibility as an objection that might be made to his analysis: "One could object that this description [of giving] is still given in terms of the self, of the subject that says I, *ego,* of intentional or intuitive perception-consciousness, or even of the conscious ego (for Freud the ego or a part of the ego can be unconscious). One may be tempted to oppose this description with another that would substitute for the economy of perception-consciousness an economy of the unconscious."[44] Nevertheless,

---

[40] For a clear and concise summary of this development, see Yunxiang Yan, *The Flow of Gifts: Reciprocity and Social Networks in a Chinese Village* (Stanford: Stanford University Press, 1996), 4–13 [hereafter Yan, *FG*].

[41] Yan, *FG,* 11.

[42] W. Lewis Hyde, *The Gift: Imagination and the Erotic Life of Property* (New York: Random House, 1983) [hereafter Hyde, *GIELP*].

[43] Hyde, *GIELP* 152.

[44] Derrida, *GT1,* 15.

in response to such an objection, he maintains that the cover of unconsciousness is insufficient to conceal the gift:

> But such a displacement does not affect the paradox with which we are struggling, namely, the impossibility or the double bind of the gift: For there to be gift, it is necessary that the gift not even appear, that it not be perceived or received as gift. . . . For there to be gift, not only must the donor or donee not perceive or receive the gift as such, have no consciousness of it, no memory, no recognition; he or she must also forget it right away and moreover this forgetting must be so radical that it exceeds even the psychoanalytic categoriality of forgetting. This forgetting of the gift must even no longer be forgetting in the sense of repression.[45]

It is ironic that Hyde understands the reckoning of value to be a "stepping out of the circle" rather than the other way around. His explication of the unreckoned aspect of the gift says exactly the opposite of what he apparently intends. But further, if we observe his stated meaning (that "unconsciousness" preserves the spirit of the gift), he still cannot escape the circle of return that puts the restriction back into his economy.

Referring as he does to Mauss, Sahlins, and Hyde, Derrida concludes that, evidently regardless of whether or not a redemptive surplus can be observed in gift exchange, the very fact of reciprocity is sufficient to undermine how the word "gift" is used in each of these studies. Derrida asks whether or not it can really be gift to which these authors refer.[46] For in each case, the gift is enclosed within the totality of a system, and is in this way subject to return. On Derrida's reading, no generosity, no excess, no lack of measure would be sufficient to transform the gift-object into a

---

[45] Derrida, *GT1,* 16.

[46] "What remains problematic is . . . the very existence of something like *the* gift, that is, the common referent of this sign that is itself uncertain. If what Mauss demonstrates, one way or the other, is indeed that every gift is caught in the round or the contract of usury, then not only the unity of the meaning 'gift' remains doubtful but, on the hypothesis that giving would have a *meaning* and *one* meaning, it is still the possibility of an effective existence, of an effectuation or an event of the gift that seems excluded. Now, this problematic of the difference (in the sense that we evoked earlier) between 'the gift exists' and 'there is gift' is never, as we know, deployed or even approached by Mauss, no more than it seems to be, to my knowledge, by the anthropologists who come after him or refer to him." Derrida, *GT1,* 26.

pure gift, for it could not satisfy the most basic condition that a gift never prompt an exchange.[47] In this way, most of the studies on the gift are open to critique.

It is easy in the face of this rather overwhelming analysis to assume—and according to Derrida many do—that his last word on the gift is that there is no gift.[48] Such a reading tends to elicit very pragmatic responses: of course there must be such a thing as a gift, and therefore this Derrida is a madman (or a shaman); if the gift is caught up in a system of exchange, perhaps exchange is not such a bad thing after all. From a theological perspective, and crude as my interpretation may sound, this is the core of the response of John Milbank in "Can a Gift Be Given?"[49] Just touching on Milbank's argument here, there are two features of particular interest: the assertion that what is needed is not "pure gift" but "purified gift-exchange"; and the defense of the gift as "delay and non-identical repetition."[50] Milbank allows that "Christianity transforms but does not suppress our 'given' social nature which is exchangist," or in other words, he argues that it is not the economic element that has to be purged from gift-giving, but rather the motivation for giving that has to be altered. The meaning of purified gift exchange is Christian agape.[51] He further allows that where the gift is returned by way of a delay or a difference it is no longer simply quid pro quo. In these terms, the gift that does not come back exactly the same escapes simple reciprocity. And there is something to be said for this argument, given that *Given Time* ponders not only giving but the giving of time.[52] For Milbank, the

---

[47] "For there to be a gift, there must be no reciprocity, return, exchange, countergift, or debt." Derrida, *GT1,* 12. It must nevertheless be pointed out that Derrida does not discourage the attempt at generosity without measure. This way of addressing the problem is discussed by Caputo, *DN,* 145–47.

[48] See his comments in "On the Gift: A Discussion between Jacques Derrida and Jean-Luc Marion, Moderated by Richard Kearney," *God, the Gift, and Postmodernism,* ed. John D. Caputo and Michael J. Scanlon (Bloomington: Indiana University Press, 1999) [hereafter Caputo and Scanlon, *GGP*], 54–78, 60 [hereafter Derrida and Marion, *OTG*].

[49] John Milbank, "Can a Gift Be Given?" *Rethinking Metaphysics,* ed. L. Gregory Jones and Stephen E. Fowl (Oxford: Blackwell, 1995), 119–61 [hereafter Milbank, *CGG*].

[50] Milbank, *CGG,* 131–32.

[51] Milbank, *CGG,* 131.

[52] Milbank reads this as the solution to the problem Derrida poses: time can be given because "it is a non-identical repetition which can never actually occur." Milbank, *CGG,* 131. See also Alan D. Schrift, "Introduction: Why Gift?" in *The*

disparity between givers and between gifts is enough to take the heat out of the exchange: God gives, and while the believer is obligated to return, he or she can never return *enough.* What is returned is not the given gift but something different altogether, albeit in response to the gift.[53] The economy is thus affirmed and even explicitly sanctioned in the realm of divine-human relations.

A pragmatic response such as Milbank's is in many senses appealing, particularly because it seems to make sense of the human condition: we may not always give with the best of intentions now, but growth in the Christian life can purify our motives and thereby undercut the negative aspects of exchange. The gift would then serve as a model for other human goods that stand in need of transformation, such as love, justice, or peace. But a number of difficulties emerge from this view. One is that it forces us to maintain an inherent contradiction in the word "gift," so that it means something that is given freely but also in response to another gift. An alternative difficulty is that it claims to enable our knowledge of the gift (I have received, I therefore give) without making it possible for us to know which gifts meet the conditions of purified exchange (was your gift entirely disinterested?). In an interesting way, this second problem places us squarely back in Derrida's court: if a gift is present—that is, if I know it as such—then I cannot know if it is free. And then there is the further, theological problem, which is that if God enters into a system of exchange, we cannot be free *not* to return the divine gift in some measure. Milbank has no apparent problem with the type of obligation a "purified" exchange system still necessarily involves, and, in fact, he embraces it.[54] But I cannot believe in a God who obliges my belief, and similarly, a God who constantly places me in debt seems not particularly loving. The incorporation of the elements of difference and delay do not solve this problem. If the gift returns in a different measure or kind or after some delay, it still undoes itself, for it can always be the result of a need for a

---

Logic of the Gift: Toward an Ethic of Generosity, ed. Alan D. Schrift (New York: Routledge, 1997), 1–22, 10–11 [hereafter Schrift, *LG*].

[53] Milbank, *CGG,* 150.

[54] "We participate in the trinitarian exchange such that the divine gift only begins to be as gift to us at all . . . *after* it has been received—which is to say returned with the return of gratitude and charitable giving-in-turn—by us." Milbank, *CGG,* 136.

certain circularity, keeping it all in the family, as it were. One can dislike Derrida's analysis of the gift, and many do, but it is impossible to argue against it without accepting some sort of compromise on its terms. Yet Derrida claims not that there can be no gift but that a gift cannot be known as such; in other words, he claims that no phenomenon of gift can be known. "I never said that there is no gift. No. I said exactly the opposite. *What are the conditions for us to say there is a gift, if we cannot determine it theoretically, phenomenologically?*"[55] Now we have come to the heart of the matter. For Derrida, the gift cannot be phenomenologically described; we cannot reach the gift through phenomenology. This judgment will place Derrida in direct opposition to Marion, for whom phenomenology remains a viable way to approach even phenomena that cannot be seen. Already the theological implications are becoming apparent. It is, then, necessary to explore further the history and limits of phenomenology.

---

[55] Derrida and Marion, *OTG,* 60; emphasis added.

2
Husserl and Heidegger

A Phenomenological Starting Point

A concise way of defining phenomenology is to say that it is characterized by two questions: What is given (to consciousness)? and How (or according to what horizon) is it given? While what is given may not necessarily be a gift, it is already evident from the framing of this definition that the question of the gift will not be irrelevant in this context. Just how that is so will become clearer in later chapters. For the moment, however, it is sufficient to note that the reading of the gift that Marion propounds aims to be a strictly phenomenological one, and therefore that in order to understand both his and Derrida's viewpoints on the question of the gift, both writers need to be situated in relation to phenomenology. The amount of literature produced by each author is extensive. Nevertheless, English-speaking readers have had far greater access to the works of Derrida, and only relatively recently did the task of translating Marion's works begin. For this reason, I have chosen to sketch in this chapter, and the following, aspects of the phenomenological background along with some of the main points in Derrida's response to phenomenology. In the subsequent chapters I will examine Marion's reading of phenomenology in more detail, allowing for a general unfamiliarity with his works.

Husserlian Phenomenology

Husserlian phenomenology arises at a time when philosophy is suffering a crisis of purpose and credibility, and it marks an attempt to reestablish philosophy as the science of the sciences by providing a sure foundation for knowledge in a specifically focused examination of what presents itself to consciousness. Its revolutionary character lies in its suspension of questions of existence and in its attempt to withdraw from the crude division of reality into subject and object. In the summary he originally made only for himself at the end of a lecture series, Husserl outlines three stages in the phenomenological method.[1] The initial stage involves finding an appropriate starting point for philosophical reflection. This, he suggests, can be achieved by adopting a form of Cartesian doubt. If we are not to drown in a sea of unlimited skepticism, there must be something that is known about which we can be sure. "Without doubt there is *cogitatio,* there is, namely, the mental process during the [subject's] undergoing it and in a simple reflection upon it. The seeing, direct grasping and having of the *cogitatio* is already a cognition."[2] Why is this cognition more certain than any other? It is more certain because it is genuinely immanent, whereas the possibility of transcendent knowledge is much more difficult to affirm.[3] In this way Husserl reaches a first principle concerning the exclusion of all transcendence: "I must accomplish a *phenomenological reduction: I must exclude all that is transcendently posited.*"[4]

At the next stage, Husserl affirms that "the Cartesian *cogitatio* already requires the phenomenological reduction."[5] He is basing his method not on the mental activity of a person but on the pure phenomenon of cognition.[6] His next question therefore concerns how this phenomenon can have access to that which is not immanent to it.[7] While it is possible to "see" various isolated phenomena, Husserl considers this an inadequate path to the sure

[1] Later prefaced to the published version of the lectures as "The Train of Thought in the Lectures," in Edmund Husserl, *The Idea of Phenomenology,* trans. William P. Alston and George Nakhnikian (The Hague: Martinus Nijhoff, 1964), 1–12 [hereafter Husserl, *IP*].

[2] Husserl, *IP,* 2.

[3] "The genuinely immanent is taken as the indubitable just on account of the fact that it presents nothing else, 'points' to nothing 'outside' itself, for what is here intended is fully and adequately given in itself." Husserl, *IP,* 3.

[4] Husserl, *IP,* 4.

[5] Husserl, *IP,* 5.

[6] "The truly absolute datum is the *pure phenomenon,* that which is reduced. The mentally active ego, the object, man in time, the thing amongst things, etc., are not absolute data; hence man's mental activity as his activity is no absolute datum either. *We abandon finally the standpoint of psychology, even of descriptive psychology.*" Husserl, *IP,* 5.

[7] Husserl, *IP,* 5.

knowledge of the universal.[8] Instead, he suggests that eidetic abstraction will yield the most helpful information about the essence of cognition. "Cognition belongs to the sphere of the *cogitationes*. Accordingly, we must through 'seeing' bring its universal objects into the consciousness of the universal. Thus it becomes possible to have a doctrine about the essence of cognition."[9] But while this brings us to the point of being able to assent to the objectivity of essences, a further clarification is required. Husserl makes a distinction between the "absolutely given" and the "genuinely immanent," observing that what is universal meets the conditions of the former but not of the latter.[10] He then refines his notion of the phenomenological reduction: "It means not the exclusion of the genuinely transcendent . . . but the exclusion of the transcendent as such as something to be accepted as existent, i.e., everything that is not evident givenness in its true sense, that is not absolutely given to pure 'seeing.' "[11] For Husserl, the stance of objectivity is achieved in relation to *Evidenz*, to "the pure viewing and grasping of something objective directly and in itself."[12] This point is crucial because it is not only in the exclusion of the *existence* of what is transcendent but also in the emphasis on its givenness that the real possibilities of the phenomenological method lie.[13]

The third stage in Husserl's description of the phenomenologi-

---

[8] "At first it seems beyond question that on the basis of these 'seeings' we can undertake logical operations, can compare, contrast, subsume under concepts, predicate, although, as appears later, behind these operations stand new objectivities. But even if what here seems beyond question were taken for granted and considered no further, we could not understand how we could here arrive at universally valid findings of the sort we need." Husserl, *IP*, 6.

[9] Husserl, *IP*, 6.

[10] Husserl, *IP*, 6–7.

[11] Husserl, *IP*, 7.

[12] Husserl, *IP*, 6.

[13] "Thus the field is now characterised. It is a field of absolute cognitions, within which the ego and the world and God and the mathematical manifolds and whatever else may be a scientifically objective matter are held in abeyance, cognitions which are, therefore, also not dependent on these matters, which are valid in their own right, whether we are sceptics with regard to the others or not. All that remains as it is. The root of the matter, however, is *to grasp the meaning of the absolutely given, the absolute clarity of the given,* which excludes every meaningful doubt, in a word, *to grasp the absolutely 'seeing' evidence which gets hold of itself.*" Husserl, *IP*, 7.

cal method involves even greater refinements. Husserl now distinguishes between "*appearance* and *that which appears,*" or as he next expresses it, between "the givenness of the appearing and the givenness of the object." This distinction is again one where "it is a consciousness which constitutes something self-given which is not contained within what is occurring [in the world] and is not at all found as *cogitatio.*"[14] The task of phenomenology thus becomes one of correlating how something is given with what it "is" that is given. Husserl summarizes the phenomenology of cognition as follows: "On the one hand it has to do with cognitions as appearances, presentations, acts of consciousness in which this or that object is presented, is an act of consciousness, passively or actively. On the other hand . . . [it] has to do with these objects as presenting themselves in this manner."[15] This accords with the distinction Husserl makes elsewhere between the noesis and the noema, bearing in mind that neither of these refers to the "really" existing object, but only to its givenness to the phenomenologically reduced consciousness.[16]

With regard to the last point, it is important to advert to the further distinction made by Husserl regarding experience as it refers to the real or empirical—theoretical experience (*Erfahrung*)—and experience as it refers to intentionality (*Erlebnis*). The former is the realm of the natural attitude (which Husserl seeks to suspend), and of natural knowledge: "Natural knowledge begins with experience (*Erfahrung*) and remains *within* experience. Thus in that theoretical position which we call the 'natural' standpoint, the total field of possible research is indicated by a *single* word: that is, the *World.*"[17] In contrast, experience as it refers to

[14] Husserl, *IP,* 9.

[15] Husserl, *IP,* 11.

[16] Edmund Husserl, *Ideas: General Introduction to Pure Phenomenology,* vol. 1, trans. W. R. Boyce Gibson (London: Allen and Unwin, 1972), §§87ff. [hereafter Husserl, *I1*].

[17] Husserl, *I1,* 52. Ricoeur, in describing *Erfahrung* according to Husserl, observes the belief that is part of the natural attitude: "Experience means more than perception in the phenomenologist's language. The sense of perception only appears by the reduction of certain characters of experience, a reduction that uncovers the deficient and incomplete aspect of experience. In experience we are already on the level of a perception shot through with a 'thesis,' that is to say with a believing that posits its object as being. We live through perception in giving credit to the vehemence of presence, if I may use such language, to

intentionality, or "lived experience," is ideal experience, although it does not relate solely to inner experience.[18] "That an experience is the consciousness of something: a fiction, for instance, the fiction of this or that centaur . . . this does not relate to the experimental fact as lived within the world . . . but to the pure essence grasped ideationally as pure idea."[19] Additionally, Husserl speaks of intentional experience (the consciousness of something) and non-intentional experience (e.g., sense data to which we do not necessarily advert).[20] "For it is easily seen that *not every real phase* of the concrete unity of an intentional experience has itself the *basic character of intentionality,* the property of being a 'consciousness of something.' "[21] This admission of two types of intentionality might be seen to maintain the priority of the constituting subject, but it can be understood more positively as a reassertion of the priority of the given phenomenon (which Marion will underline with his constant reference to what "gives itself" or "shows itself").[22] With that emphasis in place, it is possible to see why phenomenology is so revolutionary, and why it has a possible connection with theology.

---

the point of forgetting ourselves or losing ourselves in it. This believing (*doxa*) has certitude as its fundamental mode, the correlate of which is the index of actuality." Paul Ricoeur, *Husserl: An Analysis of His Phenomenology,* trans. Edward G. Ballard and Lester E. Embree (Evanston: Northwestern University Press, 1967), 40 [hereafter Ricoeur, *HAP*].

[18] Levinas explains: "We have said that intentionality is not the mere representation of an object. Husserl calls states of consciousness *Erlebnisse*—what is 'lived' in the sense of what is experienced—and this very expression connects the notion of consciousness to that of life, i.e., it leads us to consider consciousness under the rich and multiform aspects characteristic of our concrete existence." Emmanuel Levinas, *The Theory of Intuition in Husserl's Phenomenology,* trans. André Orianne, 2nd ed. (Evanston: Northwestern University Press, 1995), 53 [hereafter Levinas, *TIHP*].

[19] Husserl, *I1,* 120. He develops this understanding of experience from Dilthey. See, for example, Wilhelm Dilthey, "The Understanding of Other Persons and Their Expressions of Life" (1910), *Descriptive Psychology and Historical Understanding,* trans. Kenneth L. Heiges (The Hague: Martinus Nijhoff, 1977), 121–44, 124–25.

[20] Husserl, *I1,* 120.

[21] Husserl, *I1,* 120.

[22] I refer here to Marion's constant use of *se donne* and *se montre.* While it is usual to translate these third-person conjugations (in the impersonal sense) as "is given" and "is shown," it is of course possible to play on the ambiguity of the personal and read "gives itself" and "shows itself."

Having sketched an introduction to phenomenology as it is developed by Husserl, we can now ask how it sits in the light of the two questions with which I framed the discussion: what is given, or gives itself (to consciousness), in phenomenology, and how is it given (i.e., according to what horizon)? For Husserl, what is given are present, intentional objects, according to a horizon of the phenomenologically reduced consciousness. But there may be more than that. It may be that "non-intentional experience" is also given according to the horizon of the reduction. This is a point of ambiguity on which much will rest.

Derrida and Husserl

Derrida begins his publishing career with several major works on Husserl in which he traces the metaphysical residue inherent in Husserl's phenomenological method. In *Edmund Husserl's "Origin of Geometry"* he observes the "difference and delay" that characterize all thought, and the failure of the phenomenological reduction to overcome such *différance.*[23] More strongly, in *Speech and Phenomena* Derrida writes:

[23] "The discursive and dialectical intersubjectivity of Time with itself in the infinite multiplicity and infinite implication of its absolute origins entitles every other intersubjectivity in general to exist and makes the polemical unity of appearing and disappearing irreducible. Here delay is the philosophical absolute, because the beginning of methodic reflection can only consist in the consciousness of the implication of *another* previous, possible, and absolute origin in general. Since this alterity of the absolute origin structurally appears in *my Living Present* and since it can appear and be recognized only in the primordiality of something like *my Living Present,* this very fact signifies the authenticity of phenomenological delay and limitation. In the lackluster guise of a technique, the Reduction is only pure thought as that delay, pure thought investigating the sense of itself as delay within philosophy." Jacques Derrida, *Edmund Husserl's "Origin of Geometry": An Introduction,* trans. John P. Leavey, Jr., rev. ed. (Lincoln: University of Nebraska Press, 1989), 152. As Kevin Hart notes, Derrida's thinking of giving and the impossibility of giving is also set up in these pages: "Derrida observes that 'Being itself must always already be given to thinking [*donné à penser*], in the pre-sumption—which is also a resumption—of Method' (p. 152). And he goes on to claim that 'In the lacklustre guise of a technique, the Reduction is only pure thought . . . investigating the sense of itself as delay within philosophy' (p. 153). If the first remark anticipates a thinking of the gift and in particular the impossibility of giving in the present, the second just as surely sets death on the agenda of such a thought. Dehiscence is proper to consciousness,

> Do not phenomenological necessity, the rigor and subtlety of Husserl's analysis, the exigencies to which it responds and which we must first recognize, nonetheless conceal a metaphysical presupposition? Do they not harbor a dogmatic or speculative commitment which, to be sure, would not keep the phenomenological critique from being realized, would not be a residue of unperceived naïveté, but would *constitute* phenomenology from within, in its project of criticism and in the instructive value of its own premises? This would be done precisely in what soon comes to be recognized as the source and guarantee of all value, the "principle of principles": i.e., the original self-giving evidence, the *present* or *presence* of sense to a full and primordial intuition.[24]

While Husserl maintains the admirable ambition of suspending "the natural attitude," of doing away with all presuppositions to consider the phenomenon as it gives itself in person to consciousness, Derrida shows that this ambition is not realized in Husserl's work. Far from being value-free, it appears to be value-laden. Husserl depends on the interrelated presence of the (noematic) object to the self-present subject, on the guarantee that presence provides of evidential force. Derrida's argument that Husserl's phenomenology is essentially metaphysical relies on two problems related to the question of presence: time and language.

With regard to time, Derrida argues that the perfect presence to consciousness of the intended object, which Husserl requires to meet the conditions of *Evidenz,* is inevitably undone by the fact that presentation involves the temporally divisive movements of re-presentation and appresentation.[25] What is supposedly present

---

we are told, and it follows that death cannot be regarded as an empirical moment that leaves consciousness intact. No, death threatens transcendental life. And this threat forms the condition of possibility for discourse and history." Kevin Hart, rev. of *The Gift of Death,* by Jacques Derrida, *Modern Theology* 12, no. 4 (1996): 495–96.

[24] Jacques Derrida, *Speech and Phenomena and Other Essays on Husserl's Theory of Signs,* trans. David B. Allison and Newton Garver (Evanston: Northwestern University Press, 1973), 4–5 [hereafter Derrida, *SP*].

[25] "Briefly, it is a question of (1) the necessary transition from retention to *re-presentation* . . . in the constitution of the presence of a temporal object . . . whose identity may be repeated; and (2) the necessary transition by way of *appresentation* in relation to the *alter ego,* that is in relation to what also makes possible an ideal objectivity in general; for intersubjectivity is the condition for objectivity, which is absolute only in the case of ideal objects." Derrida, *SP,* 7.

to consciousness is never actually present, but slightly "out of sync" with the reflection that must always follow or anticipate it. For the same reason, Derrida is able to criticize Husserl's foundation of phenomenology on the self-present subject. Never present at its own origin, the subject is never able to recuperate itself.[26]

With regard to language, Derrida observes that Husserl ties it to the expression of an idea that is perfectly present: the linguistic sign is invested with meaning because it reflects the presence of the idea within the perfect self-presence of consciousness.[27] But this understanding comes undone with the recognition that language is not a purely internal system, but a means of communication. When language is used to communicate, it invariably falls away from the perfect self-presence it is supposed to express.[28] Derrida suggests that rather than ideas preceding their expression in language, language actually constitutes ideas: there can be no ideas that do not depend on the mediation of signs. Further, since language relies on the possibility of repetition, ideas are subject to the same dissemination that such repetition invites. As soon as a word is repeatable (a condition that is essential if language is to be meaningful) it bears the potential for a loss or alteration of meaning. Language therefore reflects not full presence, but a play of presence and absence: language operates as an infinite network of references that cannot be held at bay. This infinite play is implicated in Derrida's neologism *différance,* where the condition of possibility for meaning (that a word is repeatable) is also the condition of impossibility for determinate meaning, because a word can always be repeated in a different context, and because its meaning can always be deferred.[29] For this reason, according to Derrida, determinate meaning is strictly *undecidable.*

---

[26] Derrida, *SP,* 63–64.

[27] See Derrida, *SP,* chapter 4, "Meaning and Representation."

[28] Derrida, *SP,* 68–69.

[29] See the essay "Différance," which appears in Derrida, *SP,* 129–60, 129: "The verb 'to differ' seems to differ from itself. On the one hand, it indicates difference as distinction, inequality, or discernibility; on the other, it expresses the interposition of delay, the interval of a *spacing* and *temporalizing* that puts off until 'later' what is presently denied, the possible that is presently impossible. Sometimes the *different* and sometimes the *deferred* correspond [in French] to the verb 'to differ.' This correlation, however, is not simply one between act and object, cause and effect, or primordial and derived. . . . In the one case 'to differ' signifies nonidentity; in the other case it signifies the order of the *same.* Yet

Derrida does not reject Husserl's work, especially since there is no simple moving aside from or out of philosophy, but simply points out ways in which it continues to subscribe to some of the presuppositions of metaphysics. Very often he is able to indicate within Husserl places where it could have been different, hints of an awareness of something else, of an impossibility that cannot be readily overcome. This occurs, for example, where Husserl recognizes the potential disruption to self-presence that is implied in his theory of internal time consciousness.[30] Or again, there is great possibility in Husserl's understanding that intentions need not be fulfilled.[31] Caputo, in his reading of Derrida and Husserl, marks the distinction between them in terms of the radicalness of their respective reductions, and it is a telling point: "It [*Dissemination*] moves beyond the eidetic reduction, which is a reduction *to* meaning [this is Husserl's position], toward a more radical reduction *of* meaning, a grammatological liberation of the signifier, releasing it into its free play."[32] It is as though Husserl orients his reduction by a belief (perhaps a natural attitude) in ultimate meaningfulness, a commitment to the triumph of cosmos over chaos. Derrida, on the other hand, makes no such commitment in advance. It is not that we surrender all hope of meaning with Derrida, but that we are forced to recognize that no one interpretation of meaning is absolute. Yet once this is recognized, it re-

---

there must be a common, although entirely differant [*différante*], root within the sphere that unites the two movements of differing to one another. We provisionally give the name *différance* to this *sameness* which is not *identical:* by the silent writing of its *a,* it has the desired advantage of referring to differing, *both* as spacing/temporalizing and as the movement that structures every dissociation."

[30] See John D. Caputo, *Radical Hermeneutics* (Bloomington: Indiana University Press, 1987), 133 [hereafter Caputo, *RH*].

[31] Caputo observes: "That is why the Husserlian discovery which Derrida most cherishes—and this must seem a sheer perversity to Husserlian orthodoxy—is the possibility of intention *without* intuition, that is, of unfulfilled intention. Husserl saw not only that expressive intentions *can* function in the absence of their objects, but also that this is their essential function. He saw that one can speak without seeing, that one can speak without having the truth, and indeed that one can speak without avoiding contradiction. Speech, in order to be speech, in order to be 'well-formed,' is bound only by purely formal laws of linguistic configuration, organized by a theory of linguistic signification (*Bedutungslehre*). Even if speech is deprived of an object, of truth, or of consistency, it can remain good speech." *RH,* 140.

[32] Caputo, *RH,* 148.

mains possible to suggest that some interpretations can be argued more effectively than others.[33]

Heideggerian Phenomenology

From Heidegger's perspective, Husserl makes a significant contribution to philosophy with his development of the phenomenological method. However, Heidegger develops his own application of the method, coinciding with his attempt to move beyond philosophy (as metaphysics) to what he perceives to be a comprehensive ontology. Where Husserl uses phenomenology to gain access to objects as they are presented to consciousness, Heidegger uses phenomenology to gain access to the meaning of the being of those objects.[34] Heidegger's ontological goal ("to explain Being itself and to make the Being of entities stand out in full relief") is to be made possible through the application of the phenomenological procedure, but in such a way that he radically alters Husserl's original idea.[35] Heidegger notes that the purpose of phenomenology is "to let that which shows itself be seen from itself in the very way in which it shows itself from itself."[36] But he then asks, "What is it that phenomenology is to 'let us see'?" and his answer does not refer us to the given objects, but to being itself, which is given concomitantly with those objects. What phe-

---

[33] See Caputo, *DN,* 184; Joseph S. O'Leary, *Religious Pluralism and Christian Truth,* rev. ed. (Edinburgh: Edinburgh University Press, 1996), 40–42 [hereafter O'Leary, *RPCT*].

[34] I will maintain the use of the more ambiguous but thus more expressive "being" rather than "Being," except in quotations.

[35] Martin Heidegger, *Being and Time,* trans. John Macquarrie and Edward Robinson (Oxford: Blackwell, 1962), 49 [hereafter Heidegger, *BT*]. "*For Husserl,* phenomenological reduction . . . is the method of leading phenomenological vision from the natural attitude of the human being whose life is involved in the world of things and persons back to the transcendental life of consciousness and its noetic-noematic experiences, in which objects are constituted as correlates of consciousness. *For us* phenomenological reduction means leading phenomenological vision back from the apprehension of a being, whatever may be the character of that apprehension, to the understanding of the being of this being." Martin Heidegger, *Basic Problems of Phenomenology,* trans. Albert Hofstadter, rev. ed., (Bloomington: Indiana University Press, 1982), 21 [hereafter Heidegger, *BPP*].

[36] Heidegger, *BT,* 58.

nomenology enables us to see "is something that proximally and for the most part does *not* show itself at all: it is something that lies *hidden,* in contrast to that which proximally and for the most part does show itself; but at the same time it is something that belongs to what shows itself, and it belongs to it so essentially as to constitute its meaning and its ground."[37]

Heidegger's chief criticism of Husserl is that the latter interprets the being of beings in an ontic rather than a genuinely ontological fashion. Heidegger's according of a new priority to the ontological question is developed in his illustration of the insufficiency of previous ontologies, particularly that of Descartes, on which it may be suggested that the ontology of Husserl is at least partially based.[38] According to Heidegger, Descartes understands being in terms of its substantiality, its presence-at-hand: what remains constant in an entity is its real substance and hence its real being.[39] This is typical of ontologies where "entities are grasped in their Being as 'presence'; this means that they are understood with regard to a definite model of time—the '*Present.*' "[40] For Heidegger, what is given is being, but being gives itself not in presence to knowledge but in withdrawal from it.[41] The initiative is no longer with the subject who seeks to understand but with being that calls *Dasein* to thought.[42] The world and all it contains are given *in* their being. All beings are grounded in being, but being itself, which is no-thing, is without ground.[43]

Of great interest for the present study is Heidegger's use of the locution *es gibt,* which appears in *Being and Time* but is also found in later works, and which seems to become a crucial point upon

[37] Heidegger, *BT,* 59.

[38] See Husserl, *IP,* 2, or Edmund Husserl, *Cartesian Meditations,* trans. Dorion Cairns (The Hague: Martinus Nijhoff, 1970) [hereafter Husserl, *CM*].

[39] See Heidegger, *BT,* 122–32.

[40] Heidegger, *BT,* 47.

[41] See Martin Heidegger, *The Principle of Reason,* trans. Reginald Lilly (Bloomington: Indiana University Press, 1991), 70 [hereafter Heidegger, *PR*].

[42] See Martin Heidegger, *What Is Called Thinking?* trans. J. Glenn Gray (New York: Harper and Row, 1968) [hereafter Heidegger, *WCT*].

[43] Heidegger, *PR,* 70, 49. On the difficulties Heidegger's thinking of the principle of reason occasions, and on his thinking of *Ereignis* as ground, see Joseph S. O'Leary, "Theological Resonances of *Der Satz vom Grund,*" *Martin Heidegger: Critical Assessments,* ed. Christopher Macann (London: Routledge, 1992), 214–56, especially 245–46 [hereafter O'Leary, *TRSG*].

which Heidegger's thought turns.[44] The way in which *es gibt* is situated in Heidegger's thinking is outlined in the lectures he gave in 1927, published as *Basic Problems in Phenomenology:*

> Perhaps there *is* no other being beyond what has been enumerated, but perhaps, as in the German idiom for "there is," *es gibt,* still something else *is given.* Even more. In the end something is given which *must* be given if we are to be able to make beings accessible to us as beings and comport ourselves toward them, something which, to be sure, is not but which must be given if we are to experience and understand any beings at all.[45]

The ambiguity of the phrase *es gibt* means that it can be interpreted both as "there is" and "it gives." According to Heidegger's translator, John Macquarrie, the second sense is the stronger, and Heidegger's intention is clarified where, in the "Letter on Humanism," he insists that the French *il y a* ("there is") translates the *es gibt* only "imprecisely."[46] It seems that he desires to empha-

---

[44] Heidegger, *BT,* 26, 255, 464.

[45] Heidegger, *BPP,* 10.

[46] John Macquarrie, *Heidegger and Christianity* (London: SCM Press, 1994), 60 [hereafter Macquarrie, *HC*]; Martin Heidegger, "Letter on Humanism," *Basic Writings: Martin Heidegger,* rev. ed. by David Farrell Krell (London: Routledge, 1993), 217–65, 238 [hereafter Heidegger, *LH*]. Marion himself refers to this problem in *L'idole et la distance* (Paris: Grasset, 1977), 283 [hereafter Marion, *ID*]: "Ainsi la pensée qui s'essaie à penser l'Etre dans son essence en vient à laisser de côté la différence ontologique comme telle, pour en reprendre l'enjeu sous l'autre formulation du *don.* Ou plutôt du *es gibt,* que nous traduisons—ou plutôt ne traduisons pas—par un il y a, où manque justement la connotation du *Geben,* du *donner:* il faudrait transposer, et demander, devant un donné, ou une donnée (pour un problème, une question, une entreprise) comment ce donné est donné, et surtout si son caractère de donné a quelque rapport avec sa manière d'être tel étant." This text is now available in English as *The Idol and Distance: Five Studies,* trans. with an introduction by Thomas A. Carlson (New York: Fordham University Press, 2001). Marion also makes reference to the problem in *God Without Being,* trans. Thomas A. Carlson (Chicago: University of Chicago Press, 1991), 102 [hereafter Marion, *GWB*], and in *Étant donné* (Paris: Presses Universitaires de France, 1997) [hereafter Marion, *ED*] at the footnote on p. 97: "En ce qui concerne le '*es gibt*' utilisé par Heidegger, sa transposition dans le '*il y a*' français, ne peut se justifier malgré l'usage. L'analyse de *Zeit und Sein* ne vise qu'à faire jouer le pli entre le don donné (ou *Gabe*) et un donner (*Geben*), où Heidegger veut éviter qu'on confonde la donation avec un éventuel don donnant." Heidegger's distancing from the French *il y a* is interesting in the light of later French philosophers who use the *il y a* evocatively in speaking of the interminable weight of being. See, for example, Emmanuel Levinas, *Existence and Existents,* trans. Alphonso Lingis (The Hague: Martinus Nijhoff, 1978), 57

size the aspect of (generous) giving in a way that also enables him to avoid saying that being "is."[47] Derrida observes: "We translate the idiomatic locution *es gibt Sein* and *es gibt Zeit* by 'il y a l'être' in French and in English 'there is Being' (Being is not but there is Being), 'il y a le temps,' 'there is time' (time is not but there is time). Heidegger tries to get us to hear in this the 'it gives,' or as one might say in French, in a neutral but not negative fashion, 'ça donne,' an 'it gives' that would not form an utterance in the propositional structure of Greco-Latin grammar."[48] As this comment from Derrida indicates in an anticipatory way, Heidegger uses *es gibt* in speaking of both being and time.[49] But what Heidegger means when he says this is far from straightforward. What does it mean that being is given? What is the relationship between the giving of being and the giving of time, especially since neither being nor time "is" any "thing"?[50] And most importantly for the

---

[hereafter Levinas, *EE*]: "This impersonal, anonymous, yet indistinguishable 'consummation' of being, which murmurs in the depths of nothingness itself we shall designate by the term *there is*. The *there is,* inasmuch as it resists a personal form, is 'being in general.' " We are also reminded of Blanchot's "neuter." John Caputo notes the sense of generosity that Heidegger intends by *es gibt* but which is absent from the French usage of *il y a*. " 'There is' must not be confused with any generosity; it is not to be taken to mean that it 'gives' anything, as in the German 'there is/*es gibt*.' It [in this context, *khôra*] is nothing kindly and generous, and does not 'give' or provide a place, which is the trap that Heidegger falls into when he finds a 'giving' in this *es gibt* which puts thinking-as-thanking in its debt. Nor is it properly receiving, since it is unaffected by that by which it is filled. It is not even absolutely passive inasmuch as both active and passive operations take place in it. It resists every theomorphic or anthropomorphic analogy. It is not any kind of 'it' (*il, id, quod*) that is or does or gives anything." Caputo, *DN,* 94–95.

[47] Heidegger, *LH,* 238: "At the same time 'it gives' is used preliminarily to avoid the locution 'Being is'; for 'is' is commonly said of some thing that is. We call such a thing a being. But Being 'is' precisely not 'a Being.' "

[48] Derrida, *GT1,* 20.

[49] In "Time and Being" he often plays with the expression, frequently repeating "It gives Being" and "It gives time." Martin Heidegger, "Time and Being," *On Time and Being,* trans. Joan Stambaugh (New York: Harper and Row, 1972), 1–24, for example at 6 and 16 [hereafter Heidegger, *TB*].

[50] Derrida comments, with reference to Heidegger's *On Time and Being:* "From the beginning of the meditation, Heidegger recalls, if one can put it this way, that in itself time is nothing temporal, since it is nothing, since it is not a thing (*kein Ding*). The temporality of time is not temporal, no more than proximity is proximate or treeness is woody. He also recalls that being is not being (being-present/present being), since it is not something (*kein Ding*), and that therefore one cannot say either 'time is' or 'Being is,' but '*es gibt Sein*' and '*es gibt Zeit*.' It

purposes of this project, what can be made of the "it" that gives? To refer to Derrida once again, "the enigma is concentrated both in the 'it' or rather the '*es*,' the '*ça*' of '*ça donne*,' which is not a thing, and in this giving that gives but without giving anything and without anyone giving anything—nothing but Being and time (which are nothing)."[51]

It seems that there are three ways we might read the *es gibt*. One way is suggested by *Being and Time*. Here being is understood to be given by time, and therefore it could be said that *es gibt Sein* simply means that time gives being.[52] At this point in Heidegger's writing, the phrase is meaningful insofar as it is understood that being only becomes luminous in the concrete finitude of *Dasein*, and so is given according to the horizon of ecstatic temporality that is *Dasein*'s way of being.[53] A horizon is not an agent: time does not give being in the sense that it creates it, but is rather a condition of possibility for *Dasein's* transcendence toward it. Evidently this analysis can appear dependent on the initiative of *Dasein*, and Heidegger eventually moves away from this dependence, as he makes the famous *Kehre* from phenomenology to thought, "from There-Being to Being."[54] Thus the later Heidegger emphasizes

---

would thus be necessary to think a thing, something (*Sache* and not *Ding*, a *Sache* that is not a *being*) that would be Being and time but would not be either a being or a temporal thing." *GT1*, 20.

[51] Derrida, *GT1*, 20.

[52] This is anticipated on the very first page of Heidegger, *BT*.

[53] See the discussion by William J. Richardson, S.J., *Heidegger: Through Phenomenology to Thought* (The Hague: Martinus Nijhoff, 1963), 85–90 [hereafter Richardson, *HTPT*].

[54] Richardson, *HTPT*, 624. The notion of a turn can be somewhat misleading, and Heidegger himself understands his later work as continuous with the essential concerns of *Being and Time*. The preface by Heidegger that Richardson includes in his study emphasizes this sense of continuity. Richardson nevertheless accords with the judgment of many others that Heidegger's work involves two distinct phases, even if they are to be read as a unity. See Richardson's conclusion, especially at 623–28. See also the comment by David Farrell Krell in "General Introduction: The Question of Being," *Basic Writings: Martin Heidegger*, 33. The move is complicated by the fact that the thinking of being that Heidegger later attempts is still necessarily linked with *Dasein*. By way of explanation, Richardson suggests that "Heidegger's perspective from beginning to end remains phenomenological. By this we mean that he is concerned only with the *process* by which beings are lit up and reveal themselves as what they are for and to man. The lighting-process takes place in man—not through (sc. by reason of) him, yet not without him either. If the lighting-process does not take place by reason

the priority of being over *Dasein,* even though *Dasein* is the there that is necessary for thought. Thought is a yielding to being, the accomplishment of letting being be.[55] An additional problem with this first way of understanding the *es gibt* is that it does not take account of the giving of time as such, and we have already observed that this is to be a further factor in Heidegger's work.

Another way of reading the *es gibt* is suggested in the "Letter on Humanism," where Heidegger confirms that the "it" of "it gives" is being itself.[56] In other words, being gives itself, or being gives being. Again, such a pronouncement requires some interpretation. How exactly does being give itself? According to the ontology that Heidegger attributes both to the ancients and, in adapted form, to the medieval scholastics and the subsequent philosophical tradition, being gives itself as substantial presence:

> It will be manifest that the ancient way of interpreting the Being of entities is oriented towards the "world" or "Nature" in the widest sense, and that it is indeed in terms of "time" that its understanding of Being is obtained. The outward evidence of this . . . is the treatment of the meaning of Being as *παρουσια* [*parousia,* which the translators suggest is "being at," or "presence"] or *ουσια* [*ousia,* which would be "substance" in the Aristotelian tradition, or "essence," "existence," or "being" in the tradition of Plato], which signifies, in ontologico-Temporal terms, "presence" ["Anwesenheit"]. Entities are grasped in their Being as "presence"; this means that they are understood with regard to a definite mode of time—the *"Present."*'[57]

On Heidegger's reading, being is in this way modeled, as it were, on beings. Further, such an understanding often underlies the

of man, then the Light itself holds the primacy in the process; if it does not take place without him, then the There is necessary that the Light be able to light-up, and to that extent may be considered as projecting the light." Richardson, *HTPT,* 627. See also 532.

[55] Richardson, *HTPT,* 541.

[56] Heidegger, *LH,* 238. See also the translators' note at p. 255 of Heidegger, *BT:* "In his letter *Über den Humanismus* . . . Heidegger insists that the expression 'es gibt' is here used deliberately, and should be taken literally as 'it gives.' He writes: 'For the "it" which here "gives" is Being itself. The "gives," however, designates the essence of Being, which gives and which confers its truth.' " Macquarrie discusses this more fully in *HC,* 60.

[57] Heidegger, *BT,* 47.

transition that is frequently made from thinking being (as the being of entities) to thinking being as a being among beings, or even a being beyond and somehow behind beings.[58] This is what Heidegger uncovers as the difficulty, for example, in Christian metaphysics or Cartesian ontology.[59]

---

[58] "We said that ontology is the science of being. But being is always the being of a being. Being is essentially different from a being, from beings. How is the distinction between being and beings to be grasped? How can its possibility be explained? If being is not itself a being, how then does it nevertheless belong to beings, since, after all, beings and only beings *are*? What does it mean to say that being *belongs* to beings? The correct answer to this question is the basic supposition needed to set about the problems of ontology regarded as the science of being. . . . It is a distinction which is first and foremost constitutive for ontology. We call it the *ontological difference*—the differentiation between being and beings. . . . With this distinction between being and beings and the selection of being as theme we depart in principle from the domain of beings. We surmount it, transcend it. We can also call the science of being, as critical science, *transcendental science*. In doing so we are not simply taking over unaltered the concept of the transcendental in Kant, although we are indeed adopting its original sense and its true tendency, perhaps still concealed from Kant. We are surmounting beings in order to reach being. Once having made the ascent we shall not again descend to a being, which, say, might lie like another world behind the familiar beings. The transcendental science of being has nothing to do with popular metaphysics, which deals with some being behind the known beings." Heidegger, *BPP*, 17.

[59] With regard to the former, he comments: "Yet Being—what is Being? It is It itself. The thinking that is to come must learn to experience that and to say it. 'Being'—that is not God and not a cosmic ground. Being is farther than all beings and is yet nearer to man than every being, be it a rock, a beast, a work of art, a machine, be it an angel or God. Being is the nearest. Yet the near remains farthest from man. Man at first clings always and only to beings. But when thinking represents beings as beings it no doubt relates itself to Being. In truth, however, it always thinks only of beings as such; precisely not, and never, Being as such. The 'question of Being' always remains a question about beings. It is still not at all what its elusive name indicates: the question in the direction of Being. Philosophy, even when it becomes 'critical' through Descartes and Kant, always follows the course of metaphysical representation. It thinks from beings back to beings with a glance in passing toward Being. For every departure from beings and every return to them stands already in the light of Being." Heidegger, *LH*, 234. And with regard to Descartes, Heidegger is readily able to observe the confusion: "in this way of defining a substance through some substantial entity, lies the reason why the term 'substance' is used in two ways. What is here intended is substantiality; and it gets understood in terms of a character of substance—a character which is itself an entity. Because something ontical is made to underlie the ontological, the expression '*substantia*' functions sometimes with a signification which is ontological, sometimes with one that is ontical, but mostly with one which is hazily ontico-ontological. Behind this slight difference of signification, however, there lies hidden a failure to master the basic problem of Being." Heidegger, *BT*, 127.

Heidegger thinks of being as that which brings into presence but which itself withdraws.[60] Being "lights up" beings without becoming a being, since being "is" not, it "is" no-thing. In this sense, being is horizonal. "Being comes to destiny in that It, Being, gives itself. But thought in terms of such destiny this says: it gives itself and refuses itself simultaneously."[61] In answer, then, to the question about what it means that being gives itself, we could suggest that being gives itself as withdrawal. Being, which "is" no-thing, gives in a retreat from giving. Again, it is thought that provides the locus for this "letting-be," this gift of being. "In hailing the thinker into Being, Being imparts itself to him as gift, and this gift is what constitutes the essence of the thinker, the endowment by which he is."[62]

There is a further possible reading of *es gibt,* this time taking account of the material still later than the "Letter on Humanism," including the 1962 lecture "Time and Being." This reading does not exclude the others but perhaps allows them to be focused more precisely. In "Time and Being," Heidegger plays with the phrases "It gives Being" and "It gives time."[63] There is obviously still a relationship between the giving of being and the giving of time, but it is via a third "term," if such it can be called. This third term "is" *Ereignis,* which Heidegger says "will be translated as Appropriation or event of Appropriation."[64] Heidegger also indicates that " 'event' is not simply an occurrence, but that which makes any occurrence possible."[65] The event of appropriation gives being and gives time; it is the condition of possibility for being and time. It is the event of appropriation that establishes a relationship between being and the human.[66] The event of appropriation establishes a certain reciprocality between being and

---

[60] Richardson, *HTPT,* 315, 532–33.

[61] Heidegger, *LH,* 239.

[62] Richardson, *HTPT,* 599. "What is most thought-provoking gives food for thought in the original sense that it gives us over, delivers us to thought. This gift, which gives to us what is most thought-provoking, is the true endowment that keeps itself concealed in our essential nature. When we ask, then, 'What is it that calls on us to think?,' we are looking both to what it is that gives to us the gift of this endowment, and to ourselves, whose nature lies in being gifted with this endowment." Heidegger, *WCT,* 126.

[63] Heidegger, *TB,* 6, 16.

[64] Heidegger, *TB,* 19.

[65] Heidegger, *TB,* 19.

[66] See Joan Stambaugh's introduction to *On Time and Being,* x–xi.

time.[67] But appropriation "is" not, and is not itself given.[68] Derrida comments:

> This word *Ereignis,* which commonly signifies event, signals toward a thinking of appropriation or of de-propriation that cannot be unrelated to that of the gift. So from now on it will not be a matter of subordinating, through a purely logical inversion, the question of Being to that of *Ereignis,* but of conditioning them otherwise one by the other, one with the other. Heidegger sometimes says that Being . . . is *Ereignis.* And it is in the course of this movement that Being (*Sein*)—which is not, which does not exist as being present/present being—is signaled on the basis of the gift.
>
> This is played out around the German expression *es gibt,* which, moreover, in *Sein und Zeit* (1928) had made a first, discreet appearance that was already obeying the same necessity.[69]

On the third reading of *es gibt,* transcendent being is most clearly situated in its immanence.[70] There is no "being" somehow "beyond" the world, but only being given in the mode of withdrawal, in the event of appropriation.[71] Being "is" transcendent, but it is not a transcendent being. Heidegger speaks of "being as Appropriation," but what "is" this event of appropriation?[72] Once again, he struggles to express his intention. The event of appropriation is not an event in the usual sense of the word.[73] It is

[67] "[The process of] presenc-ing (Being) is inherent in the lighting-up of self-concealment (Time). [The] lighting-up of self-concealment (Time) brings forth the process of presencing (Being)." Heidegger, preface to Richardson, *HTPT,* xx.

[68] See Stambaugh's introduction to *On Time and Being,* xi.

[69] Derrida, *GT1,* 19.

[70] George Steiner comments that Heidegger's works "are an explicit rejoinder to what he calls the 'onto-theological' bias in Western thinking. Whereas the latter arrives, inherently, at the inference of the transcendent, at the attempt to locate truth and ethical values in some abstract 'beyond,' Heidegger's ontology is densely immanent. Being is being-in-the-world. There 'is' nowhere else. Being and authenticity can only be realized within immanent existence and time. For Heidegger, there is no divine sphere of immaculate ideation, no unmoved mover." George Steiner, *Heidegger,* 2nd ed. (London: Fontana, 1992), 63.

[71] "The matter at stake first appropriates Being and time into their own in virtue of their relation, and does so by the appropriating that is concealed in destiny and in the gift of opening out. Accordingly, the It that gives in 'It gives Being,' 'It gives time,' proves to be Appropriation." Heidegger, *TB,* 19.

[72] Heidegger, *TB,* 21.

[73] Heidegger, *TB,* 20.

instead "the extending and sending which opens and preserves."[74] It is the extending and sending of being.[75]

Of pertinence to this study is the way Heidegger speaks of thought as a thankful response to the gift.[76] It is important to note here not only the importance of the whole idea of giving in Heidegger's work, but also the way it is not to be characterized by reciprocity. In Heidegger's words:

> To the most thought-provoking, we devote our thinking of what is to-be-thought. But this devoted thinking is not something that we ourselves produce and bring-along, to repay gift with gift. When we think what is most thought-provoking, we then give thought to what this most thought-provoking matter itself gives us to think about. This thinking which recalls, and which *qua* thinking alone is true thanks, does not need to repay, nor be deserved, in order to give thanks. Such thanks is not a recompense; but it remains an offering; and only by this offering so we allow that which properly gives food for thought to remain what it is in its essential nature. Thus we give thanks for our thinking in a sense that is almost lost in our language. . . . When the transaction of a matter is settled,

[74] Heidegger, *TB,* 20.

[75] Caputo points out that the crucial feature of Heideggerian phenomenology is not so much that it uncovers ontological difference, but that it seeks to think difference itself, the meaning of the givenness of Being. See Caputo, *RH,* 178–79.

[76] See Heidegger, *WCT,* 139–47. "What gives us food for thought ever and again is the most thought-provoking. We take the gift it gives by giving thought to what is most thought-provoking. In doing so, we keep thinking what is most thought-provoking. We recall it in thought. Thus we recall in thought that to which we give thanks for the endowment of our nature—thinking. As we give thought to what is most thought-provoking, we give thanks" (145–46). The implications of this position are well described by Richardson: "Once we see that the original German word for thought (*Gedanc*) suggests re-cord, it is not difficult to understand in what sense it also implies thanks-giving (*Danken*). Being's supreme gift to the thinker is the very Being by which he *is* a thinker: ek-sistence. Does it not warrant acknowledgment on man's part? Such an acknowledgment in its purity, however, is not in the first place a requiting of this gift with another gift. On the contrary, the purest form of acknowledgment is simply the accepting of the gift, sc. assuming it, acquiescing in it, yielding to its demands. Acceptance, then, is the most original form of thanks. Now when There-being accepts the endowment by which the thinking comes about, sc. ek-sistence, it accepts the gift of thought as such. For There-being to accept thought as thought is to do what lies within its power to accomplish thought. This is by that very fact the fulfillment of thinking. Thinking thus conceived in the moment of fullfilment is clearly thanks-giving." Richardson, *HTPT,* 601.

> or disposed of, we say in Alemannic dialect that it is "thanked." Disposing does not mean here sending off, but the reverse: it means to bring the matter forth and leave it where it belongs. This sort of disposing is called thanking.[77]

It seems that Heidegger is concerned with the undervaluing of a gift by the offering of a gift in return. Rebecca Comay's insightful article "Gifts without Presents: Economies of 'Experience' in Bataille and Heidegger" provides a nuanced reading of this problem.[78] Comay maintains that the gratitude of thanking which is thought does not provoke a return of the gift, since in *Ereignis* the gift is at once sent and withheld. In other words, since the giving which is the sending is at the same time a losing which is the gift withheld, there "is" no gift as such that can be returned. Appropriation is expropriation; thinking is the thankful response to a gift that is no-thing.[79] "Thanking becomes simply the recursive, performative movement . . . which knows no object for its gratitude and thus has nothing with which to pay back."[80] The gift of being, in being withheld, can be given without return. With regard, then, to the questions about what is given in phenomenology and according to what horizon it is given, what is preeminently given for Heidegger is being (which "is" no-thing, and which withdraws in the giving), according to a temporal-historical horizon in the event of appropriation.

Derrida and Heidegger

The relationship between Heidegger and Derrida is a complex one: Derrida's work is enabled in some ways by that of Heidegger, yet he still engages deconstructively with Heideggerian texts.[81] De-

---

[77] Heidegger, *WCT,* 146.

[78] Rebecca Comay, "Gifts without Presents: Economies of 'Experience' in Bataille and Heidegger," *Yale French Studies* 78 (1990): 66–89 [hereafter Comay, *GWP*].

[79] Comay, *GWP,* 86.

[80] Comay, *GWP,* 89.

[81] Rodolphe Gasché underlines this complexity in *Inventions of Difference: On Jacques Derrida* (Cambridge: Harvard University Press, 1994), 78 [hereafter Gasché, *IDJD*]: "Although Derrida has claimed it to be indispensable, for instance, to place oneself within the opening of Heidegger's questions, he has also

rrida takes up Heidegger's critique of presence, to the point where he unravels the dream of full presence.[82] Yet Derrida is wary of other Heideggerian absolutes. The purity of presence may be tainted after Heidegger, but the possibility of an absolute truth lives on, unfolding as part of a destiny that is German but essentially Greek (or perhaps the reverse):[83]

> What I have attempted to do would not have been possible without the opening of Heidegger's questions. And . . . would not have been possible without the attention to what Heidegger calls the difference between Being and beings, the ontico-ontological difference such as, in a way, it remains unthought by philosophy. But despite this debt to Heidegger's thought, or rather because of it, I attempt to locate in Heidegger's text—which, no more than any other, is not homogenous, continuous, everywhere equal to the greatest force and to all the consequences of its questions—the signs of a belonging to metaphysics, or to what he calls onto-theology.[84]

---

been very critical on many occasions of Heidegger's philosophical idiom. But even this criticism, including Derrida's 'disseminative gesture,' is made, at least to a certain degree, in Heideggerian language."

[82] The extent to which Heidegger effectively overcomes presence is in question. Levinas, for example, argues that Heidegger "never really escaped from the Greek language of intelligibility and presence. Even though he spent much of his philosophical career struggling against certain metaphysical notions of presence—in particular the objectifying notion of presence as *Vorhandenheit* which expresses itself in our scientific and technological categorization of the world—he ultimately seems to espouse another, more subtle and complex, notion of presence as *Anwesen,* that is, the coming-into-presence of Being." Emmanuel Levinas in Richard Kearney, *Dialogues with Contemporary Continental Thinkers: The Phenomenological Heritage* (Manchester: Manchester University Press, 1984), 56 [hereafter Kearney, *DCCT*]. It is true, certainly, that there is an ambiguity in Heidegger with regard to his use of "presence" and "presencing."

[83] See John D. Caputo, *Demythologizing Heidegger* (Bloomington: Indiana University Press, 1993) [hereafter Caputo, *DH*].

[84] Jacques Derrida, *Positions,* trans. Alan Bass (Chicago: University of Chicago Press, 1981), 9–10 [hereafter Derrida, *Pos*]. "I believe, in numerous ways, what I write does not, shall we say, *resemble* a text of Heideggerian filiation . . . I have marked quite explicitly, in *all* the essays I have published . . . a *departure* from the Heideggerian problematic. This departure is related particularly to the concepts of *origin* and *fall.* . . . And . . . I have analyzed it as concerns time, 'the transcendental horizon of the question of Being,' in *Being and Time,* that is, at a strategically decisive point. This departure also, and correlatively, intervenes as concerns the value *proper* (propriety, propriate, appropriation, the entire family of *Eigentlichkeit, Eigen, Ereignis*) which is perhaps the most continuous and most difficult thread of Heidegger's thought." Derrida, *Pos,* 54.

One of these "signs of a belonging to metaphysics" is the Heideggerian emphasis on "gathering." "But take the example of Heidegger: well, it is at the moment in which what he calls 'ontological difference' or the 'truth of Being' seems to assure the most 'gathering' reading of philosophy that I believe it is urgent to question this very gathering, this presumption of unity, what it still excludes or reduces to silence."[85] Or in a different context, "One of the recurrent critiques or deconstructive questions I pose to Heidegger has to do with the privilege Heidegger grants to what he calls *Versammlung*, gathering. . . . Once you grant some privilege to gathering and not to dissociating, then you leave no room for the other, for the radical otherness of the other."[86]

Both the positive and the negative aspects of Derrida's relationship with Heidegger can be best illustrated for our purposes in the way Derrida reads the *es gibt*. An example of his reading can be taken from *Spurs: Nietzsche's Styles:*

> Heidegger . . . submits the question of Being itself to the enigmatic operation of the abyssal gift (*le don s'endette/le don sans dette*). In his development . . . of the *es gibt Sein* Heidegger demonstrates that the *giving* (*Geben*) and the *gift* (*Gabe*), which in fact amount to nothing (to neither a subject being nor an object being), cannot be thought of in terms of Being. Because they constitute the process of propriation, the *giving* and the *gift* can be construed neither in the bound-

---

[85] Jacques Derrida, *Points: Interviews, 1974–1994,* ed. Elisabeth Weber, trans. Peggy Kamuf et al. (Stanford: Stanford University Press, 1995), 131 [hereafter Derrida, *Po*].

[86] Jacques Derrida, "The Villanova Roundtable," in Caputo, *DN,* 3–48, 15 [hereafter Derrida, *VR*]. On the question of Heidegger and gathering, it seems to me that O'Leary's observations on the possible self-limitations of Heideggerian thought are highly relevant. See O'Leary, *TRSG.* O'Leary also, of course, questions "deconstruction's" preference for the other, asking whether or not this is just as unitary a reading of reality as Heidegger's. "Even the deconstructive version of the *Ereignis* as essentially difference, unless is it worked out in terms of a concrete pluralism, still risks projecting a unitary instance which undercuts all religions and philosophies as the unnameable other." O'Leary, *TRSG,* 246. The important point upon which O'Leary seizes here is the need for a working out "in terms of a concrete pluralism." The difficulty, as we shall see, is that unless it can in some way be concretized, all talk of otherness can tend to reduce what it aims to promote, the otherness in otherness, the plurality of othernesses. I think Derrida recognizes that alterity is only encountered in the concrete, and that is where, perhaps, a Derridean "ethics" is more effective than a Levinasian ethics.

> aries of Being's horizon nor from the vantage point of its truth, its meaning. Just as there is no such thing then as a Being or an essence of *the* woman or the sexual difference, there is also no such thing as an essence of the *es gibt* in the *es gibt Sein,* that is, of Being's giving and gift. The "just as" finds no conjuncture. There is no such thing as a gift of Being from which there might be apprehended and opposed to it something like a determined gift. . . . Still, it does not follow from this that one should, by a simple reversal, transform Being into a particular case or species of the genus *propriate,* give/take, life/death. Heidegger himself cautions against making of Being a mere incident in the event called *Ereignis* and warns of the futile nullity of a conceptual reversal of this sort between species and genus (*genre*).[87]

What is Derrida saying here? He seems to recognize that for Heidegger the *giving* of being escapes being: *Ereignis* cannot be read according to the measure of being; the giving is abyssal, without ground, beyond being and beyond the "truth of being." Heidegger would this way turn against his own metaphysical ambitions, as it were. The "process of propriation" that is *Ereignis* is in fact not anything. Caputo (quoting Derrida) comments:

> "Although this process is as if magnetized by a valuation or an ineradicable preference for the proper-ty (*propre*), it all the more surely leads to this proper-ty's abyssal structure" (*Spurs* 117). Although Heidegger is always talking about Being and *Ereignis,* he invariably ends up in a movement beyond Being, ground, presence, and truth, landing in an abyss (*Ab-grund*) of dis-propriation (*Ent-eignis*).[88]

The proper is the improper; the gift a withdrawal or loss. Caputo continues: "[Heidegger] sees the *Ent-eignis* in *Ereignis,* the dissimulation in all unveiling, what Derrida calls 'le coup de don,' striking by means of the gift, taking away by means of giving."[89]

But if we can follow Caputo's interpretation of Derrida on Heidegger further, it seems that Derrida is not entirely sure that Heidegger is willing to give up on the proper. Caputo suggests that Derrida is distracted by it, missing Heidegger's meaning:

---

[87] Jacques Derrida, *Spurs: Nietzche's Styles/Éperons: Les Styles de Nietzsche,* trans. Barbara Harlow (Chicago: University of Chicago Press, 1978), 120–21.

[88] Caputo, *RH,* 158.

[89] Caputo, *RH,* 158–59.

> *Ereignis* does not mean appropriation in the sense of the hotbed and seat of all propriety and ownness. It means *producing* ownness, sending things into their own, their proper shape in the various epochs, giving things (the Being-of-beings) the tenuous identity that is never insulated from difference. . . . It itself is beyond the distinction between proper and improper, identity and difference, because it grants these and all distinctions. It gives ownness and unownedness—and hence might be translated as "en-own-ing," endowing with ownness—just the way Dasein's "temporalizing" *gives* both authenticity and inauthenticity in *Being and Time,* grants them as effects. In my view, Derrida opens up this reading of Heidegger but then misses it himself.[90]

Caputo's reading would seem to be in accord with a later comment from Derrida, found in *Given Time.*[91] Once again, Derrida links *Ereignis* with a thinking of the gift. "This word *Ereignis,* which commonly signifies event, signals toward a thinking of appropriation or of de-propriation that cannot be unrelated to that of the gift."[92] Yet is it appropriation or de-propriation? In the forgetting, it is de-propriation, a de-propriation that enables the gift to take place.[93] But in the movement of appropriation, the gift can no longer be thought. "In the very position of this question, in the formulation of the project or the design of thinking, namely, the 'in order to' (we think 'in order to' . . . think Being and time in their 'own element' . . .), the desire to accede to the proper is already, we could say, surreptitiously ordered by Heidegger according to the dimension of 'giving.' "[94] It seems Derrida is arguing that Heidegger still *desires to accede to the proper,* and therefore to appropriate, with a thinking of donation that grasps rather than letting go. Where Derrida comments on the *es gibt,* he links it with propriation, and in so doing he reinforces his criticism of Heidegger in that the proper bespeaks ownership, thus is an attempt to seize the origin or even to be seized by it.[95]

---

[90] Caputo, *RH,* 178.

[91] Especially at Derrida, *GT1,* 18–23.

[92] Derrida, *GT1,* 19.

[93] "Forgetting and gift would therefore be each in the condition of the other." Derrida, *GT1,* 18.

[94] Derrida, *GT1,* 21.

[95] Maurice Blanchot's gloss is pertinent: "The donations which are the ways in which being gives by withholding itself . . . would be interrupted from the

Yet according to Caputo's reading, Derrida recognizes to some extent that Heidegger's propriation is not a possession but a being dispossessed. Derrida's writing is subject to the same deconstructive forces he observes elsewhere—an ambivalence that opens onto what Derrida may not mean to say.

All this is intriguing in the light of Gasché's comment on the relation between Heidegger's and Derrida's writing: ". . . so the thought of differance—the enabling and disabling structure of all thinking, the thinking of Being and the thinking of differance included—cannot strictly speaking be said to be Derrida's proper, or to be the result of a generalizing extrapolation from Heidegger's thought on difference."[96] What is Derrida's proper, and what is Heidegger's proper, and what does each writer have to say on the proper? There is a glimpse of the proper as abyss in Heidegger, which Derrida chooses to read as Heidegger's proper, and in so doing makes us aware of what is most not his own. Both Caputo and Gasché have further interesting comments to make on the thinking of difference and *différance*. If Heidegger's difference is to be understood only as the ontological difference, then there is room for Derrida to make his *différance* an "older" "indifference to difference."[97] But if Heidegger's difference itself precedes ontological difference, then the relationship between Derrida and Heidegger becomes even closer.[98]

It seems to me that the real difference between Heidegger and Derrida on *es gibt* comes down to the question of generosity, and this is brought out in Caputo's interpretation of the "Villanova Roundtable," written in the light of *Given Time*. Here Caputo points

---

moment that the *Ereignis,* the advent, arrives, ceasing to let itself be hidden by the 'donations of meaning' which it makes possible by its retreat. But if (since there is no other way of putting this) a decisive historical change is announced in the phrase 'the coming comes,' making us come into our 'most proper,' our 'own-most' (being), then one would have to be very naive not to think that the requirement to withdraw ceases from then on. And yet it is from then one [*sic*] that 'withdraw' rules—more obscurely, more insistently. For what of *eigen,* our 'own-most' being? We do not know, except that it refers back to *Ereignis,* just as *Ereignis* 'hides' *eigen* all the while showing it in a necessarily crude analysis." Maurice Blanchot, *The Writing of the Disaster,* trans. Ann Smock (Lincoln: University of Nebraska Press, 1995), 102 [hereafter Blanchot, *WOD*].

[96] Gasché, *IDJD,* 79. He refers also to Caputo.

[97] See Gasché, *IDJD,* chapter 3.

[98] See Caputo, *RH,* 179ff.

out that Heidegger fails on Derrida's terms with regard to the gift, no longer with direct reference to appropriation but to the appropriation that is implied once the gift is laden with generous intent:

> That gift without gift, without the swelling and contracting of gifting, could take place only if everything happened below the level of conscious intentionality, where no one intends to give anything to anyone and no one is intentionally conscious of receiving anything. Such austere, Grinch-like conditions are hardly met at all anywhere. Not even Heidegger's notion of the *es gibt das Sein* can meet this requirement, for Heidegger at once seizes upon the generosity embedded in the German idiom *es gibt* (*geben, die Gabe*), which is supposed to mean simply "there is." . . . On this account, the French idiom *il y a* is better and more "value-free," more neutral and indeterminate.
>
> What seems best to meet the demands of this ungenerous and ungrateful gifting is Plato's *khôra,* the absolutely indeterminate and indeterminable receptacle which cannot be determined as mother, nurse or receptacle, which is too un-kind, un-kin, and un-gendered, *a-genos,* to en-gender anything, which emblematizes or embodies (without a body) the pure "taking place" or "spacing" of *différance* itself.[99]

We are led, then, from *es gibt* back to *khôra* (and perhaps we should have half an eye at the same time to Blanchot's "neuter," or Levinas's *il y a*).[100] *Khôra,* however, opens onto many more themes than I can address at this point. With regard to the question of Derrida and *khôra,* I wish only to note at this stage that it does bear on the question of God and gift.[101] With this in mind, we turn to consider Levinas.

---

[99] Caputo, *DN,* 143; see also 94–95.

[100] With regard to the neuter, see Blanchot, *WOD,* 48–49, or 57, for example, or his *The Space of Literature,* trans. Ann Smock (Lincoln: University of Nebraska Press, 1982), 168–70 [hereafter Blanchot, *SL*]. I will discuss the Levinasian *il y a* in the next chapter.

[101] Hence, in "Sauf le nom": " 'God' is the name of this bottomless collapse, of this endless desertification of language. But the trace of this negative operation is inscribed *in* and *on* and *as* the *event.* . . . *There is* this event, which remains, even if this remnance is not more substantial, more essential than this God, more ontologically determinable than this name of God of whom it is said that he names nothing that is, neither this nor that. It is even said of him that he is not what is *given there* in the sense of *es gibt:* He is not what gives, his is beyond all gifts." Another voice responds to this passage, "*In* and *on,* you said, that implies, apparently, some *topos* . . . ," and the reply begins "— . . . or some *khôra* . . ." Derrida, *SLN,* 55–56.

3
Levinas

Levinas: A Dialogue with Husserl

The work of Emmanuel Levinas is important in this context for three reasons: first, because it is a dialogue with and a departure from the thinking of both Husserl and Heidegger; second, because it marks a further application and development of the phenomenological method; and third, because in each of the aforementioned respects it has had enormous influence on Jean-Luc Marion.[1] In my examination of Levinas I will order my comments according to these aspects of his relevance.

In 1930, Levinas produced *The Theory of Intuition in Husserl's Phenomenology,* in which he gives a largely favorable account of Husserl's development of the phenomenological method, although it is tempered with certain criticisms.[2] If Husserl's project has been to uncover that which has been given to consciousness, it is precisely on this area of givenness that Levinas concentrates his study, in a very particular way. For Levinas, it is the breadth of what is given that is important. In Husserl's work, Levinas finds a philosophical method that is potentially open to the given experience of life itself. At the same time, however, he discerns in the application of this method particular presuppositions that limit its efficacy, and it is on his concerns about these presuppositions

[1] With regard to Levinas and his relationship to phenomenology, see Kearney, *DCCT,* 50, where Levinas states: "Phenomenology represented the second, but undoubtedly most important, philosophical influence on my thinking. Indeed, from the point of view of philosophical method and discipline, I remain to this day a phenomenologist." Nevertheless, Levinas constantly goes beyond the boundaries of phenomenology, particularly as he seeks to place the encounter with "the Other" beyond what can be thematized, hence what can be "seen."

[2] Many commentators suggest that Levinas's reading of Husserl at this time is from a Heideggerian perspective, and that his criticisms are often Heideggerian in nature. See, for example, Adriaan Peperzak, *Beyond: The Philosophy of Emmanuel Levinas* (Evanston: Northwestern University Press, 1997), 40 [hereafter Peperzak, *B*].

that I will focus. These concerns have to do with the nature of intentionality, the question of representation, the process of intuition, the primacy of consciousness and perception, and the reduction of the other person (the Other) to the experience of "the Same."[3]

For Husserl, as for Franz Brentano before him, "intentionality" refers to the relationship between consciousness and its object; stated simply, consciousness is always consciousness of something.[4] But the crucial question is whether or not being conscious of something means that this something thus becomes an object of thematization. In other words, is all consciousness theoretical? This is the question that dominates Levinas's reading of Husserl.[5]

Levinas points out two ambiguities in Husserl's understanding of intentionality. There is initially an ambiguity that relates to Husserl's understanding of experience. Experience for Husserl is not primarily *Erfahrung* (experience in the sense that Derrida describes as a "movement of traversing"), but *Erlebnis,* which Husserl characterizes as "whatever is to be found in the stream of experience," or according to (the translation of) Levinas's trans-

---

[3] I will follow the approach adopted by some of Levinas's translators in rendering *autrui* as "the Other," meaning "the other person," and *autre* as "other." See Seán Hand's preface to *The Levinas Reader.*

[4] Levinas, *TIHP,* 37. Brentano himself takes up the idea from medieval theology. Peperzak describes the twofold nature of intentionality as "the *presence* of the object to consciousness or as the *presence* of consciousness to its objects." Peperzak, *B,* 41.

[5] What interests Levinas is that Husserl's understanding of intentionality seems to embrace the whole of life as it is lived, and not to artificially divide consciousness from its objects. "The most fundamental contribution of Husserl's phenomenology is its methodical disclosure of how meaning comes to be, how it emerges in our consciousness of the world, or more precisely, in our becoming conscious of our intentional rapport (*visée*) with the world. The phenomenological method enables us to discover meaning within our lived experience; it reveals consciousness to be an intentionality always in *contact* with objects outside of itself, other than itself. Human experience is not some self-transparent substance or pure *cogito;* it is always intending or tending towards something in the world which preoccupies it." Emmanuel Levinas, in Kearney, *DCCT,* 50. "Husserl propose l'intuition eidétique, l'intentionnalité, le primat de la conscience, 'le primat des essences inexactes, morphologiques, sur les essences exactes, mathématiques,' un *cogito* inséparable de son *cogitatum,* un *ego* subjugué par l'altérité dans l'intentionnalité qui est l'essence de la conscience et le fondement de la vérité." Marie-Anne Lescourret, *Emmanuel Levinas* (Paris: Flammarion, 1994), 84.

lation, "everything which takes place in the flow of consciousness."[6] Within experience as *Erlebnis,* Husserl includes sense data, or *hyle,* which need not themselves necessarily form intentional objects. This would mean that *hyle* could be described in Husserl's terms as "non-intentional" experience, according to a definition of intentionality as "consciousness of something." Sense data would therefore be that part of lived experience of which we were not (usually) consciously aware. Levinas observes, however, that Husserl eventually attributes even to *hyletic* elements the status of intentional objects, in the sense that they assume a transcendent meaning.[7] In this way, Husserl arrives at a conception of intentionality that is all-embracing. Experience (*Erlebnis*) becomes equivalent to intentionality as the self-transcending dynamic of consciousness. So the first aspect of ambiguity relates to the way that intentionality and experience are related. Are they one and the same? More precisely, does the fact that Husserl makes *hyletic* elements intentional objects expand intentionality to include what is not *theoretically* apprehended, or diminish experience to that which is thematized within it?

There is next an ambiguity that concerns Husserl's subsequent expansion of the idea of intentionality. Levinas explains that for Husserl, intentionality is "*what makes up the very subjectivity of subjects.*"[8] He then indicates that the types of objects toward which intentionality is directed can be different. "All the forms of our life, affective, practical, and aesthetic, are characterized by a relation to an object. . . . *Intentionality is different in each of these cases.* In each act the voluntary and affective elements are special ways of being directed toward an outside object, special ways of transcending oneself."[9] This is an important insight, because it

[6] Derrida, *Po,* 373; Husserl, *I1,* 120; Levinas, *TIHP,* 38.

[7] "We can distinguish in consciousness an animating act which gives to the hyletic phenomena a transcendent meaning: they signify something from the external world, they represent it, desire it, love it, etc. This act is an element which has a mode of existing identical to that of hyletic data, i.e., it is conscious and constituted in immanent time; it knows itself in the implicit manner which is characteristic of *Erlebnisse.* Yet it gives a meaning to the flow of consciousness. It intends something other than itself; it transcends itself." Levinas, *TIHP,* 39. Later Levinas suggests that "the hyletic data . . . are already constituted by a deeper intentionality proper to consciousness." *TIHP,* 47.

[8] Levinas, *TIHP,* 41.

[9] Levinas, *TIHP,* 43.

attributes meaning not only to things that can be grasped theoretically but also to values and desires. "We now see that concrete life must be taken in all its forms and not merely in the theoretical form. Correlatively, the real world is not simply a world of things correlative to perceptive acts (purely theoretical acts); the real world is a world of objects of practical use and values."[10] If Husserl now allows for different types of intentionality, he is allowing for a broader understanding of consciousness that does not equate with thematization.[11]

The examination of the nature of intentionality is related to the question of representation. Husserl's reading of representation (*Vorstellen,* an "experienced act of presentation") is such that in it consciousness objectifies its contents to itself.[12] Representations are defined by Husserl as "objectifying acts."[13] Yet this under-

[10] Levinas, *TIHP,* 44. Peperzak observes: "Husserl's renewal of philosophy through phenomenology can be summarized in the word 'intentionality.' He saw not only that all consciousness is a *cogito of* something (*cogitatum*), but also that the intentional structure of consciousness cannot be characterized as the relation between a representing subject and objects met by that subject. Feeling, walking, desiring, ruminating, eating, drinking, hammering, too, are intentions—or rather clusters of intentions, related in a specific, nonrepresentational way to specific correlates." Adriaan Peperzak, *To the Other: An Introduction to the Philosophy of Emmanuel Levinas* (West Lafayette, Ind.: Purdue University Press, 1993), 14 [hereafter Peperzak, *TTO*].

[11] Levinas develops this understanding of intentionality in "Intentionalité et métaphysique," *En découvrant l'existence avec Husserl et Heidegger,* 5th ed. (Paris: Vrin, 1967), 137–44. [hereafter Levinas, *EDEHH*]. This essay can be found in translation in Emmanuel Levinas, *Discovering Existence with Husserl,* trans. Richard A. Cohen and Michael B. Smith (Evanston: Northwestern University Press, 1998), 127–29.

[12] Levinas, *TIHP,* 57. This is in contrast to Brentano's view that representation means a neutral image of the intentional object appears in the consciousness. There are three German words that can be translated by "representation": *Darstellung* (presentation, sensible presentation, or "poetic presence"); *Vorstellung* (representation, which involves the internal representation of an image); and *Repräsentation* (material presentation, "the act of making present in a material and visual but not necessarily poetic sense"). See Azade Seyhan, *Representation and Its Discontents* (Berkeley: University of California Press, 1992), 7.

[13] Levinas, *TIHP,* 57. "The main model for every kind of intentionality is the perception, or even the vision, of an object which is there, facing consciousness as a *Gegenstand* (TIH, 135). The structure of the reflection through which consciousness knows itself is conceived of in analogy with the perception of external objects. In transcendental phenomenology, consciousness is studied as a sort of *Gegenstand,* while reflection, to which consciousness is given, is a sort of looking at something before it, a sort of *Vorstellung* (TIH, 184–85). The

standing of representation raises certain difficulties. If that of which I am conscious can only be that of which I can make an objective representation, then those experiences that defy such objectivity will also defy consciousness (and hence even experience itself). This seems an impracticable state of affairs, for surely consciousness is broader than specific, objective representations within it. Levinas overcomes this difficulty by making a distinction between "representation" and "having a sense." He gives the example of love: "The act of love has a sense, but this does not mean that it includes a representation of the object loved together with a purely *subjective* feeling which has no sense and which accompanies the representation. The characteristic of the loved object is precisely to be given in a love intention, an intention which is irreducible to a purely theoretical representation."[14]

While Husserl does not strictly confine the structure of intentionality to its representation of objects, Levinas observes within Husserl's work a tendency to emphasize this aspect of intentionality, thus relimiting what he has just expanded.[15] The second moment of ambiguity has been uncovered: there are for Husserl different types of intentionality, not all theoretical, but ultimately all coming back to the theoretical. In *Totality and Infinity,* Levinas makes his criticism plain: "The thesis that every intentionality is either a representation or founded on a representation dominates the *Logische Untersuchungen* and returns as an obsession in all of Husserl's subsequent work."[16] In the same passage, Levinas

---

'objective' (*gegenständliche*) mode of being is central for Husserl's phenomenology, and knowledge is understood on the basis of objectification; it is primarily *Vorstellung* or *representation.*" Peperzak, *B,* 41. See also John Llewelyn, *Emmanuel Levinas: The Genealogy of Ethics* (London: Routledge, 1995) [hereafter Llewelyn, *ELGE*], 77ff.

[14] Levinas, *TIHP,* 44–45.

[15] Levinas, *TIHP,* 53. "Although Husserl recognised the fact that, in addition to objectifying, presenting and representing intentions, consciousness is also constituted by affective and practical intentions, he maintained—at least in his earlier works—the primordial and exemplary role of the theoretical or doxic intentions. Notwithstanding his effort to purify consciousness from all contingent and particular features in order to reach a truly transcendental perspective, consciousness remained a panoramic view of a universe of presently given, remembered, or anticipated phenomena." Peperzak, *TTO,* 15.

[16] Emmanuel Levinas, *Totality and Infinity: An Essay on Exteriority,* trans. Alphonso Lingis (The Hague: Martinus Nijhoff, 1979), 122 [hereafter Levinas, *TI*].

goes on to ask: "What is the relation between the theoretical intentionality of the objectifying act, as Husserl calls it, and enjoyment?"[17] For Levinas, enjoyment is more fundamental than my ability to represent it. "Enjoyment is not a psychological state among others, the affective tonality of empiricist psychology, but the very pulsation of the I."[18] While Husserl explicitly states that the real world is what is experienced, and that this must include the aesthetic and the practical, his notion of representation as an "objectifying act" seems to favor the intellectualization of experience.[19] Intuition (the relationship between consciousness and ideas) becomes a purely theoretical act: everything is objectified.[20] Levinas alerts us to the problematic nature of this position, where even objects of the will "must have to some extent the mode of existence of theoretical objects."[21]

After discussing intentionality in general, Levinas turns to focus more specifically on the process of intuition itself, that aspect of intentionality "through which we enter into contact with being."[22] Husserl contrasts a "signifying act" (where "objects are meant without being given") with an "intuitive act" ("which reaches its object").[23] Levinas explains the difference as not concerning the degree of clarity, but having to do with whether or not the object is attained. "To say that intuition actualizes the mere intention which aims at the object is to say that in intuition we relate directly to the object, we reach it. That is the entire difference between aiming at something and reaching it. A signifying intention does not possess its object in any way; it only thinks it."[24] A signifying act—often, but not necessarily, a word—has a meaning, but its objective referent is not directly presented, and so its intention is "empty." Since a signifying act belongs only to the sphere of thought, it is possible that it might refer to something that is not real. On the other hand, an intuitive act encounters reality in *seeing* it. Nevertheless, signifying acts are not to be

[17] Levinas, *TI,* 122.
[18] Levinas, *TI,* 113.
[19] Peperzak, *B,* 41–43.
[20] Levinas, *TIHP,* 63.
[21] Levinas, *TIHP,* 63.
[22] Levinas, *TIHP,* 65.
[23] Levinas, *TIHP,* 65–66.
[24] Levinas, *TIHP,* 67.

discounted altogether.[25] Signifying acts on their own cannot be taken as knowledge, but when they encounter reality they become part of knowledge. This occurs where what is meant in the signifying intention is confirmed (or displaced) by an act of intuition.[26]

Husserl's understanding of intuition is completed in his idea of "fullness." When an object that is meant is also given, it has a fullness about it.[27] The word is used both to indicate the direct presence of the object to the consciousness and to indicate the contents of the intention that are present as a result of the presence of the object.[28] When the direct presence is by way of perception (i.e., a presentation), the fullness of the intention is exhibited in sensations.[29] When it is by way of memory or imagination (i.e., a re-presentation), the fullness of the intentional act is exhibited in phantasms. This leads Levinas to note the important role perception plays in Husserl's work: "Perception gives us being. It is through reflecting on the act of perception that we must seek the origin of the very notion of being."[30] It is also through reflecting on perception that we are able to speak of truth. When a signifying act corresponds with an act of intuition, it is fulfilled evidentially. "Evidence" refers to the presence of consciousness to being, and so being and truth originate in the same source.[31]

Levinas is keen to pursue any mention of intuition that occurs in valuing and willing. This possibility is raised in *Ideas 1,* where Husserl suggests that there can be "practical and axiological truths" in addition to theoretical truths.[32] Nevertheless, Husserl's

---

[25] Levinas, *TIHP,* 68–69.

[26] Levinas, *TIHP,* 74, 69.

[27] Levinas, *TIHP,* 69. "The central thought that self-givenness is the main form of being and that ideal knowledge is *adequacy* (i.e. the exact 'fitting' of the world into consciousness) is expressed in Husserl's theory of truth as the 'realization' or the fulfillment (*Erfüllung*) through intuition of the 'signifying' act which otherwise would remain empty, but also in the fundamental role of evidence for all knowledge and in Husserl's theory of judgement as the direct intuition of a more complex object." Peperzak, *B,* 41.

[28] Levinas, *TIHP,* 69.

[29] Levinas, *TIHP,* 70: "sensations are elements which, in life, represent objects, although only with the help of intentionality."

[30] Levinas, *TIHP,* 71. The reemergence of the ontological question in this way obviously points to disagreement with Heidegger.

[31] Levinas, *TIHP,* 75.

[32] Levinas, *TIHP,* 133.

analysis returns quickly to the priority of the theoretical, with his notion of "doxic theses."[33] According to this notion, even intuitions that are primarily nontheoretical must return to a theoretical point (the doxic thesis) before it can be asserted that the objects exist for consciousness.[34] Levinas locates here a possibility for phenomenology that seems to have been overlooked, that the given need not only be that which can be understood. What interests him is the possibility that there might be signification that gives meaning but which cannot be thematized as knowledge, and his detailed examination of the various elements of Husserl's work enables him to lay the groundwork for his own philosophical position. According to this position, vision (perception, theory, understanding, light) is unable to account for the richness and diversity of life as it is lived.[35] So Levinas lists three further objections to Husserl that are based around this central question: is it possible for phenomenology to reach, in reflection, life as it is, or only life as it is reflected in consciousness? Reflection naturally gives to life, Levinas suggests, a quality of "being reflected"; it seems cut off from the reality of life as it is being lived. The phenomenological reduction requires a step back that seems to

---

[33] Levinas, *TIHP,* 134: "This doxic thesis is the element of intentionality which . . . thinks of objects as existing."

[34] Levinas, *TIHP,* 134. Nevertheless, Peperzak notes a shift in Husserl's position: "Although in his *Ideen* Husserl stated even more clearly that the central place in knowledge is taken not by objectification and representation, but by 'lived experience' (*Erlebnis*), Levinas holds that Husserl continued to consider the objectifying acts to be fundamental. The doxic thesis is always included as the basic intention positing the existence of the meant object. Later on, however, Levinas puts the accent on Husserl's radical distinction between *meaning* (*Sinn, Seinsinn*) and *object,* a distinction effectively exploited by Heidegger, who thereby freed phenomenology from its representationist remnants." Peperzak, *B,* 42. The "later on" to which Peperzak refers is the 1940 essay "L'oeuvre d'Edmond Husserl," which appears in the collection *EDEHH,* 7–52. Of particular relevance are Levinas's comments at 23–24.

[35] Llewelyn comments: "In his placing of the ethical in the economy of being and in his placing of the economy of being in the non-economy of the ethical, Levinas will call into question the primacy of theory, that is to say of *theôria,* seeing." Llewelyn, *ELGE,* 57. Yet Llewelyn goes on to note the potential difficulty in Levinas's position when he constantly speaks of awakening, of the "opening of eyes." Llewelyn translates the Levinasian metaphor as a kind of "spiritual optics," or an "optics without synoptics" (58), which is complicated by Levinas's aural imagery. This leads to a problem when Levinas seeks to express the encounter with the Other.

cut across the experience it is designed to highlight, and seems removed from the empirical, the everyday, the historical.[36] Levinas then points out that the temporal structure of consciousness makes it impossible to grasp acts reflectively "in the present" (i.e., in all their fullness). Presentation is necessarily re-presentation.[37] Finally, he indicates that phenomena themselves occur differently in their immediately experienced state than in their state in reflection.[38]

Another aspect of Husserl's work that Levinas considers problematic is Husserl's emphasis on consciousness. Not only does Husserl not entirely clarify the nature of the reduced consciousness (in distinction from psychological consciousness), but he does not deal adequately with intersubjectivity.[39] While Husserl addresses the second question in the later text *Cartesian Meditations,* Levinas will also find his treatment there problematic, since it seems Husserl reduces the other person to the experience of the ego.[40] In *Totality and Infinity,* Levinas describes the problem:

> The constitution of the Other's body in what Husserl calls "the primordial sphere," the transcendental "coupling" of the object thus constituted with my own body itself experienced from within as an "I can," the comprehension of this body of the Other as an *alter ego*—this analysis dissimulates, in each of its stages which are taken as a description of constitution, mutations of object constitution into a relation with the Other—which is as primordial as the constitution from which it is to be derived.[41]

---

[36] Levinas, *TIHP,* 142: "The natural attitude is not purely contemplative; the world is not purely an object of scientific investigation. Yet it seems that man *suddenly* accomplishes the phenomenological reduction by a purely theoretical act of reflection upon life." See also Levinas, *TIHP,* 119; Peperzak, *B,* 43.

[37] "Levinas isolates a further set of problems in Husserlian phenomenology arising from the privilege it accords to presence, the present and representation. . . . Like Derrida in *La Voix et le phénomène,* Levinas submits the texts of phenomenology to thorough close examination and finds in them a fundamental contradiction: whilst predicated on the privilege of presence, they also imply that presence is originally fissured, that it is never fully possessed. The key notion of representation thus also becomes problematic: an object which is not present to itself cannot easily be re-presented to a transcendental Ego whose own self-presence is insecure." Colin Davis, *Levinas: An Introduction* (Cambridge: Polity Press, 1996), 19–20 [hereafter Davis, *LAI*]. See also Llewelyn, *ELGE,* 48ff.

[38] Levinas, *TIHP,* 137.

[39] Levinas, *TIHP,* 150–51.

[40] Husserl, *CM;* see especially Meditation Five.

[41] Levinas, *TI,* 67.

What emerges as the chief focus of Levinas's work is the thinking of this relation to the Other, this "relationless relation," which Levinas places prior to conscious thematization. In working out this relation, Levinas encounters some difficulty with the word "experience" (*l'expérience*): from his broad and inclusive sense of experience, which contrasts with Husserl's narrower, theoretical sense, Levinas moves to a more limited sense when it comes to referring to the encounter with the Other.[42]

To sum up Levinas's consideration of Husserl, it could be said

---

[42] "The epiphany of the Other subordinates the world of phenomena and experiences to responsibility. Insofar as we have learned the meaning of the words 'phenomenon,' 'experience,' 'manifestation,' 'truth,' etc., within the context of Western egology, they are all marked by the 'egonomic' mode of being described above. As an intruder into this world, the Other, or the Infinite, can neither be described as an object of our knowledge, nor as a phenomenon in the proper sense of the word. The supreme demand is not 'experienced' as a 'presence' and, in its complete difference from any observable figure, the face is *invisible.*" Peperzak, *B,* 14. "Both Kant and Levinas refuse to call the revelation of the Other's respectability an 'experience' (*Erfahrung, expérience*), because it cannot be understood as a perception ruled by the conditions of empirical schematism or phenomenological fulfillment, but for both thinkers that revelation is an exceptional sort of awareness, from which all philosophy should start." Peperzak, *B,* 199. Note that Peperzak suggests *Erfahrung* rather than *Erlebnis.* Yet Levinas also describes the encounter with the Other as "experience *par excellence.*" Levinas, *TI,* 109. See Llewelyn, *ELGE,* 85. Hart suggests that "Levinas proposes a way beyond romanticism by aligning experience and presence [and] then distinguishing experience and epiphany." Kevin Hart, "The Experience of Poetry," *Boxkite: A Journal of Poetry and Poetics* 2 (1998): 285–304, 291 [hereafter Hart, *EP*]. In other words, Levinas moves beyond speaking of the relation to the Other as experience, or at least heavily qualifies it. "The relation with infinity cannot, to be sure, be stated in terms of experience, for infinity overflows the thought that thinks it. Its very *infinition* is produced precisely in this overflowing. The relation with infinity will have to be stated in terms other than those of objective experience; but if experience precisely means a relation with the absolutely other, that is, with what always overflows thought, the relation with infinity accomplishes experience in the fullest sense of the word." Levinas, *TI,* 25. Yet see also the 1965 essay "Enigma and Phenomenon," in *Basic Philosophical Writings,* ed. Adriaan T. Peperzak, Simon Critchley, and Robert Bernasconi (Bloomington: Indiana University Press, 1996), 65–77 [hereafter Levinas, *EP*], where, for example, when Levinas speaks of God, he says: "The impossibility of manifesting itself in an experience can be due not to the finite or sensible essence of this experience but to the structure of all thought, which is correlation" (67). In "Truth of Disclosure and Truth of Testimony" (1972), published in the same collection (98–107), Levinas observes: "My responsibility for the other is precisely this relation with an unthematizable Infinity. It is neither the experience of Infinity nor proof of it: it *testifies* to Infinity" (103).

that Levinas's work rests on the very possibilities that Husserl to a large extent leaves unthought, while putting in question the foundations upon which Husserl's project is built—the certainty, the self-presence of the *cogito*. Levinas may continue to call himself a phenomenologist, but he abandons the phenomenological bias toward seeing in favor of a more radical "hearing" of a call to responsibility that comes from the Other.[43] Resisting the reduction of experience exclusively to the theoretical, Levinas maintains that theoretical consciousness does not and cannot envelop the given.

Levinas and Heidegger

Levinas initially embraces Heideggerian thought, particularly as a response to the lack he perceives in Husserlian phenomenology of a relation to life as it is lived, to existence.[44] But Levinas's attitude toward Heidegger changes as he observes the way phenomenology as ontology not only provides a positive possibility for approaching questions about embodied existence but also becomes with Heidegger a negative, all-encompassing strategy for grasping life in understanding.[45] This view of Heideggerian ontology is, perhaps, not uninfluenced by Heidegger's political forays in the 1930s, and by the sense evident in many of Heidegger's

[43] On hearing and prophecy, see Marc Richir, "Phénomène et Infini," *Emmanuel Levinas,* ed. Catherine Chalier and Miguel Abensour, Cahier de L'Herne (Paris: L'Herne, 1991), 241–61, 254–55.

[44] Levinas, *EDEHH,* 72: "la philosophie dans son fond n'est pas une connaissance contemplative au sujet de laquelle il y aurait lieu de se poser des questions de méthode préalablement, mais que, conformément à l'ontologisme de Heidegger, elle est, dans son essence la plus intime, la possibilité d'une existence concrète" ("[that] philosophy in its depth is not a contemplative knowledge on the subject of which we should firstly ask questions of method, but that, according to the ontologism of Heidegger, it is, in its most intimate essence, the possibility of a concrete existence"). Levinas positively evaluates the work of the early Heidegger in his reflections in Kearney, *DCCT,* 51–52: "I would say, by way of summary, that if it was Husserl who opened up for me the radical possibilities of a phenomenological analysis of knowledge, it was Heidegger who first gave these possibilities a positive and concrete grounding in our everyday existence; Heidegger showed that the phenomenological search for eternal truths and essences ultimately originates in *time,* in our temporal and historical existence."

[45] See the discussion by Peperzak, *B,* 49ff.

writings that the question of being is intimately linked with the destiny of the German nation.[46] Yet it is expressed most powerfully not in any personal attack on Heidegger and National Socialism, but in a philosophical (or quasi-philosophical) attack on the totality and neutrality of being.[47]

If Levinas rejects what he sees in Husserl as a tendency to reduce experience to knowledge or objectivity, he no less rejects what he sees in Heidegger as a tendency to absorb all meaning in ontology, an ontology that ultimately always comes back to the subject.[48] Expressed in the terms introduced in the first chapter of this book, the totality of being to which Levinas refers might also be known as the economy of being, where all is understood according to the horizon of "is-ness."[49] In other words, where being becomes the horizon against which all else is to be judged, and judged in terms of critical thought, then that which cannot be seen in those terms is overlooked, reduced, or ignored.[50] For

[46] With regard to Heidegger's political leanings, see Hugo Ott, *Martin Heidegger: A Political Life,* trans. Allan Blunden (London: Fontana, 1994). With regard to the philosophical implications of Heidegger's political thought, see Caputo, *DH.*

[47] With regard to Levinas on Heidegger and National Socialism, most commentators seem to advert to the criticism but are only able to substantiate it indirectly. See Peperzak, *B,* 204–5. Levinas did recently republish a brief article, "1933–1934: Thoughts on National Socialism: Reflections on the Philosophy of Hitlerism," trans. Seán Hand, *Critical Inquiry* 17 (1990–91): 62–71, although this does not help us a great deal.

[48] Levinas writes: "The well-known theses of Heideggerian philosophy—the preeminence of Being over beings, of ontology over metaphysics—end up affirming a tradition in which the same dominates the Other." Emmanuel Levinas, "Philosophy and the Idea of the Infinite," in Peperzak, *TTO,* 105. Peperzak's commentary on this text, particularly on Levinas's relation with Heidegger, is excellent at pp. 100–101. "The visage of being that shows itself in war is fixed in the concept of totality, which dominates Western philosophy. Individuals are reduced to being bearers of forces that command them unbeknown to themselves. The meaning of individuals (invisible outside of this totality) is derived from the totality. The unicity of each present is incessantly sacrificed to a future appealed to to bring forth its objective meaning. For the ultimate meaning alone counts; the last act alone changes beings into themselves." Levinas, *TI,* 21–22.

[49] On Levinas and economy, see Llewelyn, *ELGE,* 67–69. Levinas writes extensively on the "home" in *Totality and Infinity.*

[50] Llewelyn notes the importance of understanding what Levinas means by ontology: "In *Totality and Infinity* he asserts repeatedly that he is distinguishing

Levinas, "exemplifying" (if it could) that which cannot be seen in terms of being and comprehension is the Other.[51] Totalization and the possibility of its exception raises for Levinas the question of ethics, and he asserts that it is the ethical, arising in my responsibility for the Other, that precedes ontology. That Heidegger does not speak of ethics is, for Levinas, a crucial flaw in his thinking. "We therefore are also radically opposed to Heidegger who subordinates the relation with the Other to ontology (which, moreover, he determines as though the relation with the interlocutor and the Master could be reduced to it) rather than seeing in justice and injustice a primordial access to the Other beyond all ontology."[52] What Heidegger sees as a positive plenitude (*es gibt Sein*), Levinas comes to see as a suffocating totalitarianism.[53] This perspective emerges in Levinas's early texts, such as *De l'évasion,*

---

ontological structures or ways of being. Unless one grasps that when Levinas asserts this he is continuing a tradition to which Heidegger belongs, one will be perplexed as to how that book can be so critical of ontology. There is no reason why Levinas should not make ontological criticisms of fundamental ontology. But the ontology he defends in that book is not fundamental ontology in what he takes to be the sense ontology has in *Being and Time.* Levinas's ontology calls into question the fundamentality of the 'ontological difference,' the distinction between being and beings, between the ontological and the ontic, upon which *Being and Time* takes its stand. As previously noted, Levinas's ontology stands for the ontological significance of concrete empirical, hence ontic, experience. Whether or not Heidegger does too is not a question we shall reopen here." Llewelyn, *ELGE,* 108. See also chapter 1 of *ELGE,* which Llewelyn entitles "Ontological Claustrophobia."

[51] "In Heidegger coexistence is, to be sure, taken as a relationship with the Other irreducible to objective cognition; but in the final analysis it also rests on the relationship with *being in general,* on comprehension, on ontology. Heidegger posits in advance this ground of being as the horizon on which every existent arises, as though the horizon, and the idea of limit it includes and which is proper to vision, were the ultimate structure of relationship. Moreover, for Heidegger intersubjectivity is a co-existence, a *we* prior to the I and the other, a neutral intersubjectivity." Levinas, *TI,* 67–68.

[52] Levinas, *TI,* 89.

[53] "If we seek, in abstraction from Others and from the self that I always am, to describe the '*il y a*' that precedes all phenomena, what we find is not at all a generous and illuminating origin, but rather the anonymity of a dark, chaotic, and directionless rumbling without any structure or shape. Light and order proceed not from this 'Being,' but from something else: from the Other, the stranger who comes from afar, from an unreachable unknown, whose visage illuminates the world. The human Other's look is the origin of all meaning." Peperzak, *B,* 212.

De l'existence à l'existant, and *Le temps et l'autre,* particularly where (in the latter two) he explores the malevolence of Being in his phenomenological sketches of the *il y a.*[54]

One such sketch emerges in the context of a description of the experience of insomnia. Insomnia is a confrontation with the *il y a,* an experience of watchfulness for no purpose. In insomnia, I am "held by being": I find it onerous to be.[55] I do not intend any particular object, but there is a presence that I sense. "This presence which arises behind nothingness is neither *a being,* or consciousness functioning in a void, but the universal fact of the *there is,* which encompasses things and consciousness."[56] Levinas draws a distinction between attention and vigilance. In the former, the subject has internal or external objects in focus. In the latter, the subject loses its subjectivity: there are no objects, there is no freedom, there is no inside or outside, there is simply unyielding presence.[57] He notes the anonymity which this presence engenders. "It is not that there is *my* vigilance in the night; in insomnia it is the night itself that watches."[58] The I becomes object, rather than subject—it is depersonalized. This contrasts with consciousness, which "is precisely the breakup of the insomnia of anonymous being, the possibility to 'suspend,' . . . to take refuge

---

[54] Emmanuel Levinas, *De l'évasion* (Montpellier: Fata Morgana, 1982); Levinas, *EE;* Levinas, *Le temps et l'autre,* 5th ed. (Paris: Presses Universitaires de France, 1994) [hereafter Levinas, *TA*]. See the discussion by Davis, *LAI,* 22–24.

[55] Levinas, *EE,* 65.

[56] Levinas, *EE,* 65.

[57] "That does not come down to say that it is an experience of nothingness, but that it is as anonymous as the night itself." Levinas, *EE,* 65.

[58] Levinas, *EE,* 66. This is reminiscent of the "experience" described by Maurice Blanchot in the novel *Thomas l'Obscur,* new ed. (Paris: Gallimard, 1950), for example at 50–51: "Déjà, alors qu'il se penchait encore sur ce vide où il voyait son image dans l'absence totale d'images, saisi par le plus violent vertige qui fût, vertige qui ne faisait pas tomber, mais l'empêchait de tomber et qui rendait impossible la chute qu'il rendait inévitable, déjà la terre s'amincissait autour de lui, et la nuit, une nuit qui ne répondait plus à rien, qu'il ne voyait pas et dont il ne sentait la réalité que parce qu'elle était moins réelle que lui, l'environnait. Sous toutes les formes, il était envahi par l'impression d'être au coeur des choses. Même à la surface de cette terre où il ne pouvait pénétrer, il était à l'intérieur de cette terre dont le dedans le touchait de toutes parts. De tout parts, la nuit l'enfermait. Il voyait, il entendait l'intimité d'un infini où il était enserré par l'absence même des limites." Blanchot began the novel in 1932, that is, before Levinas's description of the *il y a.*

in oneself so as to withdraw from being."[59] In trying to describe the *il y a,* Levinas encounters a methodological difficulty. For the experience of the *il y a* lies both beyond phenomena and beyond the intuiting ego, and hence defies phenomenological description. Nevertheless, he suggests that we are sometimes able to glimpse ourselves divested, as it were, of subjectivity. In deliriousness or madness "we can surprise this impersonal 'consciousness' into which insomnia sinks."[60]

Levinas's use of the *il y a* is all the more interesting in the light of its relationship (or non-relationship) to the *es gibt,* since, as I have previously indicated, *es gibt* is frequently translated into French as *il y a* rather than *ça donne.* He distinguishes *il y a* strongly from its Heideggerian counterpart.[61] Why so? Why does Levinas say that "it has never been either the translation, or the marking down of the German expression and of its connotations of abundance and of generosity." Is it because he is simply not speaking of the same phenomenon (being)? Or is it because he wishes to characterize that phenomenon so differently? I am inclined to favor the latter interpretation.[62] And if it is the case that the source of plenitude or gift is not being (as the *il y a*) but what escapes being (the Other), then this does away with the Heideggerian orientation of donation altogether. It remains to be seen, nevertheless, whether or not it is possible to speak of what escapes

---

[59] Levinas, *EE,* 65.

[60] Levinas, *EE,* 67.

[61] "Une négation qui se voudrait absolue, niant tout existant—jusqu'à l'existant qu'est la pensée effectuant cette négation même—ne saurait mettre fin à la 'scène' toujours ouverte de l'être, de l'être au sens verbal: être anonyme qu'aucun étant ne revendique, être sans étants ou sans êtres, incessant 'remue-ménage' pour reprendre une métaphore de Blanchot, *il y a* impersonnel, comme un 'il pleut' ou un 'il fait nuit.' Terme foncièrement distinct du 'es giebt' [*sic*] heideggerien. Il n'a jamais été ni la traduction, ni la démarque de l'expression allemande et de ses connotations d'abondance et de générosité." Levinas, *De l'existence à l'existant,* 2nd ed. (Paris: L'édition du poche, 1990), 10.

[62] This is supported by a comment from Peperzak: "[Levinas] is not at all convinced of the generosity that other thinkers hear in '*Es gibt,*' and prefers to stress the dark, threatening, and chaotic side of the indeterminate *il y a.*" Peperzak, *B,* 167. It is also supported by Marion in *ID,* in the quote from that work at 283 which I used earlier: "Ou plutôt du es gibt, que nous traduisons—ou plutôt ne traduisons pas—par un il y a, où manque justement la connotation du *Geben,* du *donner.*"

being. In sum, contrary to Heidegger, Levinas puts forward the thesis that the history of philosophy has been dominated by ontology, and that the project of ontology is doomed to failure.[63] Instead of following the ontological path, Levinas suggests that we pursue a genuine metaphysics, one that has an eye, or perhaps an ear, for transcendence and the ethical.

A Levinasian Metaphysics

Levinas characterizes metaphysics as a radical aiming at exteriority (transascendence), an exteriority that is beyond our theoretical comprehension, beyond the realm of being and of knowledge, beyond what can be reduced to the Same.[64] This exteriority is transcendent, but it is not a transcendent object. Levinas claims that intentionality, "where thought remains an *adequation* with the object," is not the primary operation of consciousness.[65] By way of illustration, he indicates that there are many occasions when intentionality encounters a frustrating resistance in its quest to reduce all otherness to the Same. These areas of resistance include subjectivity itself (and here Levinas demonstrates the failure even of the phenomenological method he frequently employs), the Other, the future, death, the Infinite, and God. Levinas will seek to show that all these areas have a meaning that is irreducible to conscious experience. He will seek to show that

[63] Levinas, *TI*, 21ff.

[64] Levinas, *TI*, 28–29. "The metaphysical movement is transcendent, and transcendence, like desire and inadequation, is necessarily a transascendence." *TI*, 35. Levinas takes the term "transascendence" from Jean Wahl, as he acknowledges in the accompanying footnote. Wahl's influence on Levinas is significant, especially with regard to "the metaphysical experience," as Levinas makes clear in the essay "Jean Wahl: Neither Having nor Being," *Outside the Subject*, trans. Michael B. Smith (London: Athlone Press, 1993), 67–83. Levinas notes, for example, Wahl's speaking of "[a] disproportion to oneself that concretely signifies subjectivity: desire, quest, dialectic. But a dialectic without synthesis: without repose, without totality, without closure, without conclusion" (74); or that "Wahl's metaphysical experience is the *beyond* before the *here;* before the *here,* and farther away than any yonder that could be posited as another *here*" (75). *The Metaphysical Experience* is the title of one of Wahl's publications (Paris: Flammarion, 1965).

[65] Levinas, *TI*, 27.

the beyond being can signify, without our thereby grasping it in knowledge. In so doing, he will be repeatedly forced to recognize that speaking about the beyond being involves using the language of being. Therefore, in Levinas's work we find ourselves in a constant tension between saying and unsaying. In trying to say the *otherwise than being,* it must also be unsaid.[66] I will proceed by focusing on the question of signification as it relates to subjectivity, the Other, and God.

With regard to subjectivity, it seems there have been numerous attempts to establish its firm foundation. Consistent in many of these attempts has been the equation of subjectivity with self-consciousness, with presence to self. And yet subjectivity still seems elusive. The notion of subjectivity is now prone to the same critique to which other metaphysical concepts have recently been exposed. So we find that in contemporary terms, subjectivity is self-deconstructing.[67] Is it still possible to ask about the identity of the subject? A reading of Levinas would suggest that it is, provided we are prepared to relinquish the idea that subjectivity rests secure in self-presence.[68] According to Levinas, the origins of subjectivity lie prior to consciousness, in immemoriality. Subjectivity is never present at its own origin; it is not self-constituting.[69] Levinas arrives at this principle by way of an analysis of time, and he expresses it in three interconnected ways.

Especially in his earlier works, Levinas speaks of the hypostasis

---

[66] Levinas, *OBBE,* 7. Levinas adverts here to his ongoing conversation with Derrida on the problems of using language to specify what cannot be specified. See Kearney, *DCCT,* 64.

[67] See Simon Critchley and Peter Dews, eds., *Deconstructing Subjectivities* (Albany: SUNY Press, 1996) [hereafter Critchley and Dews, *DS*]; and Eduardo Cadava, Peter Connor, and Jean-Luc Nancy, eds., *Who Comes After the Subject?* (London: Routledge, 1991) [hereafter Cadava et al., *WCAS*].

[68] Levinas here responds to Husserl, who, as we have seen, places a great deal of weight on self-presence and therefore self-identity. But the distinction between identity and self-identity, which will be observed in the ensuing discussion of Levinas on subjectivity, is also a Heideggerian distinction. Heidegger distinguishes *identisch* from *selbig.* His translators point out that the two words mean virtually the same thing in ordinary German, but they seem to mean in Heidegger "identical" and "selfsame," respectively. In this way Heidegger is able to reinforce his distinction between the authentic and the inauthentic self. See Heidegger, *BT,* 150, 168. See also Martin Heidegger, *Identity and Difference,* trans. Joan Stambaugh (New York: Harper and Row, 1969).

[69] With thanks to Michael Fagenblat for his explanation in this regard.

of the subject in its emergence from impersonal being.[70] The event of hypostasis involves the taking up of being: the I becomes an ego or posited subject through taking a position. In other words, Levinas suggests a duality between the ego and the self. Because of the time lag that occurs as the ego takes up the self, the ego is always slightly out of step with itself. Another way in which Levinas asserts that the subject is not self-constituting comes out of his criticism of Husserl's notion that all acts of intuition ultimately involve some form of doxic representation. Levinas maintains that the priority attributed to theoretical consciousness does not give an adequate account of aesthetic and practical intuition. In *Totality and Infinity* he speaks of an irreducible basis of affectivity or bodiliness, an enjoyment of life or a

[70] "Hypostasis, an existent, is a consciousness, because consciousness is localised and posited, and through the act without transcendence of taking a position it comes to being out of itself, and already takes refuge in itself from Being in itself." Levinas, *EE,* 83. What does Levinas mean by this taking of a position? Llewelyn discusses hypostasis extensively in *ELGE* at 27–50. Peperzak (discussing *OBBE*) observes: "In Levinas' view, Spinoza, Hegel, Heidegger, and their numerous followers, reduce the subject to the anonymous essence, of which they are only functions, instead of recognizing the subject as 'sub-stance' or *hypostasis* whose self cannot be lost in Being. The description of *hypostasis* was already a central topic in Levinas' first book, *From Existence to Existents.* In later works, the expression does not frequently occur, but the separation between the subject—who is 'me' as well as 'ego'—and Being, remains a basic thesis. The difference between Saying and Said is a new way of stressing that separation: in Saying the subject expresses its nondialectical difference from Being, that is, from all that can be gathered in the Said." Peperzak, *B,* 117. I find Peperzak's comments helpful, although they do not explain the *how* of hypostasis. Levinas's discussion with Philippe Nemo in *Ethique et infini* (1982; Paris: Livre de poche, 1996), 37–43, suggests that Levinas is not entirely comfortable with his early attempts to discuss the separation of the I from impersonal Being. There he speaks of a later strategy, where less than the subject positioning itself, it is constituted as dispossessed in responsibility for the Other. This makes a certain amount of sense, in that individuation is always at the cost of becoming responsible, and so of being "dispossessed." Becoming an *I* is always about finding oneself already "there," or already having been "thrown," to use Heidegger's word. The split of which Levinas speaks is a valid one, and it could as easily be seen in Derrida's idea that the subject can never be present to itself. In Levinas perhaps it is not so much a matter of escaping the *il y a*—as if we could be fully separate from it—but only of finding oneself precariously suspended in it. This interpretation would accord, I think, with a reading of *EE.* Another point to note in passing is that the *il y a* has a sense of immemoriality to it, and this must lead to some confusion in making any identification of a trace or a call.

suffering need that always precedes conscious contemplation.[71] Yet bodiliness is still not the distinctive basis of my identity. A third means of illustration occurs in Levinas's treatment of the failure of phenomenology to observe the genesis of consciousness. In Husserl's phenomenology, and in a very particular sense, consciousness is constitutive of the world. But can consciousness constitute itself? Despite his best efforts to maintain that it can and does, Husserl is always left with a "primal impression," an irreducible residue of subjectivity.[72] Levinas will focus on this residue as an indication that subjectivity exceeds the boundaries of knowledge and being.[73] We are left with an approach to subjectivity that rests on diachrony, on a disturbance in time, a rupture. The ego is never perfectly synchronized with the self, is never present to itself, and does not constitute itself. My subjectivity is both immemorial in origin and invested in me from beyond me. This insight enables Levinas to make two important claims: that subjectivity is created and that my subjectivity is only awakened by the other person.

Immemoriality is frequently observed in any one of three forms in Levinas: as diachrony, as anachronism, or as the immemorial past.[74] As early as *Existents and Existence,* Levinas speaks of effort taking on "the instant, breaking and tying back together again the thread of time," the "knot" of the present, or "the engagement in being on the basis of the present, which breaks, and then ties back, the thread of infinity."[75] These images form the basis of Levinas's understanding that the present is never a pure present, but always interrupted by the past and the future. Synchrony is a dream: there is only diachrony. Nevertheless, diachrony is not simply a device that mimes the Heideggerian temporal ecstases. Through it, Levinas wants to refer not to "the past" that can be recuperated by memory in the present, but to a past "which has

---

[71] "Life is *love of life,* a relation with contents that are not my being but more dear than my being: thinking, eating, sleeping, reading, working, warming oneself in the sun." Levinas, *TI,* 112.

[72] See Ricoeur's discussion in *HAP,* especially at 110ff.

[73] Levinas, *OBBE,* 32–34.

[74] See Kevin Hart, *The Dark Gaze: Maurice Blanchot and Friends* (forthcoming).

[75] Levinas, *EE,* 33, 78, 99.

never been present." He asks: "But how, at the still temporal breaking point where being *comes to pass,* would being and time fall into ruins so as to disengage subjectivity from its essence?"[76] In other words, the past of which Levinas wishes to speak is a past where there can be no memory, a more "original" past than the simple past. "There must be signaled a lapse of time that does not return, a diachrony refractory to all synchronization, a transcending diachrony."[77] This is the immemorial past.[78] Immemoriality is behind the idea that the ego is always out of step with itself, at its very origin.[79] It has the meaning of a past that has never been present either to me or to anyone else. But immemoriality also has to do with my relationship with the Other. The Other is the locus of the call to responsibility that constitutes me, a call that is itself immemorial. "In consciousness, this 'who knows where' is translated into an anachronical overwhelming, the antecedence of responsibility and obedience with respect to the order received or the contract."[80] In this sense, immemoriality is also transcendental. Yet further, the Other can never be present to me, and in this way immemoriality assumes the sense of a past that has never been present *to me.* There are thus three names for immemoriality and three possibilities for understanding it, each of which, I believe, is valid at different moments in Levinas's work. The immemorial is the rupture in my own present by my irretrievable origin; it is the transcendental call of the Other that constitutes me at that irretrievable origin; and it is what characterizes my relationship to the Other, whose present (and whose past) escapes me irretrievably.

To return to the question of subjectivity, if the origin of subjectivity is immemorial, how can it signify? If the origin of subjectivity

---

[76] Levinas, *OBBE,* 9.

[77] Levinas, *OBBE,* 9.

[78] Levinas, *OBBE,* 24: "A past more ancient than any present, a past which was never present and whose anarchical antiquity was never given in the play of dissimulations and manifestations, a past whose *other* signification remains to be described, signifies over and beyond the manifestation of being, which would thus convey but a moment of this signifying signification."

[79] "In the identity of self-presence—in the silent tautology of the prereflexive—lies an avowal of difference between the same and the same, a disphasure, a difference at the heart of intimacy." Emmanuel Levinas, "Philosophy and Awakening," in Cadava et al., *WCAS,* 212.

[80] Levinas, *OBBE,* 13.

is prior to consciousness and irrecuperable by memory, can I speak of identity? Levinas's answer is that it is my responsibility for the Other that makes me unique. Prior to my consciousness, prior to my freedom, and in my utter passivity, the Other invests me with subjectivity by calling me to responsibility.[81] I only become *I* in responding "Here I am" to the Other who calls. Subjectivity signifies as responsibility, as my substitution for the Other as a hostage.[82]

We turn now to consider in more detail what Levinas has to say about the other person.[83] Fundamental is the sense that the Other is utterly transcendent. While much of Western philosophy tends to think of the Other in terms of the Same, that is, as an alter ego who is accessible by way of empathy or by virtue of their equality with me, Levinas makes absolute the distance of alterity. I simply cannot grasp the Other in knowledge, for the Other is infinite and overflows the totality of comprehension and of being. Infinity is "given" in my experience of the Other as utterly beyond and in excess of me. Who the other person "is" can never be present to me: our presents are never synchronous. At one stage Levinas suggests that the Other inhabits a future I can never reach, and this seems to be an effective way of describing the relationship.[84] But in his later works, he tends to focus on the past dimension of diachrony, perhaps because he wishes to emphasize the priority of the Other as the one who invests me with subjectivity. It may also be because he wishes to distance himself from Heidegger, who emphasizes the future in temporal ecstasis.[85] What are we to

---

[81] See, for example, Levinas, *OBBE,* 10.

[82] See Levinas, *OBBE,* 135.

[83] I have indicated above that Levinas distinguishes between *autre* and *autrui,* a distinction that is rendered in translation as other/Other. But Levinas also distinguishes between *même* and *autre,* the same (often the first person) and the other, and it is difficult to translate this "other."

[84] See Levinas, *TA,* and the excerpt in Hand, *The Levinas Reader,* 45. Derrida speaks of "the movement and time of friendship" as an "undeniable future anterior, the absolute of an *unpresentable* past as well as a future." Jacques Derrida, *Politics of Friendship,* trans. George Collins (London: Verso, 1997), 249–50 [hereafter Derrida, *PF*]. The link between future and immemorial past is made well here.

[85] Emmanuel Levinas, "The Trace of the Other," *Deconstruction in Context,* ed. Mark C. Taylor (Chicago: University of Chicago Press, 1986), 345–59, 346 [hereafter Levinas, *TO*].

make of this absolute transcendence? The difficulty it suggests is how the Other, completely unknowable, can nevertheless signify to me at all. Moreover, there is the problem of how I, presumably an Other for Another, signify for that Other. How does the space of our "relationless relation" function?[86]

Levinas uses two mechanisms to work out the problem of the signification of the Other, and these basically correspond to the chronology of his two major works, *Totality and Infinity* and *Otherwise Than Being or Beyond Essence.* In *Totality and Infinity,* the Other signifies in the face. The face of the Other operates in Levinas's thought like a valve. Its phenomenality is always exceeded by its removal to transcendence. He suggests this removal when he speaks of the trace in the face: it is a removal beyond being to a third order that is neither presence nor absence but otherness. Levinas calls this third order *illeity.* [87] When things are given to me in vision, I exercise power over them. But this is not so with the face, which cannot be encompassed. The alterity of the Other is not just relative, as though we were different but somehow inhabiting the same plane. And further, this alterity does not just negate the I, since such negation would again imply our mutual existence within a larger relation. Instead, the Other proceeds as an epiphany that comes to me from utterly elsewhere.[88] The Other is completely otherwise, and this difference is evinced in speech.

Here we find the beginnings of an alternative model of signifi-

---

[86] Levinas, *TI,* 80: "a relation without relation."

[87] "[A] trace signifies beyond being. The personal order to which a face obliges us is beyond being. *Beyond being is a third person,* which is not definable by the oneself, by ipseity. It is the possibility of this third direction of radical *unrightness* which escapes the bipolar play of immanence and transcendence proper to being, where immanence wins against transcendence. Through a trace the irreversible past takes on the profile of a 'He.' The *beyond* from which a face comes is in the third person. The pronoun *He* expresses exactly its inexpressible irreversibility, already escaping every relation as well as every dissimulation, and in this sense absolutely unencompassable or absolute, a transcendence in an ab-solute past. The *illeity* of the third person is the condition for the irreversibility." Levinas, *TO,* 356. See Mark C. Taylor's discussion of the trace in *Altarity* (Chicago: University of Chicago Press, 1987), 205. On Derrida's "trace," see Geoffrey Bennington, in Geoffrey Bennington and Jacques Derrida, *Jacques Derrida* (Chicago: University of Chicago Press, 1993), 74–75.

[88] Levinas, *TI,* 194.

cation, the one Levinas developed more fully in response to criticisms that "the face" was too phenomenal a device to refer us to transcendence, which is presented in *Otherwise Than Being*.[89] In that work, Levinas speaks more of the proximity of the Other in Saying, rather than the Other's face.[90] According to the "proximity" model, I am exposed to the Other. "Responsibility for the other, in its antecedence to my freedom, its antecedence to the present and to representation, is a passivity more passive than all passivity, an exposure to the other without this exposure being assumed, an exposure without holding back, exposure of exposedness, expression, saying."[91] Exposure is "saying uncovering itself."[92] In the exposure of proximity, the Other signifies through Saying. Language relates separated terms without reducing them to the Same: through words the Other can appear to be thematized, but in speaking the Other at the same time evades this thematization.[93] The Other to whom I ascribe meaning will always contest that meaning.[94] As soon as I convert the Other's Saying into an intelligible Said, I have already corrupted the epiphany. While I can have a relationship with the Other in discourse, I do not thereby compromise the Other's absoluteness. Whereas in representation I have power

---

[89] This is Derrida's criticism in "Violence and Metaphysics" [hereafter Derrida, *VM*], in Derrida, *WD*, 79–153. See also Peperzak, *TTO*, 136.

[90] Peperzak suggests the move in *TTO*, 181–82, 212, and in *B*, 80. Something of the connection between paths can be observed in Levinas's comment: "A trace is sketched out and effaced in a face in the equivocation of a saying." *OBBE*, 12. In that work, an entire chapter is devoted to the question of proximity (61ff.).

[91] Levinas, *OBBE*, 15.

[92] Levinas, *OBBE*, 15. See also Peperzak, *TTO*, 221.

[93] Levinas uses the Saying/Said distinction in *TI*, for example: "To the one the other can indeed present himself as a theme, but his presence is not reabsorbed in his status as a theme. The word that bears upon the Other as a theme seems to contain the Other. But already it is said to the Other who, as interlocutor, has quit the theme that encompassed him, and upsurges inevitably behind the said." Levinas, *TI*, 195. But it is much more important for him in *OBBE*. See, for example, 34–51.

[94] "The formal structure of language thereby announces the ethical inviolability of the Other and, without any odor of the 'numinous,' his 'holiness.' " Levinas, *TI*, 195. "The said, contesting the abdication of the saying that everywhere occurs in this said, thus maintains the diachrony in which, holding its breath, the spirit hears the echo of the *otherwise*." Levinas, *OBBE*, 44.

over the Other, in discourse the Other puts me in question.[95] The Other remains an enigma rather than becoming a phenomenon.[96]

While proximity and Saying resolve to some extent the difficulties involved with the face, the question of how I encounter the Other still remains. For Levinas wants to say that I do not inhabit the same space as the Other: the Other does not belong to the economy of Being.[97] So in Levinas's work we find that there is an emphasis on the asymmetry of the relationship.[98] The Other is always above me. "Height" is an important metaphor for Levinas: "For Desire this alterity, non-adequate to the idea, has a meaning. It is understood as the alterity of the Other and of the Most-High. The very dimension of height is opened up by metaphysical Desire. That this height is no longer the heavens but the Invisible is the very elevation of height and its nobility."[99] Levinas speaks of "curved space": "this curvature of the intersubjective space inflects distance into elevation; it does not falsify being, but makes

[95] "For the ethical relationship which subtends discourse is not a species of consciousness whose ray emanates from the I; it puts the I in question. This putting in question emanates from the other." Levinas, *TI,* 195. "To maintain that the relationship with a neighbor, incontestably set up in saying, is a responsibility for the neighbor, that saying is to respond to another, is to find no longer any limit or measure for this responsibility, which 'in the memory of man' has never been contracted, and is found to be at the mercy of the freedom and the fate, unverifiable by me, of the other man. It is to catch sight of an extreme passivity, a passivity that is not assumed, in the relationship with the other, and, paradoxically, in pure saying itself. The act of saying will turn out to have been introduced here from the start as the supreme passivity of exposure to another, which is responsibility for the free initiatives of the other. Whence there is an 'inversion' of intentionality which, for its part, always preserves before deeds accomplished enough 'presence of mind' to assume them. There is an abandon of sovereign and active subjectivity." Levinas, *OBBE,* 47. The "inversion of intentionality" of which Levinas speaks here will be most significant when it comes to Jean-Luc Marion.

[96] See Levinas, *EP,* especially the introduction to the essay by Robert Bernasconi, who observes Levinas's increased awareness of the problem of presence and ontology and his use of the device of immemoriality.

[97] On Levinas and economy, see *TI,* 175ff.

[98] Levinas, *TI,* 215.

[99] Levinas, *TI,* 34–35. "The being that presents himself in the face comes from a dimension of height, a dimension of transcendence whereby he can present himself as a stranger without opposing me as an obstacle or an enemy." Levinas, *TI,* 215.

its truth first possible"; "this 'curvature of space' expresses the relation between human beings."[100] In other words, the Other is removed from me by virtue of a curvature of space that prevents my "apprehension" (read comprehension) of him or her. According to such an image, and adapting Levinas's own metaphor of prophecy, I could hear the voice of the Other without "seeing" the Other. Yet such absolute asymmetry is problematic because it leaves no prospect for my own alterity for the Other. It breaks down the possibility of any general application of Levinas's thinking. And this is exactly how Levinas desires it to be, emphasizing my own, always greater, share of the responsibility. There can be no reciprocity. While Levinas develops a different mechanism for the functioning of a community and the need for justice (based on a "third" person), the meeting with the Other only works one way.[101] Perhaps the idea of absolute asymmetry is well suited to the contemplation of God, but it does not sit easily in the human context. Far better would be Maurice Blanchot's doubly curved space of "double dissymmetry."[102]

Turning, then, to the question of God, for Levinas meaningful speech about God tests the limits of philosophy. God signifies beyond philosophy. And yet, that does not mean the language of faith is any more helpful. The beyond being is not simply the realm of faith, and it is certainly not accessible by way of a negative theology, for negative theology is still tied to being even as its

---

[100] Levinas, *TI,* 291.

[101] Levinas, *OBBE,* 16: "The act of consciousness is motivated by the presence of a third party alongside of the neighbor approached. A third party is also approached; and the relationship between the neighbor and the third party cannot be indifferent to me when I approach. There must be a justice among incomparable ones. There must then be a comparison between incomparables and a synopsis, a togetherness and contemporaneousness; there must be thematization, thought, history and inscription."

[102] See Maurice Blanchot, *The Infinite Conversation,* trans. Susan Hanson (Minneapolis: University of Minnesota Press, 1993), 73 [hereafter Blanchot, *IC*]: *"The neutral relation, a relation without relation, can be indicated in yet another manner: the relation of the one to the other is doubly dissymmetrical. We have recognised this several times. We know—at least in one sense—that the absence between the one and the other is such that the relations, if they could be unfolded, would be those of a non-isomorphic field in which point A would be distant from point B by a distance other than point B's distance from point A; a distance excluding reciprocity and presenting a curvature whose irregularity extends to the point of discontinuity."*

absence presupposes a presence. For Levinas, both faith and philosophy are bound to ontology.[103] He opposes Infinity to the totality of being, and when he speaks about God, it is in terms of Infinity. Picking up Descartes's "Idea of the Infinite," Levinas posits that it breaks up consciousness, that it exceeds the capacity of consciousness to contain it, and that it defies the grasp of intentionality.[104] The idea of God also functions in this way.

When Levinas speaks of the idea of the Infinite, we may be less than convinced by his apparently Cartesian argument that it is introduced into thought. This surely sounds like a lapse into a proof for the existence of God, and while Levinas disputes that he is interested in proofs, if the Infinite *is* God, then we have come no further in Levinas than in Descartes. However, some important distinctions may enable us to continue with Levinas. These are distinctions that can be made between transcendence, the Transcendent (or transcendental signified), and the transcendental. The first term (transcendence) is the opposite of immanence, and so means that which lies beyond myself or is irreducible to personal experience. The second term (the Transcendent) is related to the first, in that the Transcendent is that which lies beyond consciousness. But it has been capitalized to suggest its difference from simple transcendence: the Transcendent is that which is not only not reducible to immanence, but is posited as beyond the world as such. (In Kant's sense, the [T]ranscendent is that beyond the limits of any possible experience.) The Transcendent thus easily becomes another name for God. It

[103] "A religious thought which appeals to religious experiences allegedly independent of philosophy already, inasmuch as it is founded on experience, refers to the 'I think,' and is wholly connected on to philosophy." Levinas, *GP,* 172.

[104] "It is not the proofs of God's existence that matter to us here, but the break-up of consciousness, which is not a repression into the unconscious, but a sobering up or an awakening, jolting the 'dogmatic slumber' which sleeps at the bottom of every consciousness resting on its object. The idea of God, the *cogitatum* of a *cogitatio* which *to begin with* contains that *cogitatio, signifies the non-contained par excellence.* Is not that the very absolution of the absolute? It overflows every capacity; the 'objective reality' of the *cogitatum* breaks up the formal reality of the *cogitatio.* This perhaps overturns, in advance, the universal validity and primordial character of intentionality. We will say that the idea of God breaks up the thought which is an investment, a synopsis and a synthesis, and can only enclose in a presence, re-present, reduce to presence or let-be." Levinas, *GP,* 173.

might be possible to relate Derrida's "transcendental signified" to this definition of the Transcendent, since when God is thought as the Transcendent, it is often to make possible and to guarantee the operation of "the system" from a point external to it. The third term (the transcendental) is to be understood with a Kantian-Derridean inflection (and is used in distinction from the "transcendentals" of medieval theology). The transcendental in Kant's sense is that which "establishes, and draws consequences from, the possibility and limits of experience."[105] The transcendental in Derrida's sense (to which we should rightly refer as the quasi-transcendental) is the condition of possibility and impossibility for meaning, which, without delaying further with the details here, is infinite interpretability.

The point of making these distinctions is to help in identifying what is going on in Levinas's work. Is he, in suggesting that God signifies in the Infinite, (a) affirming belief in God as the Infinite (the Transcendent causes the idea of the Infinite), or (b) suggesting that God may or may not be the source of the Infinite (the experience of the Infinite is given in transcendentality, and so its origin cannot be conclusively determined)? It seems to me that he is taking the latter option, which puts the Transcendent in question without removing it as an option for faith. There is no guarantee of the divine origin of the idea, no question of proof, no definite slippage from transcendentality to the transcendental signified, although it might be said that Levinas does move between transcendentality and God as utterly transcendent, if not the Transcendent. As we have seen, Levinas wants to indicate that the totality of being is interrupted by being's "otherwise," Infinity. And since to speak outside the realm of being is to speak outside the realm of any sort of proof, all we are left with phenomenally is the experience of interruption. So when Levinas says that the idea of the Infinite overflows consciousness, it is not that he can define the content of the Infinite, but only that he can locate a resistance to intentionality. Levinas will say that the Infinite signifies as a trace, as a mark of erasure that is suggestive but which proves nothing.[106] With regard to the question of God, then, it

[105] *The Cambridge Dictionary of Philosophy,* ed. Robert Audi (Cambridge: Cambridge University Press, 1995), 807.

[106] See Levinas, *TO,* 356–59.

seems to me that Levinas is saying that if we want to speak of God, the language of Infinity is the only one remotely available to us. As it happens, the language of Infinity or of God will refer us back to infinite relationships between people, which Levinas describes as religion.[107] But the Infinite may or may not be God. If we use Derrida's terms, it is undecidable. Further, it can as easily be introduced into consciousness by way of the Other as by God.[108] The origin of the idea rests in the same primal scene as the origin of our subjectivity. It is immemorial. So when Levinas says that we are created, and this he does frequently, he never specifies the source of that creation.

Is it possible to have a relationship with the Infinite? Levinas will answer yes, although it will be a relationship that has no ground and no goal. It will be a relationship characterized by desire, an infinite desire that cannot find satisfaction in an Infinite term. It will involve, on our part, a movement of transcendence, but not a movement that will reach the Transcendent.[109] How then does the Infinite signify, if not as the Transcendent goal of our desire? In my judgment the Infinite signifies in two ways. It signifies in the other person, as illeity, as desirability, as a trace. And it signifies in me, as goodness, as ethics, as kenotic love. This will require some explanation. If I may address the second point first, that the Infinite signifies in me, it will be easier to explore how the Infinite signifies in the Other.

The signification of the Infinite in me occurs as the conversion of desire. Although "conversion" is not a word that Levinas himself uses, I find it quite helpful in trying to understand the process he describes. My desire is for the Infinite. But the Infinite cannot be obtained in desire, for that would reduce it to immanence.

---

[107] While in relationship the distance between the self and the Other is traversed, it is still maintained as distance. In conversation, the egoism of the I remains, but the right of the Other over me is recognized in apology. Totality is fractured not through the exercise of thought as such, but through the encounter with the face and through speech. The connection that is so formed Levinas calls "religion." This connection, in which the Other is able to remain completely other, resists too the totalization of history. See Levinas, *TI,* 40.

[108] See the *avant propos* to Emmanuel Levinas, *De Dieu qui vient à l'idée,* 2nd ed. (1986; Paris: Vrin, 1992), especially at 11–12. See also Levinas, *GP,* 179ff., where he reworks his ideas starting from proximity.

[109] See Levinas, *GP,* 177.

My desire must therefore become disinterested: I must desire the Infinite without desiring it. How is that possible? It is possible only if my desire is converted. This conversion occurs when my desire for the Infinite becomes desire for what Levinas says is "the undesirable par excellence—the Other."[110] My substitution for the Other, my love for the Other, which Levinas insists is "without Eros" and which we might suggest is thus kenotic, my ethical response to the Other—this is the meaning of goodness.[111] Thus we are enabled to explain why Levinas also refers to the Infinite as "the Good beyond Being." The Infinite signifies in goodness. In the Infinite we are referred to the Good.

There is no doubt that we will hear echoes of Christian theology here, and I am not altogether sure that Levinas, although Jewish, wishes to exclude them. In fact, Levinas frequently quotes from the New Testament. And the richness of his own scriptural tradition shows itself in his subsequent discussion of what we would identify as theological themes: glory, witness, inspiration, and prophecy. He tells us: "The subject as a hostage has been neither the experience nor the proof of the Infinite, but a witness born of the Infinite, a modality of this glory, a testimony that no disclosure has preceded."[112] In my responsibility for the Other, I can never be responsible enough. My responsibility increases asymptotically: as I am called to empty myself more completely, to substitute myself for the Other more fully, the glory of the Infinite is amplified. Levinas insists that inspiration, or prophecy, is the way the Infinite passes in the finite, and in passing, constitutes my very psyche immemorially. My awakening to subjectivity, which is an ethical response to the cry of the Other, bears witness to the glorious passing of the Infinite, testimony prior to disclosure.[113]

The signification of the Infinite in the Other occurs as illeity. Illeity indicates the way that the face of the Other opens onto Infinity: the reference it contains to the third person suggests not that we are to think of the Infinite *as* a third person *behind* the

---

[110] Levinas, *GP*, 177. Note that "autrui" in the French text indicates that the Other is indicated, rather than the "other" given in the translated version.

[111] Levinas, *GP*, 178.

[112] Levinas, *GP*, 182.

[113] Levinas, *GP*, 184.

Other, but that in the third person, Infinity passes in the Other. Levinas tells us: "We have designated this way for the Infinite, or for God, to refer, from the heart of its desirability, to the non-desirable proximity of Others, by the term 'illeity.' " By illeity, Levinas invokes "the *he* in the depth of the you," the desirable in the undesirable.[114] In this way we see that the two moments of signification are joined. The Infinite signifies both in the conversion of my desire and in what we might call, with some reservations, a conversion of desirability.

The passing of the Infinite in the finite can only ever signify as a trace. It is immemorial: it will always already have passed when we are able to advert to it.[115] The Infinite is never present to us, never in range of proof, never able to be grasped in knowledge. That it is God who has passed as the Infinite will ultimately be a question for faith. According to Levinas, if we are able to speak of God, then ethics is the meaning to which we might refer, not because ethics is a practical replacement for spiritual commitment, but because it is in the heart of ethics that God signifies. For Levinas there is no other way to desire God than in desiring the Other, for whom I am utterly responsible.

After such a long excursus on the thought of Levinas, what might be said specifically on Levinas and the questions of what is given, and according to what horizon? Levinas both continues and departs from the tradition he inherits from Husserl. Both emphasize the givenness of phenomena, but Levinas wants to allow for the possibility of phenomena that are not given according to any horizon. Further, this exclusion of any horizon against which, for example, the Other is given, means that Levinas rejects the Heideggerian emphasis on being's ultimacy. Consequently, being is not seen as the source of all goodness and plenitude, even as it gives itself. Instead, Levinas refers us to "the good beyond being" (Plato's *to agathon epekeina tes ousias*). With regard to the possibility of a signification that cannot be reduced to the

---

[114] Levinas, *GP*, 178.

[115] "Immemorial" here will be in the sense of relationally immemorial—God is never present *to me* as such. But we could think the passing of God as transcendentally immemorial as well, if we choose to suggest that the call to responsibility might come from God and therefore might constitute me. This would be in accord with Levinas's thinking of "creatureliness."

dimensions of any horizon, Levinas utilizes the figures of the trace, the Saying, the immemorial, and the Infinite to suggest meaning without comprehension. Additionally, he emphasizes not the visual (usually associated with understanding) but the aural (rich with connotations of prophecy): this is perhaps behind his move from the signification of the face to the signification of the Saying.

Derrida and Levinas

To hear Derrida speak of Levinas is to hear him speak with the greatest reverence of someone whose influence upon him has been immeasurable.[116] That is not to say that Derrida is not also critical of Levinas's work, but it is clear that, especially insofar as Levinas seeks to embrace the ethical, Derrida has come to think in solidarity with him.[117] In the course of my discussion of Levinas I have already made several references to Derrida, and I wish to limit my discussion here to two interrelated points, each arising in "Violence and Metaphysics." I would like to consider the general idea of a "beyond" in Levinas and how this might be read by Derrida. Then I would like to consider one of the specific criti-

---

[116] Derrida, *Ad,* 16: "je voudrais seulement rendre grâce à celui dont la pensée, l'amitié, la confiance, la 'bonté' . . . auront été pour moi, comme pour tant d'autres, une source vivante, si vivante, si constante, que je n'arrive pas à penser ce qui lui arrive ou m'arrive aujourd'hui, à savoir l'interruption, une certaine non-réponse dans une réponse qui n'en finira jamais pour moi, tant que je vivrai" ("I would like only to thank the one whose thought, friendship, confidence, 'goodness' . . . will have been for me, as for so many others, a living source, so living, so constant, that I can't think what happens to him or to me today, that is to say the interruption, a certain non-response in a response which will never end for me, as long as I live"). The admiration goes both ways: see Levinas's essay on Derrida in *Proper Names,* trans. Michael B. Smith (London: Athlone Press, 1996) [hereafter Levinas, *PN*].

[117] Derrida initially sees that deconstruction threatens ethics. See the discussion in *La Communication* (Montréal: Edition Montmorency, 1973), 426. Yet he comes to see an ethical bent in deconstructive activity itself. See, for example, Simon Critchley, *The Ethics of Deconstruction: Derrida and Levinas* (Oxford: Blackwell, 1992) [hereafter Critchley, *EDDL*]; or Critchley's essay "Derrida: Private Ironist or Public Liberal?" *Deconstruction and Pragmatism,* ed. Chantal Mouffe (London: Routledge, 1996), 19–40 [hereafter Mouffe, *DP*]. See also the discussion by Richard Kearney in "Derrida's Ethical Return," *Working Through Derrida,* ed. Gary B. Madison (Evanston: Northwestern University Press, 1993), 28–50.

cisms he makes of Levinas concerning the signification of the face.

Thinking beyond any horizon necessarily implies thinking something according to a newer horizon. Could it be said of Levinas that in thinking beyond being he simply reinscribes a further horizon for the given, the horizon of the good or the ethical? This criticism has several dimensions. It relates to Levinas and the use of horizons, and as we have seen, Levinas tries to avoid thinking in horizonal terms. With his allusion to "curved space," he tries, I suspect, to give the sense that the Other cannot be framed by any horizon. In *Totality and Infinity* he observes: "Since Husserl the whole of phenomenology is the promotion of the idea of *horizon,* which for it plays a role equivalent to that of the *concept* in classical idealism; an existent arises upon a ground that extends beyond it, as an individual arises from a concept."[118] And he includes Heidegger, who "posits in advance this ground of being as the horizon on which every existent arises, as though the horizon, and the idea of limit it includes and which is proper to vision, were the ultimate structure of relationship."[119] That he tries to exclude reference to a horizon, nevertheless, does not mean that Levinas himself does not employ one. For Levinas asks that we encounter the Other according to responsibility, and this condition effectively becomes the horizon in which relationship is made possible. Yet at the same time, Levinas consistently refuses to specify that horizon. One never knows, with Levinas, what responsibility means, for that would be to put in place a meta-ethics, something like a Kantian categorical imperative; it would be to destroy the possibility of a unique and irreducible response. If Levinas puts a horizon in place, he simultaneously allows it to be suspended by the transcendentality that inhabits all experience and which will characterize respect for the Saying.

The criticism also relates to the thinking of the correlates inside/outside, here/beyond, or being/being's otherwise. Derrida observes: "However it [Levinas's project] is also a question of inaugurating, in a way that is to be new, quite new, a metaphysics of radical separation and exteriority. One anticipates that this meta-

[118] Levinas, *TI,* 44–45.
[119] Levinas, *TI,* 67–68.

physics will have some difficulty finding its language in the medium of the traditional logos entirely governed by the structure 'inside-outside,' 'interior-exterior.' "[120] Levinas assigns himself the task of thinking beyond being, but he will find himself inscribed within being by the very language he uses to defy it. There is no escaping the violence.[121] He seeks to address this criticism in *Otherwise Than Being or Beyond Essence,* admitting that "betrayal" is inevitable, but insisting that the otherwise than being does show itself, even if unfaithfully.[122]

The criticism finally relates to Derrida's comments on the "hyperessential," which, especially insofar as it concerns God, I submit comes down to the difference between Levinas and Derrida in thinking infinity. Caputo describes these two ways with characteristic lucidity:

> Infinity for Derrida is not symbolic but hyperbolic infinity, as opposed to Levinas, for whom it is expressly something metaphysical and even theological, something ethico-theo-logical. The Levinasian gesture that requires deconstruction, even demythologization, is to reify this infinity, to make it a metaphysical being—which Levinas then cannot call Being and will not call a mere fiction. The Levinasian gesture is like the Heideggerian to just this extent: that it attributes actuality or reality to what it valorizes, that it claims this infinity is real, *ad literam, ad infinitum.* But in Derrida, the quasi infinity of undeconstructible justice is neither Being nor otherwise than Being; the excess is not the excess of Being but the excess of linguistic performance, an excess within the operations made possible and impossible by *différance,* in response to the singularity lying on the edge of *différance.* In Derrida, infinity means a hyperbolic responsiveness and responsibility, a hyperbolic sensitivity.[123]

The two types of infinity that are being considered are, first, an infinity that bears a relation to transcendence, and possibly to the Transcendent; and second, an infinity that is related purely to transcendentality. In other words, it marks a return to the prob-

[120] Derrida, *VM,* 88.

[121] Derrida, *VM,* 91–92. See also Jacques Derrida, "How to Avoid Speaking," trans. Ken Frieden, *Derrida and Negative Theology,* ed. Harold Coward and Toby Foshay (Albany: SUNY Press, 1992), 73–142, 133 n. [hereafter Derrida, *HAS*].

[122] Levinas, *OBBE,* 6.

[123] Caputo, *DH,* 200.

lem of transcendentality versus the Transcendent. Is Levinas merely positing the Transcendent as the transcendental signified? It seems to me that the solution to the problem can only be found in two alternatives: either in a dogmatic assertion of a faith position (one way or the other, for atheism requires as much faith as theism); or in the acceptance of undecidability, of an uncertainty that becomes the very condition of possibility for faith itself. According to the former, revelation overrides doubt (or a kind of empirical positivism makes belief impossible). According to the latter, I cannot prove the existence of the Transcendent, who appears according to no horizon of mine. But if God were to give Godself to me, then I could know God only in the traces that mark the human economy (marked as it is with transcendentality), or perhaps as an enigma.[124] These are the choices with which Levinas deals and, as we will come to see, the choices with which Marion is faced.[125]

And Derrida? Writing more and more in the area of religion, Derrida does not exclude the possibility of a choice for God made in faith, provided it is not a faith that deludes itself that it can know its "object" other than according to transcendentality. In "Sauf le nom," for example, he explores the possibilities of a negative theology read otherwise than according to the idea of an absent presence.[126] Negative theology is like a memory, testifying

---

[124] Levinas, *EP,* 77: "The relationship with the Infinite then no longer has the structure of an intentional correlation. The supreme anachronism of a *past* that was never a *now,* and the approach of the infinite through sacrifice—is the Enigma's word." On the enigma, see Theodor W. Adorno, *Aesthetic Theory,* trans. Robert Hullot-Kentor (London: Athlone Press, 1997), 120ff.

[125] And according to Graham Ward, Marion overrides his post-metaphysical preoccupations and comes down in favor of Christian dogmatism. See his "The Theological Project of Jean-Luc Marion" in *Post-Secular Philosophy: Between Philosophy and Theology,* ed. Phillip Blond (London: Routledge, 1998), 229–39 [hereafter Blond, *PSP*].

[126] In "How to Avoid Speaking" Derrida observed that " 'negative theology' seems to reserve, beyond all positive predication, beyond all negation, even beyond Being, some hyperessentiality, a being beyond Being." Derrida, *HAS,* 77. Derrida in that essay was largely responding to the idea that deconstruction was a type of negative theology, and negative theology did not come out too well as a result. Responding to Derrida, Kevin Hart rehabilitates negative theology, deconstructing positive theology. Hart notes that the "hyper" in "hyperessentiality," as it is used by Denys the Areopagite, has a negative rather than positive meaning, and that it suggests a rupture of essentiality rather than a surplus. See

to a yet immemorial event that leaves a mark on language.[127] One of the authorial voices in the essay describes it as a "passion that leaves the mark of a scar in that place where the impossible takes place."[128] It carries a wound, just legible, and bears witness to an unknowable God who has nothing save a name.[129] And the name is that of the unnameable nameable, the nameable beyond the name.[130] This reading of negative theology is far more Levinasian in tone, in the sense that any "God event" would be immemorial, leaving but a wound or a scar or a trace.[131] But it is also consistent with Derrida's thinking of the aporia or the rupture, a thinking that avoids the more obvious pitfalls of Levinas's language of "beyond."[132]

Returning to Derrida's criticism of Levinas, this time concerning the phenomenality of the face, he suggests that while Levinas wants to treat the face as a "nonphenomenal phenomenon," he cannot but recognize it phenomenally.[133] The face inevitably becomes the *alter ego:* "*either* there is only the same, which can no longer even appear and be said, nor even exercise violence (pure infinity or finitude); *or* indeed there is the same *and* the other, and then the other cannot be the other—of the same—except by being the same (as itself: ego), and the same cannot be the same (as itself: ego) except by being the other's other: alter ego."[134] Additionally, the face cannot mark a trace of the nonphenomenal Other without that trace being in some way phenomenal, and

---

Kevin Hart, *The Trespass of the Sign* (Cambridge: Cambridge University Press, 1989), 202 [hereafter Hart, *TS*].

[127] Derrida, *SLN,* 54.

[128] Derrida, *SLN,* 59–60.

[129] Derrida, *SLN,* 60, 55–56.

[130] Derrida, *SLN,* 58.

[131] "Immemorial" here would possibly refer us more to the transcendental than to the Transcendent, bearing in mind that Derrida does not equate God with *différance* and hence not with the quasi-transcendental. Derrida's question "And what if God were an effect of the trace?" still rings in my ears. See Derrida, *VM,* 108.

[132] The recent volume *God, the Gift, and Postmodernism* situates the debate between Marion and Derrida and the question of negative theology very well. See especially the essay by John D. Caputo, "Apostles of the Impossible," at pp. 185–222 of that collection [hereafter Caputo, *AI*].

[133] Derrida, *VM,* 128.

[134] Derrida, *VM,* 128. See the discussion by Richard Beardsworth in *Derrida and the Political* (London: Routledge, 1996), 133ff.

so subject to "original contamination by the sign."[135] Derrida's criticism is powerful, and Levinas clearly takes it up, because he responds to it by moving from the use of the face as the valve of transcendence to the proximity of Saying. But I am inclined, nevertheless, to want to think further on the phenomenality of the trace and the undecidable possibilities it bears. Marion will seize on this very point: that the invisible somehow manifests itself in the visible, although it will need to be demonstrated that he takes adequate account of the factor of undecidability, which seems to me to be decisive. With this background in mind, I turn now to examine Marion's reading of phenomenology.

[135] Derrida, *VM,* 129.

4

Refiguring Givenness

PHENOMENOLOGY has been broadly characterized as the study of phenomena as they give themselves to consciousness, but clearly there are many interpretations of what such a study might entail. For Husserl, it seems phenomenology aims to observe what is given in presence to consciousness; for Heidegger, phenomenology has as its object the uncovering of what gives itself in "presencing"; for Levinas, phenomenology, in its failure, alerts us to what gives by exceeding conscious thematization. Paying heed to each of these three styles as well as others, Marion develops his phenomenological approach. In doing so, he maintains that what he achieves rests strictly within phenomenological bounds: Marion quite deliberately and strongly indicates his resistance to a theological reading of his later works, *Réduction et donation* and *Étant donné*.[1] At the same time, however, these works open onto a consideration of revelation as it might be said to enter the phenomenological sphere. The question that is asked of these works is whether that entry is indeed possible. Taken together with his earlier and more explicitly theological texts, this questioning can be developed further along the lines of whether the entry of revelation can be described as gift, and to what extent it can be specified. This chapter has as its focus the main features of Marion's initial formulation of a phenomenology of givenness, particularly as it is reliant on or departs from the phenomenologies of Husserl, Heidegger, and Levinas, but also as it interacts with the work of his contemporaries: Michel Henry, Jean Greisch, and Dominique Janicaud, among others.

[1] See the "Réponses préliminaires" in *Étant donné,* where Marion denies that he is theologically motivated in *Réduction et donation,* and in the book he is introducing; see also pp. 16–17 n. More strongly, see Derrida and Marion, *OTG,* 70.

Réduction et donation: The Recovery of Husserl

In *Réduction et donation,* Marion offers a careful—and in many ways, insightful—reading of Husserl, whose work is frequently eclipsed by that of his most famous student, Heidegger.[2] The title of Marion's work indicates why Husserl is so important for him: Marion's use of the word *donation* is an attempt to echo the German *Gegebenheit,* "givenness," a phenomenological emphasis that Marion finds in Husserl and which favors what is given over the consciousness that might be understood to make such giving possible.[3] Marion affirms that phenomenology represents a way for philosophy to proceed after Nietzsche's radical questioning of metaphysics. Husserl's project, as Marion understands it, is to examine the possibility of the unconditional givenness of present objects to consciousness. However, the problem he sees in Husserl's approach is that the desire for objectivity interferes with the stated goal of "returning to the things themselves," which seems to result in an overemphasis on intuition.[4] And since Husserl locates donation in the present, it becomes impossible for him to consider the nonpresent.[5] Marion nonetheless claims that Husserl ultimately values givenness over intuition, that intuition depends on a signification that precedes it, and that such dependence proves the priority of givenness over objectivity (and, it might be suggested, over presence). In this way, Husserl breaks the bonds of metaphysics, and both Heidegger's and Derrida's criticisms of his work are overstated.[6] That signification precedes intuition can be illustrated by

[2] Jean-Luc Marion, *Réduction et donation: Recherches sur Husserl, Heidegger, et la phénoménologie* (Paris: Presses Universitaires de France, 1989) [hereafter Marion, *RED*]. This work is available in English as *Reduction and Givenness: Investigations of Husserl, Heidegger, and Phenomenology,* trans. Thomas A. Carlson (Evanston: Northwestern University Press, 1998) [hereafter Marion, *RAG*], but the translations used are generally my own unless otherwise indicated.

[3] *Donation* can be rendered in English as "donation" as well as "givenness," although the translation in *RAG* uses "givenness," a use upon which Marion has insisted. "Donation" keeps open the play between donation as an act (Ms. X made a donation to Community Aid Abroad) and donation as a fact (there was a donation left at the front door). In other words, "donation" retains the possibility of a giver, and the distinction between act and fact is one Marion himself makes in *ED,* 97ff.

[4] Marion, *RED,* 7–8, 15; *RAG,* 1–2, 7. He argues this in detail in chapter 2.

[5] Marion, *RED,* 89; *RAG,* 56.

[6] Marion, *RED,* 28–33; *RAG,* 15–19.

two examples: the possibility of phenomenological deception, and the fact that the "I" has a meaning even though it cannot be fully intuited.[7] The second point is crucial for Marion's rehabilitation of Husserl, and I will explore it in further detail.

Marion perceives two weaknesses in Husserl's ontology, one of which is that according great privilege to objectivity requires that this objectivity be subordinated to a transcendental I. Priority is given to consciousness as the realm of "absolute being."[8] Yet this priority ironically enables Marion to argue that the I actually eludes being.[9] Marion insists that the I, which is seen to be phenomenologically constitutive, does not present itself but is only signaled in the phenomenological reduction, and is so excepted both from the realm of "what is" and from what it "means to be," although evidently it is not bereft of all meaning. Since the I precedes objectivity, it also precedes the ontology that makes objectivity possible: it "is" an exception to being.[10] Marion explains: "The anteriority of the I with regard to every object and of subjectivity with regard to objectivity designates a deviation on this side of ontology: phenomenology occupies this deviation; it presents itself thus in the strictest sense as the instance of that which has not yet to be in order to exercise itself."[11] Ontology only has a conditional legitimacy: it is subject to the I that makes

[7] Marion, *RED,* 46; *RAG,* 27–28.

[8] Marion, *RED,* 233–34; *RAG,* 156–57.

[9] This idea in Marion corresponds with Levinas's location of a "gap" in subjectivity, where the "I" never coincides with itself and cannot recuperate its immemorial origins. Similarly, it can be related to Derrida's observation that the subject can never be totally self-present. Marion differs from Derrida in his location of the I "beyond" being, with a certain Levinasian turn of phrase. In my judgment, Marion's analysis of subjectivity is excellent. It can be examined in the texts to which I have already referred (Cadava et al., *WCAS;* Critchley and Dews, *DS*), as well as in the current context, and in book 5 of *ED.*

[10] Marion, *RED,* 235: "Si d'une part le Je précède l'objectité, le monde et la réalité, si de l'autre l'ontologie traite exclusivement de l'objectité des objets, ne doit-on obligatoirement conclure que le Je s'excepte de l'être et qu'une phénoménologie qui le reconnaîtrait précéderait toute ontologie? C'est un fait que Husserl a tiré cette conséquence: 'Ainsi en arrive-t-on a [*sic*] une philosophie première qui soit antérieure même à l'ontologie . . . et consiste en une analyse de la structure nécessaire d'une subjectivité.' " *RAG,* 157–58.

[11] Marion, *RED,* 236: "L'antériorité du Je sur tout objet et de la subjectivité sur l'objectité désigne un écart en deçà de l'ontologie; la phénoménologie occupe cet écart; elle se présente donc au sens le plus strict comme l'instance de ce qui n'a pas encore à être pour s'exercer." *RAG,* 158.

the reduction. The reduction not only puts in parenthesis ontology as such, but also the whole question of being. Yet the I itself is only attested to in making the reduction, and if the reducing I is excluded from being, where is it located?[12] Heidegger would say that Husserl fails because he leaves the being of the I undetermined. Marion suggests instead that "the I, thus the phenomenological reduction with it, *is not.*"[13] This would mean that the I "is" outside being. In spite of Heidegger's critique, Husserl actually makes a leap outside the horizon of being; in other words, he takes phenomenology further than Heidegger—beyond the question of being: "the *ultimate* possibility of phenomenology would not consist more in the question of being than it exhausts itself in the objectivity of the constituted object: beyond the one and also the other, a last possibility could still open up for it—that of posing the I as transcendent to the reduced objectivity, but also to the being of the being, to place it, by virtue of the reduction taken to its ultimate consequences, outside being."[14] Recognizing that Husserl does not thematize this possibility, Marion argues that his use of the reduction nevertheless pushes us toward it.[15] The transcendence of the I signifies in the making of the reduction, but it does not have to be thought according to being.

If one of the keys to *Réduction et donation* is seen to be the possibility that phenomenology can deliver more than the objects of metaphysics, the other is that this seemingly unlimited potential depends for its success on the extent and rigor of the reduction that is applied. The whole purpose of the book is to attempt to arrive at an unconditional reduction. In the manner already indicated, Marion is able to go beyond what he calls the "transcendental" reduction, which is associated with Husserl in the tradition of Descartes and Kant. But Marion is also able to over-

---

[12] Marion, *RED,* 236; *RAG,* 158.

[13] Marion, *RED,* 240: "le Je, donc la réduction phénoménologique avec lui, n'*est* pas." *RAG,* 161.

[14] Marion, *RED,* 241: "la possibilité *ultime* de la phénoménologie ne consisterait pas plus dans la question de l'être, qu'elle ne s'épuise dans l'objectité de l'objet constitué; au-delà de l'une et aussi de l'autre, une dernière possibilité pourrait encore s'ouvrir à elle—celle de poser le Je comme transcendant à l'objectité réduite, mais encore à l'être de l'étant, de se poser, en vertu de la réduction conduite à ses dernières conséquences, hors de l'être." *RAG* 161–62.

[15] Marion, *RED,* 245–46; *RAG,* 165.

come what he terms the "existential" reduction, evidently linked with Heidegger, and which will now be investigated further.

Réduction et donation: Going beyond Heidegger with Levinas

Marion's reading of Husserl is that the return to the things themselves tends to take us back to the things in their objectivity, when this need not be the case. As we have already begun to see, his reading of Heidegger is that the return takes us back to the things in their being, and similarly he deems this to be an unsatisfactory approach to phenomenology.[16] Heidegger's strength, in Marion's judgment, lies in his recognition that being is *given,* in one sense according to, but very much in excess of, categorical intuition. Being cannot be intuited in its fullness: the categorical intuition of being remains only as a mark of an anonymous givenness. Yet does phenomenology drive us inevitably and solely to a consideration of being? If there is givenness that exceeds consciousness, is this being giving itself to thought, or does givenness precede even being?

Marion agrees with Heidegger to the extent that he understands Husserl to have gone beyond his stated phenomenological objective—to return to the things themselves—in focusing on objectivity and givenness in presence.[17] Marion thus agrees that phenomenality need not just be defined in terms of presence: phenomenology is not simply a means of examining that which is manifest as present, but also that which is unapparent.[18] In fact,

[16] Marion, *RED,* 9, 58–59; *RAG,* 2–3, 36–37.

[17] Marion, *RED,* 79ff.; *RAG,* 49ff.

[18] Marion, *RED,* 90. Marion does not quote the German as it relates to presence, only to monstration. If we consider the parts of *BT* to which he is referring (¶7), we find that Heidegger is here not considering the question of presence explicitly, but is speaking about manifestation and hiddenness. Given that Heidegger raises the question of being as it shows itself (59), and that he has spoken about the misapprehension of being as "presence" (*Anwesenheit*), understood according to "the Present" (*die Gegenwart*) (47), it seems that these meanings will lie behind Marion's understanding of *la présence.* Interestingly enough, Marion insists that in order for the examination to be thoroughly phenomenological, Heidegger will have to arrive at an "intuited presence" of being. See *RAG,* 167.

it is because phenomena are sometimes not readily given that phenomenology is necessary. Heidegger's phenomenology of being emerges for this reason: being is no-thing, it is the unapparent, the not-present, the enigmatic, which cannot be approached as some-thing behind other phenomena but which concerns their very phenomenality.[19] Yet driven by the concern about whether or not phenomenology must lead us to being, Marion puts in question the means by which Heidegger arrives at the sense of being. Heidegger adopts a two-phased reduction. The first phase is the Husserlian one, where the natural attitude is suspended and the phenomenon brought into focus. In the second phase, the initial suspension of the ontological question is then converted into a renewed focus on the sense of being that is given in the reduced phenomenon. But Heidegger's accomplishment of the second phase is, according to Marion, dependent on at least one of two mechanisms, and this is where he will pressure Heidegger. For Heidegger can only arrive at being either by a consideration of *Dasein,* the being that is itself ordered to the uncovering of a sense of being, or by a consideration of being as the nothing, which is achieved in the phenomenological examinations of anxiety and boredom.[20] If Marion can show that neither of these mechanisms inevitably leads to being, then he will be able to argue that givenness has the priority, even over being. Being will not have the last word.

According to Marion's analysis, Heidegger's attempt to arrive at being via *Dasein* fails for two reasons. The first is that Heidegger misinterprets the significance of *Dasein.*[21] The second reason is that ontological difference effectively still remains unclarified in *Being and Time.* Initially, it appears that Heidegger's major phenomenological breakthrough is in his thinking of ontological difference.[22] But as Marion's analysis unfolds, it becomes evident

[19] Marion, *RED,* 91ff.; *RAG,* 57ff.

[20] Marion, *RED,* 104–18; *RAG,* 66–76.

[21] Marion develops this theme in chapter 3 by way of a detailed consideration of Descartes, on whom he is a recognized specialist. See also his "Heidegger and Descartes," trans. Christopher Macann, in *Martin Heidegger: Critical Assessments,* ed. Christopher Macann (London: Routledge, 1992), 178–207.

[22] Marion, *RED,* 163ff.; *RAG,* 108ff. Marion goes on in some detail to show a much higher degree of dependence of Heidegger on Husserl in this regard than might first be thought.

that the sense of ontological difference brought out in *Being and Time* is obscured by other considerations. *Being and Time* is not about acceding to being, but acceding to the sense of being.[23] Here the interrogation of *Dasein* represents a phenomenological breakthrough, yet the desired sense of being is never really attained. This is because Heidegger cannot arrive at the difference between the being of the being and the sense of being in general.[24]

Since the approach to being by way of *Dasein* fails in *Being and Time,* Marion examines a later approach, developed by Heidegger in *What Is Metaphysics?*[25] Here Heidegger tries to access the phenomenon of being by way of the nothing. Since being can be no thing, no actual being, it may bear a certain similarity to nothing, which is other than an object.[26] The nothing is not about a negation of any particular phenomenon, but the negation of the totality of being (*l'étant*): not a negative phenomenon, it is a phenomenon of the negative.[27] How is it possible for us to be given the totality of being, in order that it might be negated? Marion observes the distinction between the apprehension of being in its totality and finding oneself at the heart of being in its totality. The latter becomes possible according to various affective tonalities of *Dasein,* such as *ennui* (boredom, tedium, annoyance, world-weariness), joy, love and anxiety.[28] *Ennui* has the effect of

[23] Marion, *RED,* 194; *RAG,* 129.

[24] Marion, *RED,* 196–97; *RAG,* 131–32. This question will become very important in chapter 6 of *RED* because it demands the separation of being from its inherence in beings.

[25] "What Is Metaphysics?" was delivered in 1929 and first published in 1930 by Friedrich Cohen in Bonn. An English translation appears in *Basic Writings: Martin Heidegger,* 89–110. The epilogue and introduction, added by Heidegger in 1943 and 1949, respectively, do not form part of this version. The epilogue is reproduced as part of the earlier translation in Martin Heidegger, *Existence and Being,* trans. R. F. C. Hull and Alan Crick, 2nd ed. (London: Vision, 1956), 353–92. Marion's reading of this text is heavily influenced by the epilogue, and to a certain extent, also by the introduction.

[26] Marion, *RED,* 253; *RAG,* 170. It can appear that the pursuit of the nothing is a pointless exercise, especially if it is regarded as itself a being, or as simple negation. See the critiques by Carnap and Bergson that Marion repeats at *RED,* 254–56; *RAG,* 170–72.

[27] Marion, *RED,* 257–58; *RAG,* 172.

[28] Marion, *RED,* 258; *RAG,* 173. Marion notes that joy divides itself into joy and love.

rendering distinctions between beings unclear. All is confused in a strange indifference: "Thus, by the mood of *ennui*, Dasein accedes to the totality of being [*l'étant*] as a phenomenon given in person, without reserve or condition; being in its totality gives itself to be seen, precisely because *ennui* renders indifferent the qualitative and quantitative differences between beings. Dasein thus finds itself thrown as such in the middle of being in its totality."[29] Nevertheless, Heidegger clearly has a preference for anxiety over *ennui* as a more fundamental affective tonality.[30] Like *ennui*, anxiety leads to a lack of differentiation between beings. But whereas in *ennui*, *Dasein* is left lingering in a kind of fog of indifference, in anxiety, being in its totality not only becomes indistinct but also threatening. *Dasein* is menaced by no particular being, but by being as a whole.[31] What does the nothing manifest? In Marion's opinion it manifests only ambiguity. Since anxiety itself is ambiguous, so is the nothing. It does not seem to manifest the phenomenon of being. The nothing shows itself not as a distinct phenomenon, but on the surface of beings.[32] It is observed through the double movement of *renvoi* (sending back) that it provokes, driving *Dasein* from the menace of all being and toward the fact of being in its entirety.[33]

At the heart of Marion's analysis is the criticism that just that to which anxiety drives us remains at the mercy of Heidegger's indecision. For it is not until 1943 that Marion finds it clearly articulated that anxiety drives us to the nothing and thus to

[29] Marion, *RED*, 260: "Ainsi, par la tonalité de l'ennui, le Dasein accède-t-il à l'étant dans son ensemble comme à un phénomène donné en personne, sans réserve ni condition; l'étant en totalité se donne à voir, précisément parce que l'ennui rend indifférentes les différences qualitatives et quantitatives entre les étants. Le Dasein se trouve donc bien jeté comme tel au milieu de l'étant dans son ensemble." *RAG*, 174.

[30] Marion, *RED*, 262; *RAG*, 175: "au-delà de l'ennui, qui montre la totalité de l'étant, l'angoisse dispose à son Rien. L'ennui ne reçoit donc qu'un rôle provisoire et de transition, sur une route qui mène de l'étant à son Rien par l'intermédiaire de sa totalisation" ("beyond *ennui*, which shows the totality of being, anxiety opens onto nothingness. *Ennui* thus only receives a provisional and transitional role, on a way which leads from being to its nothing by the intermediary of its totalization").

[31] Marion, *RED*, 263; *RAG*, 175.

[32] Marion, *RED*, 264–65; *RAG*, 176.

[33] Marion, *RED*, 265–67; *RAG*, 177.

being.[34] Marion's conclusion is in fact that anxiety does not naturally provide access to the phenomenon of being, and that in order for the nothing to be read as being, an appropriate hermeneutic needs to be uncovered.[35] The problem is that anxiety renders all beings indistinct, and that as such it renders beings mute: the nothing simply renders nothing.[36] Heidegger's eventual solution comes in the form of the call of being. Being calls us by its own power, even in the nothing. This provides the means for interpreting nothing as being, and the attempt to access the phenomenon of being by way of anxiety becomes incidental.[37] It is in *Ereignis,* the "event of Appropriation," that the call of being is exercised. But such a call can only be given in a response.[38]

Does the interpretation of the nothing as being provide access to the phenomenon of being? There is no imperative that *Dasein* hear or respond to the call: "If being only renders itself accessible by the claim which it exercises, if this claim can only demand a response in exposing itself to a deaf denial of gratitude, the ontological hermeneutic of the nothing *can* fail, since in order to accomplish itself it *must* be able to fail."[39] The ontological hermeneutic of the nothing has to be able to fail. Marion has thus uncovered what he calls a "counter-existential" of *Dasein,* which suspends *Dasein*'s destination toward being:

> The nothing to which *Dasein* ultimately accedes cannot lead to being itself, insofar as this *Dasein* discovers itself there, but not necessarily for and by being, but as, for and by an indistinction more originary than all ontic indetermination: the indecision before "anticipatory resolution" itself follows from the indecision of being to give itself immediately as a phenomenon. In other words: does the white voice of being's call, call in the name of being, or, by its

[34] Marion, *RED,* 267–72; *RAG,* 178–81.

[35] Marion, *RED,* 272; *RAG,* 181.

[36] Marion, *RED,* 275; *RAG,* 183.

[37] Marion, *RED,* 278: "puisque la revendication de l'être seule fait expérimenter l'être, l'analytique existentiale de l'angoisse devient désormais au moins insuffisante à manifester le 'phénomène d'être,' voire totalement superfétatoire." *RAG,* 185.

[38] Marion, *RED,* 279; *RAG,* 186.

[39] Marion, *RED,* 283: "Si l'être ne se rend accessible que par la revendication qu'il exerce, si cette revendication ne peut demander réponse qu'en s'exposant à un sourd déni de 'gratitude,' l'hermeneutique ontologique du Rien *peut* échouer, puisque pour s'accomplir elle *doit* pouvoir échouer." *RAG,* 188.

> indistinct silence, couldn't it let a new abyss appear, anterior, or at least irreducible, to being?
>
> Such a possibility will only find real phenomenological legitimacy if we are able to manifestly produce this counter-existential. We would suggest that it is recognized as *ennui:* Heidegger had invoked it, cursorily, to render being in its totality accessible, before resorting to anxiety in order to attain the nothing.[40]

Marion maintains that *ennui* has the power not only to disengage us from being in its entirety, but also to liberate us from the call by which being makes its claim on us. He describes this powerful *ennui* as a fundamental human condition. It is akin to an overwhelming realization of facticity, and it marks a difference from self, or a disgust with all that would normally be desired. It is neither nihilistic nor a negation.[41] *Ennui* dissolves all passion. In the state of *ennui,* I desert not only the world, but myself.[42] Contrary to what Heidegger intended, *ennui* suspends the claim of being on *Dasein.* How? For *ennui* to suspend the call of being would imply both that being could be given phenomenologically, and that *Dasein* could be affected not only ontically by *ennui,* but ontologically. Now, being is given in two ways: in the call of being that takes place in *Ereignis,* and as that which makes us wonder. *Ennui* functions by making *Dasein* deaf to the call and blind to wonder. In other words, *ennui* can render *Dasein* inauthentic, leading it to the possibility of not heeding its destiny in being.[43]

---

[40] Marion, *RED,* 283. "le Rien auquel accède ultimement le *Dasein* peut ne pas le conduire à l'être même, en sorte que ce *Dasein* se découvre là, mais non nécessairement pour et par l'être, mais comme pour et par une indistinction plus originaire que toute indétermination ontique: l'indécision devant la 'résolution anticipatrice' découle elle-même de l'indécision de l'être à se donner immédiatement dans un phénomène. Autrement formulé: la voix blanche dont l'être revendique revendique-t-elle au nom de l'être, ou, par son indistinct silence, ne pourrait-elle pas laisser paraître un nouvel abîme, antérieur, ou du moins irréductible, à l'être?

"Une telle possibilité ne trouvera d'authentique légitimité phénoménologique que si nous pouvons produire manifestement ce contre-existential. Nous suggérons de le reconnaître comme l'ennui: Heidegger l'avait invoqué, cursivement, pour rendre accessible l'étant dans son ensemble, *avant* de recourir à l'angoisse pour atteindre le Rien." *RAG,* 188.

[41] Marion, *RED,* 284–86; *RAG,* 189–91.

[42] Marion, *RED,* 287–88; *RAG,* 191–92. Marion passes here from *Dasein* to I without comment.

[43] Marion, *RED,* 289–92; *RAG,* 192–95.

Is there a possibility that the suspension of the call of being by *ennui* might leave us open to hearing a different call, a call prior to that of being? Marion mentions as examples the Christian call "from the Father," quoting Heidegger, and the call that comes to us in the face of the Other, as Levinas describes it.[44] *Ennui* would operate phenomenologically as a reduction, not to beings, or being, but to the call. "After the transcendental reduction and the existential reduction, occurs the reduction to and from the call. That which gives itself only gives itself to the one who devotes him- or herself to the call and only under the pure form of a confirmation of the call, repeated because received."[45] Such a call would precede being. But it would also precede *Dasein,* and even the I. Drawing heavily on Levinas, Marion speaks of the call that is made to *me,* and to which I respond "Here I am" (*me voici*).[46]

Marion names the one who is called "the interlocuted."[47] As the interlocuted, I have no power of self-determination. The what or the who that summons me bears an alterity that is prior to my intentionality, prior to my subjectivity, and prior to the ego.[48] I cannot anticipate or comprehend the call. It strikes me by surprise, escaping the closed circle of my being.[49] Yet while that which calls me renders me destitute, it does not annihilate me. There is still a me who is there to respond. The call seems to expose me to the necessity of making a judgment about it. Before any other question, the call renders it essential that I decide about the claim that is made on me. "It is necessary to respond to a question of fact: What claim originarily surprises it? The fact of

---

[44] Marion, *RED,* 294–95; *RAG,* 196–97.

[45] Marion, *RED,* 296: "Après la réduction transcendantale et la réduction existentiale, intervient la réduction à et de l'appel. Ce qui se donne ne se donne qu'à celui qui s'adonne à l'appel et que sous la forme pure d'une confirmation de l'appel, répété parce que reçu." *RAG,* 197–98.

[46] Marion also notes that this possibility can be observed in Heidegger, where the "there" of *Dasein* ("being there") precedes its being. Marion, *RED,* 299; *RAG,* 200.

[47] Marion, *RED,* 300; *RAG,* 200.

[48] Marion, *RED,* 300; *RAG,* 200–201.

[49] Marion, *RED,* 300–301; *RAG,* 201–2. This is reminiscent of Derrida's description of the secret that "makes us tremble," in *The Gift of Death,* trans. David Wills (Chicago: University of Chicago Press, 1995), 53–55 [hereafter Derrida, *GD*]. It is to be noted that by escaping being this alterity also escapes presence, so that Marion's rehabilitation and development of Husserl is complete.

that claim, in the paradoxical manner of an a priori that is essentially after the fact, decides the horizon where any theory of the *interloqué* will become legitimately thinkable. A facticity therefore precedes the theory, but it is no longer a matter of my facticity as *Dasein;* it is a matter of the absolutely other and antecedent facticity of the claim convoking me by surprise."[50] To this question of who or what it is that summons, Marion answers undecidably. We cannot with certainty name the caller, and that is as it must be. It becomes a question of recognizing that there is a claim being made upon me and of risking a response.[51]

Contrary to Heidegger, Marion argues that the phenomenon of being is not given according to the phenomenon of the nothing, but according to being's own call. And yet the call of being can itself be suspended by *ennui.* So Marion claims that there is the potential for an undecidable call to precede being. Whether or not this prior call can itself be suspended, he does not contemplate. What is crucial is how the phenomenological method has been harnessed to arrive at a more radical givenness than that of being. The more strict the reduction that is employed, the better we are able to observe what is given. What is reduced also becomes the measure of the one who so reduces. So he is able to arrive at his three reductions: the transcendental reduction, the existential reduction, and the reduction to the call, which can be analyzed in terms of four questions: *to whom* is *what given,* according to *which horizon,* and *what is thereby excluded?* The transcendental reduction, placed in the framework of these questions, concerns how an intentional and constitutive I is given constituted objects, according to a regional ontology that has as its horizon objectivity, and excludes that which cannot be reduced to this objectivity. The existential reduction concerns how *Dasein* (understood in terms of being-in-the-world, and brought before being in its entirety by anxiety) appears to be given different man-

[50] Marion, *RED,* 301: "Il faut répondre à une question de fait: quelle revendication le surprend originairement? Le fait de cette revendication décide, à la manière paradoxale d'un *a priori* essentiellement après coup, de l'horizon où toute théorie de l'interloqué deviendra légitimement pensable. Une facticité précède donc la théorie, mais il ne s'agit plus de la facticité mienne du Dasein; il s'agit de la facticité absolument autre et antécédente de la revendication me convoquant par surprise." Translation taken from *RAG,* 202.

[51] Marion, *RED,* 302; *RAG,* 202.

ners of being, ontological difference, and the phenomenon of being, according to the horizon of time, and excludes that which does not "have to Be." The reduction to the call concerns how the interlocuted (the me, prior to the I or to *Dasein*) is given the gift of surrendering to or withdrawing from the claim of the call, according to no other horizon than that of the call itself, and excludes nothing, since it is transcendental.[52]

In *Réduction et donation,* Marion seeks to push the boundaries of phenomenology in order to allow for the possibility that being might give not only itself, but also that which "is not" according to the horizon of being. Marion's argument has three essential aspects. First is his belief that being can be exceeded: with the example of the I he indicates an exception to being, and with the example of *ennui* he indicates an exception to the call of being. Second is his emphasis on the quality of the reduction: a complete reduction (one that goes further than to what "is" and even beyond sheer "isness" itself) will yield the givenness of whatever inclines to give itself, beyond the control and initiative of a constituting subject. Finally, there is his pointing to a new horizon, the horizon of the call itself, the meaning of which will in due course be further investigated.

A Critical Engagement with *Réduction et donation*

Having outlined Marion's position as regards Husserl, Heidegger, and, to some extent, Levinas, as it is argued in *Réduction et donation,* several questions arise. It is important to address them prior to considering *Étant donné,* for it is only in the light of these questions that the nature of his responses in that work will become clear. These questions cluster around three poles, although they invariably overlap: the phenomenological, the metaphysical, and the theological. So, to what extent has Marion operated within the limits of that discipline known as phenomenology? Has Marion gone beyond metaphysical language and concepts, or has he simply reinscribed them at a higher level? And what are the theological implications of Marion's phenomenology?

[52] Marion, *RED,* 302–5; *RAG,* 203–5.

The Reduction to Givenness and the Limits of Phenomenology

In an article contributed to a special edition of the *Revue de Métaphysique et de Morale* dedicated to *Réduction et donation,* Michel Henry makes the point that of four possible founding principles of phenomenology, the reduction to givenness is the only one that can achieve an appropriate phenomenological end.[53] For Henry, that end is the experience of life, and the means to that end is not the exposition of being or beings but of the "how" of phenomenality, the mode of givenness of phenomena.[54] The reduction to donation is the most radical reduction because it allows us to arrive at (without our comprehending it) what gives us to ourselves: auto-affection, or "Arch-Revelation." The focus of phenomenology is therefore not on that which can be made present in representation (that which "appears"), but on that which exceeds representation in its "appearing," which is invisible. While this article is a response to Marion's work and has its own particular emphases (the call is always determined as the "call of Life"; there is no possibility of response; the call is immanent), we can see why Marion names Henry as one of his greatest influences.[55] Marion and Henry belong to those who are promoting the renewal of phenomenology. But is this phenomenology phenomenological in the tradition of Husserl? Is the reduction to givenness, which is frequently a reduction to what "is not" or "is not seen," legitimately phenomenological? This question arises as an issue not only in the context of *Réduction et donation* but in the broader context of phenomenological studies in contemporary France, and it has a number of aspects.

In the previous chapters, phenomenology was described as the study of what gives itself to consciousness and how it is given. It quickly became clear that according to the way Husserl developed his science, givenness was dependent on the presence of the given object to consciousness. Marion underlines this condition when

---

[53] Michel Henry, "Quatre principes de la phénoménologie," *Revue de Métaphysique et de Morale* 96, no. 1 (1991): 3–26, 21–25 [hereafter Henry, *QPP*].

[54] This thesis is developed as Henry's "phénoménologie matérielle," and an extended treatment of it can be found in his work of the same name (Paris: Presses Universitaires de France, 1990); see also his *L'essence de la manifestation* (Paris: Presses Universitaires de France, 1963).

[55] Henry, *QPP,* 24. Marion made this disclosure in personal conversation.

he observes, in relation to Heidegger and the "phenomenon of being": "In strict phenomenology, the ultimate instance of decision remains 'the principle of principles,' namely the givenness that is justified unconditionally by intuited presence; it is before this latter instance that it might be decided whether a 'phenomenon of Being' eventually gives itself."[56] In Marion's analysis, and as we have seen, Heidegger's attempt to deliver being in this way fails, particularly because the call that is to deliver it is and must be of undecidable origin. This is similar to the way in which Levinas, by exceeding being, cannot deliver an individual, concrete Other, and cannot deliver a God who can be known in the Infinite, but only guessed at. And it is precisely because of issues such as these—although my examples lie at one end of the continuum—that Derrida is able to suggest the failure of phenomenology as such. Phenomenology fails to deliver a "phenomenon" that can be any more than a representation—that is to say, any more than an interpretation. Phenomenology is a hermeneutics. Yet in *Réduction et donation,* Marion both repeats the failure of phenomenology by delivering a call that is "otherwise than being," and infinitely interpretable, and asserts that this delivery remains within the tradition of Husserlian phenomenology. In other words, the great achievements of *Réduction et donation* are cast in phenomenological terms, when it seems they may belong beyond phenomenology completely. Now, the question is perhaps only a technical one, but it has important implications. For if, as Marion seems to be suggesting, we can describe as a (given) phenomenon that which nevertheless cannot be grasped by intuition, he is attempting to maintain a privileged position for phenomenology prior to hermeneutics. If, on the other hand, he has gone beyond the limits of phenomenology, then what gives itself otherwise remains an interruption to, rather than a legitimate object of, the Husserlian science.

It is relevant to note at this point the particular way in which Marion understands "presence." Early on in *Réduction et donation* he debates Derrida's reading of Husserl along the lines that "presence" does not mean "able to be grasped by intuition," but "given."[57] Therefore, according to his definition, there can "be"

[56] Marion, *RED,* 250; translation from *RAG,* 167.
[57] Marion, *RED,* 56–57; *RAG,* 34–35.

such a thing as a "present phenomenon" that signifies without fulfillment. Exciting as the potential of this definition might be, there is a problem here that refuses to go away. For the signification that is not fulfilled will always and necessarily be left open. It therefore cannot be described *as such;* not yet any "thing," it defies the capacity of the phenomenologist to go any further than signaling its "presence," which for Marion is in the mode of excess. The difficulty is exemplified in the passage quoted above with regard to Heidegger and being as a phenomenon. Marion tells us that "it is before the latter instance [i.e., "the givenness that is justified unconditionally by *intuited presence*"] that it might be decided whether a 'phenomenon of being' eventually gives itself" (emphasis added). In other words, in order to determine whether or not being gives itself, its givenness has to be not only present but intuited as such—that is, its meaning as being must be determinable. Yet if it exceeds intuition, how are we to determine that it is being? Heidegger suggests that this determination occurs by means of the call. But as Marion points out, with great insight, the call that is to lead us to being has itself no determinate meaning. We have indeed reached the limits of phenomenology.

This leads us to contemplate Marion's use of the word "horizon." In *Réduction et donation,* Marion speaks of a new "phenomenological horizon not determined by being," and the "horizon of the call."[58] Now, a horizon is a type of border, or limit. Husserl speaks of the horizon as the background from which things are extracted as particular objects of consciousness.[59] Expressing this in more Kantian terms, a horizon would be a condition of possibility for knowing anything at all, since the horizon forms the frame for knowledge of individual things. And thinking of horizon as context leads us to Heidegger's usage, where it is less a question of the horizon being something that moves, expands, or changes (in a factical or existentiell sense) than something that is the always and already given existential limit within which *Dasein* works.[60] Such a contextual or horizonal limit can be observed in his discussion of "being-in-the-world," for example.[61] In each of

[58] Marion, *RED,* 241, 305; *RAG,* 161, 204.
[59] See Husserl, *I1,* for example at §27.
[60] See the note by Heidegger's translators in *BT,* 1 n.
[61] Heidegger, *BT,* 33.

these cases, the horizon is a border that includes or allows for particular possibilities, which fences an economy of thought and action. Yet it seems to me that Marion is seeking to take us beyond the limits of the economies of objectivity, of being, of metaphysics, and of intuition. What he seeks is a completely unlimited horizon.[62] What he seeks, in fact, is an appearing that does not have any horizon against which it can be measured. The question is, can anything appear without "appearing as something"?

Expanding the Resonances of Gegebenheit

We turn briefly to observe a problem that arose in discussion after the release of *Réduction et donation* and has continued to be a problem even after *Étant donné.* This relates to Marion's use of *Gegebenheit.* Joseph S. O'Leary questions whether or not Marion is justified in translating it as *donation.* "He . . . reduces the plural and diverse terminology of 'givenness' in Husserl and others to a single somewhat grandiose notion of 'donation.' All this facilitates the entry of the biblical God into phenomenology, as the one who grants being."[63] Evidently, since Marion comes to insist on "givenness" rather than "donation" in English, the problem is somewhat eased.[64] However, O'Leary's comment opens onto two further difficulties. The first of these concerns the extent to which Marion is preparing a theological end for his phenomenology, and since this will be discussed at length, I do no more than raise it here. The second difficulty concerns the extent to which Marion is justified in linking Husserl and Heidegger in the way he does through a reading of *Gegebenheit.* In the words of one questioner (who remains anonymous) in the *Revue:* "If it is legitimate to distinguish and to oppose *in a common phenomenological horizon* the transcendental reduction of Husserl from and to the reduction to the 'phenomenon of being' of Heidegger, the passage to the third reduction—in the way that you propose it—remains more problematic, save that you play with a certain equivocity in the very term 'donation,' the same one that drives

[62] Marion, *RED,* 305; *RAG,* 204.
[63] O'Leary, *RPCT,* 191.
[64] Although John D. Caputo notes the difficulties this creates; *AI,* 221 n. 23.

[us] from the *Selbstgegebenheit* to the constellation of the *Geben,* of the *Gabe* and of the *es gibt.*"[65] Marion's response in this setting is strong: both Husserl and Heidegger foster and maintain the ambiguity of givenness and the terms that can be semantically associated with it. His reading therefore rests not only on an equivocal reading of their works, but on the very equivocity he finds there.[66]

Renewing the Metaphysical; Presupposing the Theological: Laruelle

Another of the difficulties associated with *Réduction et donation* is described by François Laruelle.[67] Laruelle's general criticism of Marion is that in this work he simply stays within the bounds of "philosophy," but more specifically, he argues that Marion uses phenomenology-as-philosophy to assert particularly Christian ends. For "philosophy" we can read "metaphysics," and so Laruelle is suggesting that Marion remains trapped within onto-theology:

> J.-L. M does not want to abandon philosophy—his Greek element—but only to be torn from it by a Call—by God rather than by another thought than the philosophical. He wants to be Christian from the point of view of the real, and philosophy—yet a last time, but it is definitive or un-exceedable—from the point of view of thought: he wants to continue to reduce and describe. He makes of philosophy a last negative-condition—of the Christian, his own manner of going beyond the onto-theological method of metaphysics; he chains humanity to God and God to philosophy in place of chaining humanity to itself and of leaving philosophy to its non-human destiny. Either it is a philosophy that makes *in extremis* the leap (of) the Call—but we scarcely believe it—; or it is a Christian who is condemned to do (in spite of himself) philosophy from which he asks that one tears him without making him leave it.[68]

---

[65] Question one to Jean-Luc Marion, in "Réponses à quelques questions," *Revue de Métaphysique et de Morale* 96, no. 1 (1991): 65–76, 65 [hereafter Marion, *RQQ*].

[66] Marion, *RQQ*, 68–69.

[67] François Laruelle, "L'Appel et le Phénomène," *Revue de Métaphysique et de Morale* 96, no. 1 (1991): 27–41 [hereafter Laruelle, *AP*].

[68] Laruelle, *AP*, 37–38: "J.-L. M. ne veut pas abandonner la philosophie—son élément grec—mais seulement en être arraché d'un Appel—par Dieu plutôt que par une pensée autre que la philosophique. Il veut être chrétien du point

Laruelle explains that from the very beginning, Marion sets up his project in terms of its legitimate continuation of the philosophical tradition, taking on the very *telos* of that tradition, which is to uncover the self-givenness of things.[69] He maintains that Marion's work is driven by the hermeneutic of "the Call": his phenomenology is only intelligible in terms of the call, but the decision to employ this hermeneutic already betrays his own Christian interests and exposes Marion's philosophical presuppositions.[70] Further, Marion's use of phenomenology as "the philosophy of our time" illustrates his quite traditional "philosophical faith."[71]

According to Laruelle, Marion makes two highly significant decisions: to emphasize donation as absolute, and to identify reception with donation, manifestation with the given, phenomenology with ontology.[72] Laruelle asserts that Marion's *identification* of each of the dialectical poles in these pairs enables him to resolve them in favor of a higher principle; once again, we are referred to the call.[73] However, this means that the call always remains relative to something else: "still, a *condition* remains for the Unconditioned."[74] Marion conditions his method with the philosophical decision to make the call a transcendent term that tears us from the empirical. In so doing, Marion separates himself from the position of Henry (which Laruelle reads as radical immanence without transcendence), as well as from Levinas (which Laruelle reads as transcendence without the problem of the immanence of

---

de vue du réel, et philosophie—encore une dernière fois, mais elle est définitive ou indépassable—du point de vue de la pensée: il veut continuer à reduire et décrire. Il fait du philosophe une dernière condition-négative—du chrétien, sa manière à lui de dépasser la structure onto-théologique de la métaphysique; il enchaîne l'homme à Dieu et Dieu à la philosophie au lieu d'enchaîner l'homme à lui-même et de laisser la philosophe à son destin non-humain. Ou bien c'est un philosophie qui fait *in extremis* le saut (de) l'Appel—mais nous ne le croyons guère—; ou bien c'est un chrétien qui est condamné à faire malgré lui de la philosophie à laquelle il demande qu'on l'arrache sans la lui faire quitter."

[69] Laruelle, *AP*, 28.

[70] Laruelle, *AP*, 29, 34–35. Of note here is that Laruelle uses "l'Appel" where Marion uses "l'appel." I will use the lowercase except in quotations. To what extent is Laruelle's criticism couched in terms of what he wants to find?

[71] Laruelle, *AP*, 29.

[72] Laruelle, *AP*, 30–31.

[73] Laruelle, *AP*, 31–33.

[74] Laruelle, *AP*, 33: "toutefois, une *condition* subsiste pour l'Inconditionné."

reception). For Laruelle, Marion's retaining of a dyadic structure marks his dependence on "philosophy."[75] This cannot but condition the way Marion deals with the call itself.[76] In Laruelle's judgment, the ultimate possibility for phenomenology has been posited as a reality prior to the phenomenological investigation, and on the basis of revelation. It has been made absolute.[77] "The Call is the Christian kernel which will order this [the reduction], the real heart of all relief and of all reduction—thus the *pure form* of the relief."[78] However, the call falls outside phenomenality. Further, since the call rests on a philosophical decision, there is no guarantee that it escapes the fold to which phenomena are subjected: in other words, the call cannot be identified without being subject to undecidability, and need not be ultimate.[79] Marion's phenomenology fails, and for much the same reason that (according to Laruelle) all philosophy must fail, and is in need of deconstruction.[80] "The *telos* of phenomenology is always betrayed: because it is precisely only a *telos* and because to philosophize is to betray the reality of the One."[81]

To what extent are Laruelle's criticisms valid? He is not alone

---

[75] Laruelle, *AP*, 34: "Mais elle ne le fait qu'en témoignant d'une volonté de conserver jusqu'au bout la matrice la plus fondamentale de la philosophie—celle de la Dyade, du Pli ou du Doublet—alors que tout l'intérêt des solutions 'Levinas' et 'Henry' avait été de la liquider et de venir—chaque fois sur un mode très différent—à une pensée réellement simple ou sans pli." ("But it only witnesses to a will to conserve to the end the most fundamental matrix of philosophy—that of the Dyad, of the Fold or of the Doublet—whereas all the interest of the Levinasian or Henrian solutions had been to liquidate it and to come—each time in a very different mode—to a thought really simple or without fold.")

[76] Laruelle, *AP*, 34–35: "On verra d'ailleurs plus tard que la philosophie et ses décisions continuent à conditionner de manière extérieure l'Appel lui-même, parce que l'Appel est seulement un *arrachement* à la philosophie, à ses formes 'restreintes' (ontico-ontologiques) plutôt qu'un suspens radical de toute philosophie possible; et que *l'ennui* ne va pas jusqu'à la véritable *indifférence*, qu'il n'a pas encore la plus grande force réductrice possible."

[77] Laruelle, *AP*, 35.

[78] Laruelle, *AP*, 36: "l'Appel est le noyau chrétien qui commandera celle-ci [la réduction], le coeur réel de toute relève et de toute réduction—donc la *forme pure* de la relève."

[79] Laruelle, *AP*, 38.

[80] Laruelle, *AP*, 36.

[81] Laruelle, *AP*, 37: "Le *telos* de la phénoménologie est toujours trahi: parce que ce n'est justement qu'un *telos* et parce que philosopher est trahir le réel de l'Un."

in ascribing to Marion a theological motive for developing a phenomenology of givenness, and for that reason I will address other aspects of his critique before returning to the theological one. Does Marion remain trapped within the bounds of metaphysics? As it was observed above, Marion's horizonal language opens him up to the criticism of his thinking metaphysically, and Laruelle's reading of a dyadic structure supports this criticism. At the same time, however, if we read Marion in line with his Levinasian background, and take seriously his attempts *not* to identify a "Caller" with any certainty, then he is transgressing metaphysics, if not escaping it (which would in any case be impossible, as Derrida has shown). It is hard to see how Laruelle can justify his distinction between Marion and Levinas on the grounds that the reception of the call somehow destroys its alterity, while the welcoming of the Other does not, unless in *both* instances there is a slippage from transcendental to transcendent that enables identification. And Marion's addressing of the question of subjectivity, under the figure of the interlocuted, suggests that he is well aware of the metaphysical traps that await in his analysis, and able to deal with them. To further establish Marion's "post"-metaphysical credentials we would need only to look at his previous works. But to do this would leave us in something of a bind. For it is undoubtedly in the light of Marion's previous works that Laruelle is able to make the charge that Marion is theologically (and therefore, in his mind, metaphysically) motivated. In *God Without Being* and *L'idole et la distance* we find plenty of material to support Marion's transgressing of metaphysics, but we also find much that would sustain Laruelle's opinion that Marion keeps both the philosophical and the Christian faith. The question is, to what extent does that enable us to criticize his phenomenology in *Réduction et donation*?

Does Marion arbitrarily choose the call as a means of guiding his phenomenology (and does he make it absolute)? The response might be yes to both parts of the question, if we are to assume that Marion has a Christian project in mind. But we might also interpret Marion far less suspiciously if we remember that he is not the first person to use the device of the call. The call of being is an increasingly persistent theme in Heidegger, and the summons from the Other (equally the call to responsibility, or the election by the Other) is a constant refrain in Levinas. If all Marion is doing is trying to allow for a valve in the economy of being or of beings, then the call can function in this way without necessarily pointing to a transcendent God.

Janicaud, Derrida, and Le tournant théologique

However, in spite of Marion's later avowal that *Réduction et donation* is a phenomenological, not a theological, work, criticisms of his work relating to its theological presuppositions continue to be made on various grounds. Perhaps that is because, as we have seen and will see further, the work of an author rarely stands on its own, and many of Marion's phenomenological insights have been expressed in a theological context. But it is also because Marion's work is but one of a number of works that emerge from a particular climate in French philosophy. The theological criticism is thus directed not only toward Marion, but also to a whole "school," if they might be so brought together. In 1991, Dominique Janicaud published a slim volume titled *Le tournant théologique de la phénoménologie française,* where he argues that recent French phenomenology has departed from the Husserlian emphasis on immanence, in favor of the study of the breaking up of immanence by transcendence. "Is this trait [of French phenomenology] the rupture with immanent phenomenality? The opening onto the invisible, to the Other, to a pure givenness or to an 'archrevelation'?"[82] To this question Janicaud responds with a resounding yes. Further, he argues that such openings are inherently theological ones. Tracing the genealogy of this trait, the origins of which seem to lie in Heidegger's phenomenology of the inapparent, Janicaud identifies its emergence most strongly in writers such as Levinas, Marion, Henry, and Jean-Louis Chrétien (we might also add later works by Jean-Yves Lacoste and Louis-Marie Chauvet to the list). The analysis he then pursues relies on an

[82] Dominique Janicaud, *Le tournant théologique de la phénoménologie française* (Combas: Éditions de l'éclat, 1991), 8 [hereafter Janicaud, *TTPF*]; all translations of Janicaud used here are mine. The text is now available in translation in Dominique Janicaud, Jean-François Courtine, Jean-Louis Chrétien, Michel Henry, Jean-Luc Marion, and Paul Ricoeur, *Phenemenology and the "Theological Turn": The French Debate* (New York: Fordham University Press, 2000), 1–103.

argument that these writers have pursued a methodological transgression of Husserlian phenomenology. That transgression relates to the disruption of the noetic-noematic correlation as well as to what Janicaud maintains is the essential neutrality (or atheism) of Husserl's method.[83] To remain faithful to phenomenology requires a faithfulness to Husserl's scientific approach, which means that it is illegitimate to ask questions about that which exceeds consciousness and, indeed, clearly partisan to do so.

Chapter 3 of *Le tournant* is devoted to a discussion of Marion in response to *Réduction et donation.* Recognizing that the latter work is "more discreet" in its theological interests than earlier works of Marion, Janicaud nevertheless makes the claim that Marion's work is ideologically driven.[84] Janicaud begins by observing that the question has to do with "the status of phenomenology (and of the phenomenological) between a 'surpassed' (or challenged) metaphysics and a possible theology (at once prepared and retained)."[85] Marion asserts that phenomenology is the legitimate successor of philosophy-as-metaphysics; Janicaud, on the other hand, questions whether or not this is or need be the case. Why, he asks, has "the thesis of 'the metaphysical extraterritoriality of phenomenology' and that which it allows or authorizes been pushed so far"?[86] Janicaud argues that phenomenology is inherently metaphysical, a criticism Marion addresses carefully and well in his article "Metaphysics and Phenomenology: A Relief for Theology."[87] But Janicaud further sees no necessary connection between the three reductions that Marion proposes, insisting that Marion's hermeneutic depends on a misreading of Husserl and Heidegger, along the lines of Levinas.[88] He asks: "What remains of phenomenology in a reduction that 'properly speaking *is not*'?"[89] Marion's reduction to the call, Janicaud maintains, sets us

[83] See, for example, Janicaud's discussion of Levinas at *TTPF,* 35–36.
[84] Janicaud, *TTPF,* 51ff.
[85] Janicaud, *TTPF,* 40.
[86] Janicaud, *TTPF,* 41.
[87] Jean-Luc Marion, "Metaphysics and Phenomenology: A Relief for Theology," trans. Thomas A. Carlson, *Critical Inquiry* 20 (1993–94): 573–91. This article originally appeared in French as "Métaphysique et phénoménologie: Une relève pour la théologie," *Bulletin de Littérature Ecclésiastique* 94, no. 3 (1993): 189–206.
[88] Janicaud, *TTPF,* 43–48.
[89] Janicaud, *TTPF,* 48.

up for a theological response to the question of the call's origin. The confusion and surprise of the interlocuted that Marion describes, the phenomenological "emptiness" or gap, or negative phenomenology upon which Marion insists—these are simply parts of his structuring a philosophical system toward religious ends, a structuring Caputo will later describe as "a smuggling of the invisible into the visible."[90] This reading of Marion is reinforced with a reference to another of his works—this time on Descartes—where philosophy is made destitute by theology (Descartes's thought is transgressed by that of Pascal).[91] It is also supported with a reference to Marion's response to questions put to him in the *Revue,* where Marion himself draws a thread between his earlier, theological works and what he achieves in *Réduction et donation.*[92] Janicaud concludes, therefore, that "his phenomenological gap is only explained by a double reference that each forewarned reader is aware of: the problematic of the overcoming of ontology (or of metaphysics), the properly theological or spiritual dimension. It is the overlapping of the two schemes under the cover of phenomenology that is here contested."[93] Along with Jean-Louis Chrétien, Janicaud deems Marion guilty of abandoning phenomenological neutrality.[94]

It is interesting to observe that Janicaud's critique corresponds in some ways to that of Derrida, although for entirely different reasons. The basic thrust of Derrida's criticism of Marion is that while Marion attempts to suspend the horizon by suggesting that the origin of the call cannot be ultimately determined, he does tend toward identifying the caller as the Christian God:

> To limit ourselves here to the most basic schema, let us say that the question, if not the discussion, would remain open at the point of the determination of the call or of the demand, there where the

[90] Janicaud, *TTPF,* 48–49; Caputo, *AI,* 208. See also the discussion by Eric Alliez in *De l'impossibilité de la phénoménologie: Sur la philosophie française contemporaine* (Paris: Vrin, 1995), 60ff.

[91] See Jean-Luc Marion, *Sur le prisme métaphysique de Descartes* (Paris: Presses Universitaires de France, 1986); *On Descartes' Metaphysical Prism,* trans. Jeffrey L. Kosky (Chicago: University of Chicago Press, 1999).

[92] Marion, *RQQ,* 66–68.

[93] Janicaud, *TTPF,* 51.

[94] Janicaud, *TTPF,* 53. For a response to Janicaud, see Jacques Colette, "Phénoménologie et métaphysique," *Critique* 548–49 (January–February 1993): 56–73.

> circle seems to turn between the call of Being (*Anspruch des Seins*), the call of the father (*Anspruch des Vaters*), the primacy of which Heidegger contests, and a "call which is brother to the one Heidegger dismisses," namely, the one that "Levinas will not fail to take up." Nor, I will add, does Marion, who seems to me also to make "*the* call as such," "the pure form of the call," conform to the call of the father, to the call that returns to the father and that, in truth, would speak the truth of the father, even the name of the father, and finally of the father inasmuch as he gives the name.

A little further on he continues:

> Having *declared* that it excludes any determinable content, why does Marion determine "the pure form of the call" (and therefore of the gift) as call "in the name of the Father"? As unique call, despite "the gap between the two calls (the one Christian, the other Jewish)" that it is "important to maintain"? Is it possible to hear a "pure form of the call" (and first of all must one presume such a purity? And if one does, on what basis?) that would still not be from Being, nor from the father, nor in the fraternal difference of the "there," if one can put it that way, between the Jew and the Christian, nor therefore in the language of the "Hear, O Israel: The Lord our God is one Lord" (*Deuteronomy* 6:4) in which, Marion tells us, they "both have their source" (p. 295)?[95]

Derrida's reading of Marion uncovers what we might, borrowing from Caputo, describe as "the dream of pure presence without *différance*."[96] It is a dream characterized by a fear of dissemination, or expressed more positively, by a longing for an origin (for "the return to the father"), a longing for purity (for "the *pure* form of the call"), and a longing for unity (for "*the* call as such").[97] Nevertheless, whether or not this reading is a fair one, given the limits of the passage on which it relies, is a legitimate question.

It has already been pointed out that Marion now sees *Réduction et donation* as a strictly phenomenological work, without an overt or covert theological agenda. But there is no doubt that the phenomenology he puts in place has possible openings onto theology, most specifically at the point of the call. The arguments

---

[95] Derrida, *GT1,* 52 n.

[96] John D. Caputo, *The Prayers and Tears of Jacques Derrida: Religion without Religion* (Bloomington: Indiana University Press, 1997), 20 [hereafter Caputo, *PTJD.*

[97] Emphasis added.

outlined above come down to the following: first, to the extent that Marion's work is not phenomenological, it is theological (Janicaud); and second, to the extent that it is phenomenological, it is onto-theological (Laruelle, Derrida). Why do these positions turn around the theological outcomes, which Marion is later so anxious to avoid? Perhaps it is time, in the light of what Marion writes in the preface to *Réduction et donation* ("[these investigations] maintain an indirect, but no doubt necessary tie with older works that, without knowing it, presupposed them"), to examine the theological trajectory in which *Réduction et donation* can be situated.[98]

The judgment that Marion has in mind a transcendent Caller in *Réduction et donation* is quite probably made on the basis of works such as *God Without Being* and *L'idole et la distance.* There are a number of passages to which we can refer. In *God Without Being,* for example, we read:

> The ontic difference between being and nonbeing admits no appeal; in the world, it acts irrevocably, without appeal. From elsewhere than in the world, then, God himself lodges an appeal. He appeals to his own indifference against the difference between being and nonbeing. He appeals to his own call. And his call sets this indifference into play so that the call not only calls nonbeings to become beings . . . but he calls the nonbeings as if they were beings.[99]

Or again:

> The decision of beingness depends neither on the categories of a philosophical discourse nor on Being deploying itself in ontological difference, but on instances separated by the limit between "the world" and the "call" of the God who gives life. And curiously, for an informed reading at least, the nonbeingness of that which nevertheless is results from the "world," whereas God outside-the-world prompts the beingness of nonbeings.[100]

Marion speaks of "two sources of glory and of glorification: the funding of the 'world' or the call of Christ."[101] Further, he goes

[98] Marion, *RAG,* xi.
[99] Marion, *GWB,* 87–88.
[100] Marion, *GWB,* 93.
[101] Marion, *GWB,* 94.

on to identify the call as the gift: "And from now on one can delimit even more closely the game that, indifferent to ontological difference, thus causes beings to elude being: it is called the gift. The gift that gave rise to the operations of preceding readings—call, give life, as if, father, and so on—*gives* Being/beings."[102]

This understanding of call at least partially develops what Marion presents in *L'idole et la distance* in terms of "*la distance,*" a concept that apparently defies conceptuality and so is left undefined, although not completely undescribed.[103] In that text, distance occurs both between myself and others and between myself and God.[104] It therefore functions as a guarantee for the maintenance of a sort of Levinasian alterity.[105] Distance escapes representation, possessing an anteriority that is reminiscent of immemoriality.[106] It precedes even ontological difference.[107] But most interestingly for our purposes, distance forms what Marion names the "paternal horizon," which is non-objectifiable and unthinkable.[108] In this early work (*L'idole et la distance* appeared in 1977) it is distance (the horizon of the father) that cuts across being (or, it could be said, the call of being). By the time of *God Without Being* (1982), it is God's call that cuts across being according to the horizon of the gift. And, as we have seen, by the time

---

[102] Marion, *GWB,* 100.

[103] Marion, *ID,* 244: "Bref, l'antériorité et l'extériorité herméneutiques de la distance la dispensent de toute définition relevant du 'langage-objet' (ou supposé tel). Parce qu'elle définirait, la distance ne se définirait pas." Distance is, of course, one of the themes to which Hans Urs von Balthasar heavily subscribes.

[104] Marion, *ID,* 247.

[105] Nevertheless, this distance does not seem to have the same notion of "curved space" for which Levinas allows.

[106] Marion, *ID,* 254: "La distance . . . échappe elle aussi à toute représentation, puisque tout objet représentable, comme tout sujet représentateur, dépendant déjà d'une distance définitivement antérieure."

[107] Marion, *ID,* 264.

[108] Marion, *ID,* 254: "Plus, l'horizon paternel de la distance se soustrait, par définition, à toute inquisition qui prétendrait l'objectiver. Ce dont il s'agit, en effet, avec lui, c'est précisément de l'in-objectivable de l'impensable qui outrepasse la négation même des pensables, de l'irreprésentable qui esquive la négation même du représentable." ("Further, the paternal horizon of distance withdraws, by definition, from all questioning that would purport to objectify it. What it has to do with, in effect, is precisely the unobjectifiable of the unthinkable that goes beyond even the negation of what is thinkable, the unrepresentable that avoids even the negation of the representable.")

of *Réduction et donation* (1989), it is the horizon of the call, a call that is undecidable but which could be the call of the father, that exercises itself before the claim of being.

Let us add to this brief survey the fact that, in the "Réponses à quelques questions," which is part of the *Revue* in 1991, Marion is apparently prepared to consider the connection between his earlier works and *Réduction et donation.* He is also prepared to discuss the possibility of a phenomenon of revelation, observing that "to my knowledge, this locution does not occur in *Réduction et donation,* but a lucid reader cannot help but guess that the question of revelation governs this work quite essentially."[109] And in the subsequent essay, "The Final Appeal of the Subject," Marion concludes: "More essential to the *I* than itself, the gesture that interlocutes appears, freely but not without price, in the figure of the claim—as that which gives the *I* as a *myself* rendered to *itself.* Grace gives the *myself* to *itself* before the *I* even notices itself. My grace precedes me."[110] One could make a case that we are referred here to the Christian God, the divine Giver.

The Omission of the Es Gibt

The idea that Marion has in mind a divine Giver brings us to consider a final question with regard to *Réduction et donation,* one that is raised in the *Revue* by Jean Greisch.[111] Given his interest in donation, why does Marion not refer, in this work, to the Heideggerian material on *es gibt?*[112] The answer could lie in the earlier texts *L'idole et la distance* and *God Without Being.* In the former, Marion devotes several pages to a discussion of the *es gibt.* Begin-

[109] Marion, *RQQ,* 73; my translation. We could add to this list Marion's comments in "Metaphysics and Phenomenology: A Relief for Theology"; or in "Le phénomène saturé," in Jean-François Courtine, Jean-Louis Chrétien, Michel Henry, Jean-Luc Marion, and Paul Ricoeur, *Phénoménologie et théologie* (Paris: Criterion, 1992) [hereafter Courtine et al., *PT*], 79–128 [hereafter Marion, *PS*]; trans. by Thomas A. Carlson as "The Saturated Phenomenon" in *Philosophy Today* 40 (Spring 1996): 103–24.

[110] This essay appears in its fullest translated form in Critchley and Dews, *DS.* The quote is from p. 104.

[111] Jean Greisch, "L'herméneutique dans la 'phénoménologie comme telle,' " *Revue de Métaphysique et de Morale* 96, no. 1 (1991): 43–63 [hereafter Greisch, *HPT*].

[112] Greisch, *HPT,* 56. See also O'Leary, *TRSG,* 251.

ning with the question about what "brings into presence," he speaks of the "gift" of presence, the bringing into presence that is accomplished in the *il y a.*[113] It is about meditating, he suggests, not on that which there is, but on the fact that there is a "there is," which gives in withdrawing.[114] It is about focusing not on the given, but on givenness, or donation. Referring to "Time and Being," Marion observes the play between *donner* (*Geben*—to give), *donation* (*Gabe*—the gift) and the *es* (*Il*—it).[115] He notes that metaphysics masks the sense of giving, and that it is necessary to think *donation* from within *donner* and vice versa.[116] Importantly, Marion emphasizes that Heidegger has in mind no verbal subject, no cause, no "indeterminate power," when he speaks of the *es.*[117] The *es* is named *Ereignis,* but *Ereignis* is nothing other than the giving that links being and time, which withdraws in their being given. In its withdrawal, however, the *Ereignis* reveals itself according to its key characteristic: expropriation.[118]

> Thus the *Ereignis,* which achieves and goes beyond in this ontological difference, never accedes as much to its proper sense than in disappropriating itself, since this is also how it makes "something else" accede to its characteristic. Its "absence" recovers its highest "presence," its withdrawal coincides with its proximity, since its retreat alone assures us of acceding to the "approaching proximity, *Nahheit.*"[119]

Ereignis can never be objectified, and Marion emphasizes the similarity between it and what he calls *distance.*[120] Further, he suggests

---

[113] As I have already indicated, Marion observes that this is often the accepted French translation, while maintaining a preference for *ça donne.* Marion, *ID,* 283.

[114] Marion, *ID,* 284.

[115] Marion, *ID,* 285.

[116] Marion, *ID,* 286.

[117] Marion, *ID,* 287.

[118] Marion, *ID,* 288–90.

[119] Marion, *ID,* 291: "Donc l'*Ereignis,* qui achève et outrepasse en cela la différence ontologique, n'accède jamais autant à son propre qu'en se désappropriant, puisque c'est ainsi qu'il fait accéder 'autre chose' à son propre. *L'Ereignis,* dans l'abandon, assure le *donner,* et dans le *donner* le donne à penser. Son 'absence' recouvre sa plus haute 'présence,' son retrait coïncide avec sa proximité—puisque seul ce retrait nous assure d'accéder à la 'proximité approchante, *Nahheit.*' "

[120] Marion, *ID,* 291.

that *Ereignis* is like "paternal" distance, although in that case *Ereignis* would need to be read *according to* distance.[121] He explores such a reading, coming to the conclusion that "the *Ereignis* can thus be understood in two ways, not unifiable, not contradictory, not concurrent: as such, the last word of being, and as *medium* or *analogy* of the trinitarian play (the gift of creation sending to and deepening itself in the original filiation)."[122] The analogy is particularly strong in the case of withdrawal.

Marion's treatment of *es gibt* in *L'idole et la distance* is quite positive. Because *Ereignis* precedes and so defies ontological difference, it achieves the indifference to difference that is Marion's chief interest.[123] Its possible relationship to "paternal distance" is left open: there is no necessary ideological contradiction between them at this point, although *God Without Being* will read differently in this regard. But most importantly for our purposes, there is in *L'idole et la distance* the beginning of the link between the *es gibt* and a divine Giver. This link will prove crucial to Marion's theological position, and hence it threatens to undermine his philosophical interests. In *God Without Being,* during a lengthy passage concerning the *es gibt* where Marion elaborates two interpretations of giving, we discover his strong desire not only to think a donation *anterior* to that of being, but to specify a Giver, a desire that would forbid the suspension of the horizon of donation. And in this desire it is possible to recognize why Marion does not revisit the *es gibt* in *Réduction et donation:* his earlier interpretation of it would cauterize his later argument.

In *God Without Being,* Marion construes God as gift in contrast to God as being. His strategy involves not only showing that a metaphysical understanding of being is inadequate for God (along with Heidegger), but in showing that the Heideggerian elevation of being apart from (but implicitly above) God itself fails and can be theologically dismissed. As part of the latter move, Marion must once again deal with the *es gibt.* He begins with the

---

[121] Marion, *ID,* 292.

[122] Marion, *ID,* 296: "L'*Ereignis* peut donc s'entendre de deux manières, non unifiables, ni contradictoires, ni concurrentes: comme tel, dernier mot de l'Être, et comme *médium* ou *analogon* du jeu trinitaire (le don de création renvoyant à et s'approfondissant dans la filiation originelle)."

[123] Marion, *ID,* 301.

question of the relationship of the gift to being (*l'Être*) and being (*étant*), commenting:

> No one more than Heidegger allowed the thinking of the coincidence of the gift with Being/being, by taking literally the German *es gibt,* wherein we recognize the French *il y a,* there is: superimposing one and the other, we would understand the fact that there should be (of course: being) as this fact that *it gives, ça donne.* Being itself is delivered in the mode of giving—from one end to the other along the path of his thought, from *Sein und Zeit* to *Zeit und Sein,* from 1927–1962, Heidegger does not cease to meditate on this equivalence. Do we not delude ourselves, then, by claiming to discover in the gift an instance anterior to Being/being that distorts the ontological difference of Being/being? Does not that which we apprehend as "otherwise than being" constitute precisely its most adequate and most secret thought?[124]

In response to this questioning, he maintains that "gift" and "giving" must be thought differently (not from each other, but from the Heideggerian conception), and not beginning with being/being. Marion gives two possible definitions of the gift/giving:

> On the one hand there is the sense of the gift that leads, in the *there is,* to the accentuating of the *it gives* starting from the giving itself, thus starting from the giving in so far as it does not cease to give itself; in this case, the *it* that is supposed to give does not provide—any more than does the impersonal *il* on the threshold of the *il y a*—any privileged support.[125]

This is Heidegger's interpretation, involving no giver as such. It is interesting that Marion compares this giving to "what gives" in a painting, not only because visual art has a very important place in Marion's work, but because he speaks here of giving as appropriation.[126] What gives in a work of art is neither painter nor canvas, but something else altogether that allows itself to be "seen": this is Marion's regular phenomenological refrain. But here he interprets the painting as idol rather than as icon—"gift as appropria-

[124] Marion, *GWB,* 102.

[125] Marion, *GWB,* 102–3.

[126] Marion speaks of art in *GWB* in his discussion of idols versus icons, and in *La croisée du visible,* 2nd ed. (Paris: Presses Universitaires de France, 1996) [hereafter Marion, *CV*].

tion, without any distance."[127] The question of expropriation is left hanging.

The second interpretation Marion offers of the gift/giving distinction is as follows (and I quote at length, because in this passage Marion reveals a number of significant ideas):

> On the other hand, the gift can be understood starting from giving—at least, as it is accomplished by the giver. The gift must be understood according to giving, but giving [*donation*] must not be understood as a pure and simple giving [*donner*]. Giving must be understood by reference to the giver. Between the gift given and the giver giving, giving does not open the (quadri-) dimension of appropriation, but preserves distance. Distance: the gap that separates definitively only as much as it unifies, since what distance gives consists in the gap itself. The giving traverses distance by not ceasing to send the given back to a giver, who, the first, dispenses the given as such—a sending destined to a sending back. Distance lays out the intimate gap between the giver and the gift, so that the self-withdrawal of the giver in the gift may be read on the gift, in the very fact that it refers back absolutely to the giver. Distance opens the intangible gap wherein circulate the two terms that accomplish giving in inverse directions. The giver is read on the gift, to the extent that the gift repeats the giving of the initial sending by the giving of the final sending back. The gift gives the giver to be seen, in repeating the giving backward. Sending which sends itself back, sending back which sends—it is a ceaseless play of giving, where the terms are united all the more in that they are never confused. For distance, in which they are exchanged, also constitutes that which they exchange.[128]

Here Marion expresses his position with admirable clarity. Giving, *es gibt,* is to be understood in terms of a giver, or rather, *the* giver. And soon after, Marion identifies this giver: "Doubtless we will name it God, but in crossing God with the cross that reveals him only in the disappearance of his death and resurrection."[129] Granted, we are in a book that has a theological orientation, but there is no undecidability about this giving. "God" may be "crossed out," but it is certainly God who orients the giving that

[127] Marion, *GWB,* 104.
[128] Marion, *GWB,* 104.
[129] Marion, *GWB,* 105.

exceeds being. Marion tries to protect God from reductionism not only by withdrawing God from intelligibility (by using the device of crossing out), but by introducing the horizon of distance. Distance serves to separate the terms (Giver and giving/gift, but thereby also Giver and recipient). The question is whether or not distance can separate the terms sufficiently to allow for infinite interpretability. It seems to me that in making God an absolute term, Marion has potentially compromised his reading of *es gibt.* But at the same time, within the horizon of "distance" he utilizes a mechanism that might otherwise be called "the trace," and which functions to protect the aneconomic quality of the interruption ("Distance lays out the intimate gap between the giver and the gift, so that the self-withdrawal of the giver in the gift may be read on the gift").

In response to the question of Jean Greisch, it may be that Marion avoids dealing with the *es gibt* question in *Réduction et donation* because he has already spelled out its implications elsewhere. Since he wishes to preserve the undecidability of the call, he cannot afford to insert his theological reading of *es gibt* into this context.

On the face of it, it seems that the problems raised by Laruelle, Janicaud, Derrida, and Greisch are confirmed by the theological material that precedes *Réduction et donation.* But this is too simple a solution to a complex problem. We have, on the one hand, Marion insisting retrospectively that *Réduction et donation* is not a theological book, a view that is confirmed by the letter (if not the spirit, according to some) of the text. But we have, on the other hand, an explicit confirmation by Marion that *Réduction et donation* fits in the context of his other works, which are either theological, or Cartesian, or both. And we also have his confirmation that "to my knowledge, this locution [phenomenon of revelation] does not occur in *Réduction et donation,* but a lucid reader cannot help but guess that the question of revelation governs this work quite essentially." How are we to resolve this tension? One way of interpreting it might be as follows. In *Réduction et donation,* Marion is not writing an explicit work of theology: it demands no theological commitments and does not articulate theological themes. Instead, he sets out to develop a phenomenology, one that is expanded to encompass not only what is given in fullness of intuition but also that which gives itself without the completion of signification. Nevertheless, in so doing he is working at the border of phenomenology and theology because he wants to allow for the possibility that less usual "objects" (that is, we learn more fully in *Étant donné*, phenomena of revelation) might be brought within the realm of phenomenological study.[130] Now, to the extent that Marion works at this interface, his work is very relevant for a renewed consideration of the relationship between philosophy and theology, particularly as it is opened by phenomenology. But the problems that arise at this interface are many, and they are articulated to a greater or lesser degree by the objections to his work that are represented above. It is not simply a question of Marion's having theological presuppositions in writing *Réduction et donation*, because the answer to that question is both yes and no. We have seen instead that beneath this general charge lie more specific questions that relate to the nature of phenomenology as such. Claiming that Marion has a theological agenda may be accurate, but it will also be confusing unless the main game is kept in mind. In fine, can phenomenology as a methodology sustain more than can be comprehended? If yes, then the theological connections might be validly developed. If no, then it seems that Marion's work fails, and further that there is no point pursuing phenomenology's relationship with theology. We are left, in the context of the present study, apparently unable to resolve the phenomenological problem of the gift, and therefore unable to resolve the challenge this problem poses to theology without recourse to dogmatic override. It is for this reason that this study, oriented as it is by that theological challenge, is driven chiefly to consider phenomenological concerns. To see how Marion reorients his phenomenology with an eye to his critics in *Réduction et donation*, we turn to the developments of *Étant donné*.

---

[130] There is an ambiguity in Marion's work between the use of the terms *revelation* and *Revelation*. Here I will use the capitalized term when I am speaking of a specific event occurring in faith, in the Christian tradition.

5

Being Given

In Defense of Givenness

Étant donné, published in 1997, represents the fullest account of Marion's phenomenology to date. Divided into five books, this monumental work repeats but also clarifies and extends the achievements of *Réduction et donation,* responding to many of the criticisms leveled at that project. At the moment we are concerned largely with the first book, which focuses on the formula reached in the final pages of *Réduction et donation* and developed in the article "L'autre philosophie première et la question de la donation": "as much reduction, as much givenness."[1] It is the same formula that Henry affirms in his article in the *Revue.*[2] Much as the title *Réduction et donation* leaves open a useful ambiguity, *Étant donné* allows Marion to implicate different phenomenological questions. While he plays with various alternatives, Marion ultimately suggests that we read "being given" as "it gives itself," making *étant* auxiliary to *donné,* and so focusing on the giving.[3]

---

[1] Carlson's translation of "autant de réduction, autant de donation" in *Reduction and Givenness* is "so much reduction, so much givenness." Marion, *RAG,* 203. I prefer "as much" for *autant* because it keeps the sense of proportion between the extent of the reduction and the yielding of givenness. For the intervening article, see Jean-Luc Marion, "L'autre philosophie première et la question de la donation," Institut Catholique de Paris, *Philosophie 17: Le statut contemporain de la philosophie première* (Paris: Beauschesne, 1996), 29–50, 49 [hereafter Marion, *LAPP*], 39.

[2] Indeed, Marion indicates that it is because of Henry's "validation" of the formula that he "dares" to raise it to a "principle" of phenomenology. Marion, *ED,* 24.

[3] Marion effects a shift from *givenness* to *étant-donné,* a move that is explicated by Carlson, again as translator, in a footnote to Marion's article "Metaphysics and Phenomenology: A Relief for Theology," 583: " 'The given of Being' [*le donné d'être*] defines every being as 'a being-given' [*un étant donné*]. With the hyphenation of *étant-donné,* which we translate as *being-given,* Marion creates a single term that resonates on several levels. On the one hand, one can read the simple construction wherein a noun, *l'étant* or *un étant,* is modified by an adjec-

Marion seems to echo Heidegger here—the given attests to its givenness, rather than its entitiveness; the given folds back on its givenness, which is "the fold of the given."[4] *Étant donné* is driven by two questions—and these we note well: whether or not phenomenology can go beyond metaphysics, and whether or not Revelation can be considered as a phenomenon. In this sense, *Étant donné* is heir not only to *Réduction et donation* but also to a slim but significant volume published in 1992: *Phénoménologie et théologie,* a collection of essays by Michel Henry, Paul Ricoeur, Marion, and Jean-Louis Chrétien, with an introduction by Jean-François Courtine. Many of those named by Janicaud are represented in this list.[5] While the phenomenon of revelation is under consideration, Marion insists—in response to his critics—that he is not suggesting we have to posit a transcendent donor, that he is not restoring metaphysics, and that he is not restoring the place of the transcendental subject, but simply allowing for the primary self-giving of "that which shows itself."[6]

It is perhaps in response to those same critics that Marion undertakes an extensive defense of his reduction to givenness, tracing the link between them (reduction and givenness) to Husserl's *The Idea of Phenomenology.* Using four textual examples, he argues from Husserl that (a) it is not the appearing alone that validates a phenomenon as a given, but its reduced character; (b) that the phenomenological reduction operates to exclude the transcendence of what is not given absolutely, or (c) that transcendence and immanence are redefined in relation to the reduction; and (d) that the reduction allows for the transcendent to become immanent. In other words, all the examples qualify *Gegebenheit* in terms of the quality of the reduction. Marion observes: "The link between reduction and givenness is found to be established, and

---

tive, *donné,* thus yielding *the given being* or *a given being.* On the other hand, one can also read the common French locution "étant donné (que)," which in its normal usage means 'being given' (that) or 'seeing that.' Phenomenology allows one to think the being-given in every given being, and thus the precedence of givenness over beings and their Being. The term *givenness* itself can convey at least three interrelated senses: giving, givenness, and the given."

[4] Marion, *ED,* 6–7.

[5] Courtine et al., *PT.*

[6] Marion, *ED,* 10–11.

by Husserl himself. A phenomenon only becomes absolutely given according to the extent to which it is reduced."[7] And in the same way that Marion reemphasizes the credibility of his reading of Husserl, he reexamines the Heideggerian material with a view to legitimating his association of both thinkers with a reduction to givenness. Marion's echoing of Heidegger is therefore not accidental, and where he excluded discussion of the *es gibt* (which he translates *ça donne*) from *Réduction et donation,* here he reflects on it in depth.[8]

In *Being and Time,* the *ça donne* accompanies and precedes being's opening out according to the horizon of time, the only nonontic example of what makes being accessible. Being comes to *Dasein* under the figure of givenness. Heidegger affirms that the phenomenality of being (*l'être*) does not show itself in being (*en étant*) or as a being (*un étant*), but according to givenness.[9] Nevertheless, there is still an overt dependence on *Dasein.* Not until the later text "Time and Being" does Heidegger recognize that being cannot be thought according to its own horizon, and hence discover the need to talk about a new horizon, that of givenness. Marion explains:

> To think "it gives" being (and time), to transpose being into the regime of givenness, nevertheless implies nothing arbitrary; firstly because it is necessary to recognise the impossibility of holding being in the horizon of being (only a being is, being *is* not), thus the obligation to assign to it a new horizon; subsequently because givenness, as soon as its first description, allows a reading of the most essential trait of being in its difference with being, its withdrawal.[10]

[7] Marion, *ED,* 24–25.

[8] Marion argues that the translation "*il y a*" "in effect masks all the semantics of givenness which nevertheless structure the '*es gibt.*' " *ED,* 51 n.

[9] Marion, *ED,* 50–53.

[10] Marion, *ED,* 54: "Penser que 'cela donne' l'être (et le temps), transposer donc l'être en régime de la donation n'implique pourtant aucun arbitraire; d'abord parce qu'il faut reconnaître l'impossibilité de tenir l'être dans l'horizon de l'être (seul l'étant est, l'être n'*est* pas), donc l'obligation de l'assigner à un nouvel horizon; ensuite parce que la donation, dès sa première description, permet de lire le trait le plus essentiel de l'être en sa différance d'avec l'étant, son retrait."

This withdrawal (of the gift) is an essential part of the giving.[11] Between the giving and the gift there must be a difference that maintains ontological difference. Thus we do not really think being so much as its retreat.[12]

Does Heidegger succeed in thinking givenness? Marion begins his response by saying that the *cela* is not to be thought as an enigmatic power, that it must not be thought, according to Heidegger, as a cause. It has to remain indeterminate. Heidegger is bracketing all transcendence: it is the giving, not the "it," that is important. Yet Heidegger gives the *cela* the name *Ereignis,* and Marion argues that this actually obscures the donative aspect. *Ereignis* does end up functioning as an indeterminate power, since Heidegger does not preserve the indeterminacy of the "it." Marion also wonders whether, if being disappears in the event, it meets the phenomenological exigency that it be exposed in the *cela donne.* Does the thinking of the *Ereignis* represent a phenomenological advance or a backward step? For Marion, *Ereignis* dissimulates givenness. Asking whether the retreat leads back to givenness, being, or *Ereignis,* Marion asserts that it goes back to givenness, but that Heidegger does not want to confirm this emphasis. Heidegger and Husserl thus effectively reach the same point. Although they make use of givenness, they do not affirm it as the key, but instead focus on other principles: objectivity and *Ereignis.* Marion's solution is to link givenness with reduction, a reduction that would not delimit any horizon. Givenness would in this way become its own horizon.[13]

Having reasserted the legitimacy of his reading Husserl and Heidegger in terms of givenness, Marion then explores what givenness as a horizon might mean. Givenness only ever appears indirectly, in the fold of the given.[14] As an example, he considers a painting, looking for ways in which its givenness might become apparent.[15] The painting might be seen as present-to-hand, yet

[11] Marion, *ED,* 55: "pour donner le don, le donner doit s'en retirer" ("to give the gift, the giving must withdraw").

[12] Marion, *ED,* 54–56.

[13] Marion, *ED,* 56–60.

[14] Like objectivity in its link with the object, or Being in its difference from being.

[15] Marion, *ED,* 60–62.

Marion maintains that the painting is more than the sum of its dots. It subsists beyond its visibility: its appearance is not only in its subsistence. Another way of looking at the painting is to suggest that it is ready-at-hand. This is a better option because it gives a sense of craftspersonship. It is subsistent, but there is something to see in it besides what is visible. The painting implies a painter or several painters, as well as spectators, an intention to paint, materials used, and so forth. In other words, it demands a decision to want to see more than the subsistent visible. However, this understanding is limited to functional operations and ends.[16] The painting is not really anything if it is taken in the manual sense.[17] A third path is to suggest that the painting be considered in its entitiveness. This is the Heideggerian approach, where art captures the truth of the being. But does it? Marion suspects that Heidegger remains tied to metaphysics here, since art is ordered to an end, be it beauty or truth.[18] He suggests instead that beauty appears independently of the being of a painting. We see something as beautiful not because of its own thingness but because it captures a *sense* of things. The beauty is irreal. Marion offers the possibility that the work of art, far from capturing the truth of the being, actually frees itself from it.[19] In the end, the painting *is not.*[20] The paradox of a painting is that it is not, and yet it appears all the more. In what, then, does the phenomenality of the painting consist? Marion uses Baudelaire to explain: what a painting requires is melody. The nonvisual analogy is used to express something that cannot be expressed in terms of real visibility. When a painting lacks melody it lacks its event-principle, its effect,

[16] The painting functions as (a) an aesthetic object of pleasure, (b) an object of value in the marketplace, or (c) an object of critical judgment. None of these assessments really grasps the painting as it gives itself. Marion, *ED,* 63–65.

[17] Marion, *ED,* 65–67.

[18] Marion, *ED,* 67–69.

[19] Once again he gives three examples. The painting is indifferent to the ontic circumstances of its appearance—it can be reprinted many times, but its beauty will be affirmed only by other criteria. It does not appear because it is, but because it exposes itself; physical reality alone is not sufficient to make it remarkable. To see a painting, it is not sufficient just to see it. The excess of the painting imposes itself on me, gives itself to me. Further, paintings demand revisitation. The painting does not consist of its thingness but in its mode of appearing, which can repeat itself at each viewing in a new mode.

[20] Marion, *ED,* 69–72.

which is the invisible life of the painting.[21] The effect defines the phenomenality of the painting—its givenness. That invisibility can give itself is not contradictory, but becomes possible when we bracket those things that do not belong to a given's pure phenomenality: its objectivity and its thingness. Invisibility makes visible. So it becomes possible to speak of other things that give themselves without objectivity, such as time, life, and one's word; or without being, such as death, peace, and sense. Marion uncovers here a new class of phenomena, vindicating his idea of a reduction to pure givenness.[22] It is at this point that we begin to see how revelation will become significant as a potentially invisible phenomenon.

The idea that the phenomenon can be reduced to a pure given is subject to two objections, which Marion reduces to one. He observes that there are some phenomena that define themselves by their irreducibility to givenness, such as death and nothingness, and asks whether or not there are two types of phenomenality, one that reduces to the given and the other that does not. What would this mean for the universality of givenness? Then he asks whether his reduction, which goes beyond the reduction both to objectivity and to "beingness," is really the ultimate in reductions.[23] "These two questions (universality, primacy) join themselves into one: how to justify the privilege given to givenness?"[24] We follow his response to these objections in some detail, for it is highly significant for both phenomenology and theology. Marion begins by saying that no thing is, or affects us, except insofar as it is given to us.[25] He maintains that this is even the case with regard to the nothing—givenness by denegation—a givenness by absence or lack. It is a matter of discerning the type of givenness rather than the fact of givenness. The nothing gives

[21] Marion, *ED,* 72–73. Marion uses Cézanne to describe the effect: it engages the soul, rather than perception or emotion. "L'effet fait vibrer l'âme de vibrations, qui, bien évidemment, ne représentent aucun objet, ni aucun étant, et ne peuvent elles-mêmes se décrire ou se représenter sur le mode des étants et des objets." *ED,* 75.

[22] Marion, *ED,* 73–78.

[23] With regard to the reduction to beingness, Marion uses *étantité* and connects it to Heidegger.

[24] Marion, *ED,* 79.

[25] Marion, *ED,* 79–80.

itself in anxiety, and this is not only a negative giving but a positive one.[26] The obscurity of the non-appearing gives itself (a) as the incomprehensible, where it gives the excess of the infinite (like Denys and Descartes); (b) as the weakness of intuition, where it gives the ideal of reason (Kant, Husserl); and (c) according to the negative, where it gives dialectic (Hegel). Emptiness gives itself in deception of the anticipation of perception, in desire.[27] These are, in fact, givennesses without a given. Husserl has already suggested that this is the case with nonbeing, counter-sense, and contradiction. In other words, Marion argues, givenness is not the same as intuition. There can be a given that does not fulfil intuition.[28] Marion suggests that deconstruction thus rests on "*la donation différée.*"[29] Rather than non-givenness, Husserl speaks of enlarged givenness, although Husserl is to be interpreted carefully on the question of "representation." Everything is given, but sometimes in an empty manner. Additionally, there can be no exceptions to givenness, so it makes no sense to speak of a non-givenness or a negative givenness, since these must be first donated.[30]

Marion notes the further objection that givenness presupposes the givenness to someone (ego, consciousness, subject, *Dasein,* life). This would mean that givenness would except those whom it affects. In the case of death, there would be no recipient and therefore no givenness. Yet according to Heidegger, death determines *Dasein,* which is paradoxical. For Heidegger, death is *Dasein*'s possibility par excellence, and defines its proper possibility. Death does not abolish the *Dasein* to which it gives, but gives to *Dasein* its ultimate determination of being, which is being-toward-death.[31] Death gives impossibility; it gives the experience of fini-

[26] It gives itself by the intuition of essences or by categorial intuition.

[27] Marion, *ED,* 81–82.

[28] This is also a Levinasian insight.

[29] Marion, *ED,* 82. This is very important in terms of the failure of the reduction.

[30] Marion, *ED,* 81–84.

[31] Marion, *ED,* 84–86. Of course, Heidegger's understanding of death is in this way very different from that of Levinas, for whom death always refers to the death of the Other. "This is the fundamental difference between my ethical analysis of death and Heidegger's ontological analysis. Whereas for Heidegger death is *my* death, for me it is the *other*'s death." Levinas in Kearney, *DCCT,* 62. In Derrida's discussion of Heidegger, Levinas, and death in *GD* at 41–47, he

tude as an existential determination of *Dasein*.[32] So according to Marion, even death and nothingness are given in givenness, indubitably.[33] Now, the indubitability without condition of givenness would become unacceptable if it were conceived in a substantial mode. Instead, it can only be conceived as an act, and not a personal one, but a phenomenological one that cannot be separated from the reduction. Thus Marion holds that to affirm the universality of givenness it is sufficient to try to deny it. It is always confirmed in its retreat.[34]

Having affirmed his reading of Husserl and extended his reading of Heidegger, Marion is able to present a strong case for the legitimacy of a reduction to givenness. But there remains a final issue to deal with: whether or not he has gone too far in using "givenness" to coordinate a number of words that have distinct meanings and usages (*es gibt, geben, gegeben, Gabe, Gebung, Gegebenheit*). Once again, he declares that it is not about exploiting an ambiguity but about stating a fact. The ambiguity is certainly there, but he does not find it necessary to exclude an idea that simply coordinates these different meanings. Looking further at the inevitable ambiguity of *la donation,* Marion explains that it has an ineluctable duality. It means the given gift, but it has also a sense of givenness that disappears in the given. Ambiguity is really

---

compares death as a moment of authenticity and the responsibility we bear for the other's death. Blanchot picks up on the solipsism inherent in Heidegger's perspective of death as ultimate possibility of impossibility. See Blanchot, *SL,* especially in the section entitled "The Work and Death's Space": "Can I die? Have I the power to die? This question has no force except when all the escape routes have been rejected. It is when he concentrates exclusively upon himself in the certainty of his mortal condition that man's concern is to make death possible. It does not suffice for him that he is mortal; he understands that he has to become mortal, that he must be mortal twice over: sovereignly, extremely mortal." *SL,* 96.

[32] Marion, *ED,* 86–87.

[33] It is a little like Descartes's argument for the existence of the cogito, except that the indubitability factor is different. Concerning the indubitability of the ego, it is possession that is invoked, whereas the indubitability of givenness has to do with abandonment. Givenness abandons itself in favor of the given. The indubitable is never a being but a universal act. How? Not as a transcendental (if indubitability were a transcendental it would impose itself prior to experience; transcendentals fix experience—givenness exceeds it). The indubitability of givenness is not like that of the ego, but its inverse, although it does not destroy it. Marion, *ED,* 87–89.

[34] Marion, *ED,* 89–90.

the essence of givenness, and trying to do away with the reversion of the given to givenness would mean doing away with the given itself.[35] *Gegebenheit* is, as his critics have pointed out, very difficult to render, but Marion claims that his choice to translate it by *la donation* is faithful to Husserl's use.[36] This is because "givenness" keeps the two senses of givenness: the result of givenness (the given) and givenness as a process (to give).[37]

Rethinking the Gift

In the second of the five books that make up *Étant donné,* Marion addresses the question of the gift by placing it in the context of givenness. It forms a direct response to Derrida's analysis of the gift on two fronts: Marion asserts both that phenomenology is possible and that, from a phenomenological perspective, the gift is also possible. In what follows I will draw material from two sources, both *Étant donné* and the earlier (in French) "Esquisse d'un concept phénoménologique du don," only more recently available in English as a chapter in Merold Westphal's *Postmodern Philosophy and Christian Thought.*[38] The theological setting of the article (hereafter referred to as "the Sketch") has a particular pertinence to our discussion, while *Étant donné* presents the material with greater lucidity.

Marion introduces the second book of *Étant donné* again with a

---

[35] Marion, *ED,* 91–97.

[36] This may well be the case in French, but when it is retranslated into English there is a problem.

[37] Marion notes that Löwith uses two different words (*donnée* and *présence*) but asks how we are to decide between them on any given occasion. Importantly, he also asks whether or not givenness is to be equated with presence. Marion, *ED,* 97–99. He claims that the translation of *Gegebenheit* by *donnée* is inadequate. Marion, *ED,* 99–100.

[38] "Sketch of a Phenomenological Concept of the Gift." It appeared in French as "Esquisse d'un concept phénoménologique du don" in *Archivio di filosofia,* Anno 62, nos. 1–3 (1994): 75–94 [hereafter Marion, *E*], and is now translated by John Conley, S.J., and Danielle Poe as part of *Postmodern Philosophy and Christian Thought,* ed. Merold Westphal (Bloomington: Indiana University Press, 1999), 122–43 [hereafter Marion, *SPCG*]. All translation mine unless indicated. *Étant donné* represents a more developed form of the argument, as Marion indicates in *SPCG,* 143 n.

reply to his critics. His interest in givenness is not theologically motivated, and it has no necessary metaphysical implications. Yet a juxtaposition of this text with the introduction of the Sketch is revealing. In the Sketch, Marion professes his interest in the links between the gift and revelation. The latter is characterized by an excess of intuition that gives it the appearance of a gift. We might see here something of the influence of Paul Ricoeur, who speaks of religious "feelings" (*sentiments*) "belonging to an economy of the gift, with its logic of superabundance, irreducible to the logic of equivalence."[39] For Marion, both revelation and the gift can be thought from the horizon of givenness, which is the horizon of phenomenology.[40] In the article, he undertakes his analysis of the gift with a view to coming to an understanding of revelation. But returning to *Étant donné,* we see the theological interest subject to far greater limitations. In this text, the phenomenological considerations are paramount: the task is to think givenness other than according to the model of efficient causality, a task that will involve thinking givenness along the lines of the gift.[41]

Noting that the gift has commonly been understood in terms of causality (giver gifts gift to recipient) and that such a (metaphysical) understanding defeats the gift, Marion asks whether or not the gift must remain an aporia. This leads him to an exposition and evaluation of Derrida's analysis of the gift. The merit of Derrida's discussion, he notes in the Sketch, is that it makes evident the connection between the problem of the gift and the problem of givenness. Using the Aristotelian terms of causality (which Derrida himself does not), Marion describes the metaphysical gift economy that Derrida has observed: "the donor gives the gift as an efficient cause, using a formal cause and a material cause (which is the gift) following a final cause (the good of the recipient and/or the glory of the donor); these four causes permit givenness to satisfy the principle of sufficient reason."[42] Mar-

[39] Paul Ricoeur, "Expérience et langage dans le discours religieux" [hereafter Ricoeur, *ELDR*], in Courtine et al., *PT,* 15–38, 16. It is of interest that Ricoeur uses the phrase "economy of the gift" but connects it with "superabundance" rather than "equivalence." Are we to read him in terms of Bataille on economy?

[40] Marion, *E,* 75; *SPCG,* 122–23.

[41] Marion, *ED,* 108.

[42] Marion, *E,* 76–77: "le donateur donne le don comme une cause efficiente, utilise une cause formelle et une cause matérielle (ce qui est comme le don) suivant une cause finale (le bien du donataire et/ou la gloire du donateur);

ion very deliberately links the metaphysical principles of causality and reason with the character of economy that undermines the gift.

Marion then examines each of Derrida's arguments. First there is the demand for a lack of reciprocity. The recipient must not make any return to the giver: the gift (or givenness) disappears as soon as it enters into a situation of exchange. Once again, Marion relates this to the need to satisfy the principle of sufficient reason, "that of identity and the fourfold causality which the economy follows in its metaphysical regime."[43] Derrida's next argument is an extension of the first: the recipient must not only not return anything to the giver but must remain unaware of the gift received. Here Marion makes an apparent modification to Derrida's point: "The recipient only profits from a gift—sheer gratuity—if he does not interpret it immediately as gift having to be given back, a debt to repay as soon as it is possible."[44] The word *immediately* is of interest, because upon my reading Derrida is less concerned with an immediate return than with any return as such.[45] Marion has observed a connection with time, but it is not the same connection Derrida makes, as we will later observe. He also questions Derrida's belief that a refused gift is annulled in the same way as one that is accepted, arguing that there are many gifts that go unrecognized, such as life and love, and possibly also death and hate.[46] Marion's interpretation of this lack of

---

ces quatre causes permettent à la donation de satisfaire au principe de raison suffisante." *SPCG,* 124; *ED,* 109.

[43] Marion, *E,* 77: "celui d'identité et la causalité quadriforme que suit, en son régime métaphysique, l'économie." *SPCG,* 124. This analysis is largely repeated in *ED,* 108–10.

[44] Marion, *E,* 77: "Le donataire ne bénéficie d'un don—pure gratuité—que s'il ne l'interprète pas immédiatement comme don devant être rendu, dette à rembourser dès que possible." *SPCG,* 125; *ED,* 111.

[45] Derrida's reading of Mauss on the possibility of delayed repayment is of interest here. Derrida notes the *différance* that is "*inscribed in the thing itself*" by the requirement of delay (*GT1,* 40). But this does not seem to remove, for Derrida, Mauss's gift from the cycle of economy. Perhaps an argument could be mounted, and this may be Marion's insight, that the delay or différance is sufficient to disrupt the complete return of the gift. In other words, by the time the gift is recognized in a counter-gift, a return to the identity of the gift is impossible.

[46] Marion, *E,* 78; *SPCG,* 125; *ED,* 111 n. Marion says that the true gift is one where there is no object: "When one gives life, there is no object, when one gives death, there is no object, when one gives forgiveness, one gives no object.

recognition is that the gift exceeds consciousness: a misunderstood gift remains perfectly given, since this meets the condition of no recognition.[47] By virtue of this possibility, Marion suggests that the gift thus does not depend on the recipient, and even goes so far as to say that the recipient can be phenomenologically suspended.[48]

The third of Derrida's arguments, Marion notes, concerns the donor, who must also forget the gift. Remembering is at the risk of self-congratulation: any reward would return the gift to the donor. Marion refers the donor's awareness of the gift to the ego, the transcendental and constitutive I, and since the gift is not where there is an ego, the donor can be suspended in a way similar to the recipient.[49] Derrida's last argument relates to the gift itself: for there to be gift, the gift cannot appear as gift. Marion

---

It is [the law of] the gift that one doesn't hold to an object." Jean-Luc Marion, personal interview, 21 November 1996 [hereafter Marion, Sorbonne interview].

[47] "Le donataire ne sait pas et n'a pas à connaître quel don lui advient, précisément parce qu'un don peut et doit surpasser toute claire conscience" ("The recipient does not know and does not need to be acquainted with whatever gift happens to him or her, precisely because a gift can and should surpass all clear consciousness"). Marion, *E,* 78; *SPCG,* 125; *ED,* 111. This is a crucial point in the debate between the two authors. Derrida is seeking not to reduce the gift to consciousness, and he does this by maintaining a radical anteriority and endless undecidability. Marion likewise does not wish to reduce the gift to consciousness, but he does so by taking the path of excess, where intentionality has a content but no object, much as with Descartes's idea of the infinite. Do these two paths ultimately coincide? To the extent that Marion is prepared to name his excess, perhaps not. With regard to the misunderstood gift, it seems Derrida may agree to some extent. However, Derrida distinguishes between a misunderstood gift (not recognized as gift) and an unappreciated gift (received as gift but not wanted). Marion does not always deal consistently with this issue, and his text can appear self-contradictory, as he goes on to say that a refused gift is still fully given. See Jacques Derrida, "At This Very Moment in This Work Here I Am," originally in *Textes pour Emmanuel Levinas,* and then in Jacques Derrida, *Psyché: Inventions de l'autre* (Paris: Galilée, 1987), 159–202, translated by Ruben Berezdivin for inclusion in the collection *Re-reading Levinas,* ed. Robert Bernasconi and Simon Critchley (Bloomington: Indiana University Press, 1991), 11–48 [hereafter Derrida, *ATVM*].

[48] "La donation suppose donc l'*époké* du donataire." Marion, *E,* 78; *SPCG,* 125; *ED,* 111–12. This seems a large step to take. Marion appears to be trying to say that whether or not a gift is given does not depend on the recipient. But at the same time, a recipient remains one of the conditions of im/possibility of the gift. Marion will make much of phenomenological bracketing, but I am not altogether certain that it always works.

[49] Marion, *E,* 78; *SPCG,* 125; *ED,* 112–13.

makes much of this "apparition" of the gift (*l'apparition*): it is the visibility (what he redefines in *Étant donné* as the "permanent visibility," or subsistence in presence or objectivity) of the gift as such that annuls it.[50] Yet he observes that Derrida here recovers Heidegger's "phenomenology of the inapparent."[51] For Marion, the non-appearance of the gift does not impede the phenomenological task: if the gift itself does not appear, there can still be a phenomenology of giving. Marion therefore finds baffling the paradox that Derrida embraces, which he expresses in *Étant donné* as an aporia: "Either the gift presents itself in presence, and disappears from givenness, to become inscribed in a metaphysical system of exchange; or the gift does not present itself, but thus no longer becomes visible at all, thus closing all phenomenality of givenness."[52] The two objections of Janicaud and Derrida with regard to givenness (its being implicated in metaphysical schemes of causality or subsistence in presence) are reflected in the gift.

Marion's solution is to think, along the lines of Levinas, a gift that excepts itself from being and therefore from presence thought as subsistence.[53] Yet Marion pushes the analysis further, and here his real point of disagreement with Derrida will emerge. He quotes Derrida's observations: "the truth of the gift . . . suffices to annul the gift," and "the truth of the gift is equivalent to the non-gift or to the non-truth of the gift."[54] Reading these statements via a process of formal argument, he arrives at two possible ways of understanding them. Following one way, he suggests that non-gift and non-truth are equivalent, and that therefore the gift is the truth. Alternatively, he suggests that the statements mean to oppose the gift and the truth, making them mutually exclusive. Marion tends toward accepting the first interpretation, while proposing that Derrida would probably favor the second.[55] In the debate at Villanova, and in response to this very point, Derrida maintains: "I would say that, in fact, if I had to

[50] Marion, *ED,* 113–14.
[51] Marion, *E,* 79.
[52] Marion, *E,* 79–80; *SPCG,* 126; *ED,* 113–15.
[53] Marion, *ED,* 115–16.
[54] Marion, *E,* 80–81; *SPCG,* 127–28, quoted from Derrida, *DT1,* 42. In translation it is from Derrida, *GT1,* 27.
[55] This discussion all takes place in the text of the Sketch, but the association of the gift and the truth is relegated to the footnotes of *Étant donné.*

choose, it would not be so simple. . . . I am referring to a traditional concept of truth, that is, an ontological-phenomenological concept of truth, as revelation or unveiling or adequation. From that point of view, I would say that there is no truth of the gift, but I do not give up on truth in general."[56] Taking a further step, Marion notes that Derrida distinguishes between a gift that is something determinate (which Marion identifies as the annulled gift) and a gift that gives the condition of the given in general but which actually gives nothing.[57] Since the latter gift gives no-thing, it seems to fulfil the conditions of possibility and impossibility of the gift.[58] But Marion rejects this option, too, because he sees in it a hint of the metaphysical (he reads "condition" as "foundation"). He also rejects it because he maintains that the modification of the object of the gift from given to condition of the given allows neither for the passage from the gift to givenness nor for the freeing of givenness from the economic system.[59] Now, Marion has indicated two points of disagreement with Derrida: on the question of the truth of the gift, and on the question of the gift as condition of giving. At this juncture, therefore, it seems he may wish to argue for a gift that can appear (even if not in the present) and which can be determinate. But then he changes tack. According to Marion's analysis, Derrida's gift can only be thought outside presence, outside subsistence, and outside truth, and is therefore impossible. That is unless, he argues, Derrida's gift does not deserve the name of "gift."[60] Instead of rejecting outright

---

[56] Derrida and Marion, *OTG*, 72.

[57] Marion, *E*, 81; *SPCG*, 128.

[58] And suits the giving of what does not exist, such as life, death and time. On this point I read Derrida slightly differently, placing the aforementioned gifts in the more general category rather than as conditions of the given, except, perhaps, time.

[59] Marion, *E*, 81; *SPCG*, 129–30; *ED*, 117–18.

[60] Marion, *E*, 82; *SPCG*, 129–30. In the Sorbonne interview he notes: "I have explained that Derrida says that if a gift is perfect, it is necessary that no one receives it, that no one gives it, and that no thing is given. According to him, the concept of the gift is a contradictory concept. Well, my response is that the gift isn't a contradictory concept. In the gift, always, if there is a gift, there is a giver and a receiver, but rarely the two at once. And in a true gift . . . there is no gift-object." Marion argues slightly differently with regard to truth in *ED*, 116–19, where he maintains that the gift can only be thought in dispensing with the truth of the gift as subsistence or presence—that is, he aligns himself a little more with Derrida.

what Derrida says about the gift, Marion affirms that no gift can be that which takes place in an economy, and that as a consequence there must be other conditions of possibility of the gift. He argues that all previous thinking of the gift has been done according to the horizon of exchange and in terms of causality, whereas he will think the gift according to the horizon of givenness. Looking toward Aquinas, where the gift is properly a givenness without return, or that which loses itself, Marion asserts that gratuity alone cannot suffice to define the gift.[61]

It is at this point that the methodologies of the Sketch and *Étant donné* diverge. Where the Sketch continues by reducing the gift to the way it is experienced by the donor and the recipient, *Étant donné* proceeds by bracketing each element of the causal mechanism of the gift in turn. The latter path is much less complex, although the former descriptions should not be abandoned, because they offer valuable insights into what Marion sees as the gift "itself." Therefore, while I will continue this study of Marion's articulation of the gift by way of *Étant donné*, I will also refer to the Sketch insofar as it augments this articulation.

Marion's argument is essentially as follows: if we disconnect at least one of the three causal mechanisms of the gift, the gift ceases to form part of a metaphysical construction and can be phenomenologically considered according to its givenness. By "causal mechanisms," which is my description and not Marion's, I mean those elements that regularly constitute gift-giving: a donor, a recipient, and a gift. So, Marion's first step in this process is to disconnect or bracket the recipient (*le/la donataire*), which means that we also consider the gift from the perspective of the donor. As we have seen in Derrida's analysis, if the recipient precedes the gift (by expectation or demand) or remains after it (in gratitude), the gift is doubly disqualified because it becomes the effect of a cause or involves reciprocity. If, on the other hand, the gift is considered from the perspective of the donor as pure loss, as something that cannot be returned because the specific recipient remains unknown, then it functions outside a causal or economic horizon.[62] Giving takes place when we give *as if* the gift cannot be

[61] Marion, *E,* 82–83; *ED,* 118–21.
[62] Marion, *ED,* 124–26.

returned. This is the case when I give without knowing the identity of the recipient: when I give to a charitable organization, the end recipient of my generosity will in all likelihood remain unknown to me. Then there is the instance of my giving to an enemy who does not return or even accept the gift. Here giving is in vain, without reason, an experience of sheer loss.[63] There remains the question, however, of whether or not a gift that is denied, not accepted, or not recognized is still a gift. Marion allows that it is because it remains lost, abandoned by the giver and not accepted by the recipient. And in the world of the lost, Marion suggests a new figure of resistance: the ungrateful one, one who not only refuses to pay back the debt engendered by the gift but also will not accept the debt in the first place. The ungrateful one proves, he suggests, that the gift can be fully given even without the consent of the recipient.[64] As a further possibility, Marion conceives of a giving that has a universal destination and is so unspecified. From a theological perspective, this occurs in the parable of the sheep and the goats, where everyone is a potential recipient (the recipient becomes universal) because Christ, to whom I (really) give, is invisible. Alternatively, if I sacrifice myself on behalf of a community (give my life for my country, for humanity, for children), not only is no individual a recipient, but no "thing" is given.[65] Finally, I may not know whether or not I give. As a donor, I can never be conscious of the effect I produce on possible recipients. I cannot see myself as others see me. The sportsperson, the artist, and the lover all give to those beyond them, but they do not see what they do: the giver withdraws from the gift. It is, so to speak, the right hand giving without knowing what the left hand is doing.[66]

Before leaving the discussion of the donor (suspension of the recipient), it is worthwhile returning to the Sketch to examine how Marion portrays the gift there. For what he is really doing in that context is trying to consider how the gift looks from the donor's point of view. Marion suggests that giving, for the donor, never signifies merely a transfer of property. It consists instead in

[63] Marion, *ED*, 128–29.
[64] Marion, *ED*, 130–31.
[65] Marion, *ED*, 134–35.
[66] Marion, *ED*, 139–41

the marking of an occasion or feeling. The gift-object simply serves as a support to the "real" gift; it is a symbol of that gift, always inadequate to the fullness of what it signifies. So according to Marion, there is a distinction between the gift and the gift-object. This marks a significant departure from Derrida, who includes that which the gift-object symbolizes as part of the gift as such. In other words, for Derrida the gift is annulled in its recognition, whether it be real or ideal:

> Thus the gift never coincides with the object of the gift. Better, one could suggest as a basic rule that the more a gift shows itself to be precious, the less it is achieved in an object, or, what is equivalent to it, the more the object reduces itself to an abstract role of support, of occasion, of symbol. Conversely, the gifts that give most never give anything—not a thing, not an object; not because they disappoint the expectation, but because what they give belongs neither to reality nor to objectivity.[67]

Marion's point, then, is this: the gift is not the gift-object, but that which the object (always inadequately) signifies.

If the gift is not the gift-object, what is it? A gift becomes such, not at the moment when it is given, but at the moment when the donor considers it able to be given. A gift becomes a gift only when it becomes *donable,* which might be rendered "donatable" or, following Conley and Poe, "givable." Now if something becomes givable, it does not itself gain anything: being givable is not a real predicate. The gift-object undergoes no change in itself as a result of its becoming givable. The transformation occurs totally within the donor. Marion goes on to explain that the gift begins

[67] Marion, *E,* 85: "Ainsi, le don ne coïncide pas avec l'objet du don. Mieux, on peut suggérer comme une règle de fond que, plus un don se montre précieux, moins il s'accomplit comme un objet, ou, ce qui y revient, plus l'objet s'y réduit au rôle abstrait de support, d'occasion, de symbole. Réciproquement, les dons qui donnent le plus ne donnent jamais *rien*—aucune chose, aucun objet; non qu'ils déçoivent l'attente, mais parce que ce qu'ils donnent n'appartient ni à la réalité, ni à l'objectité." *SPCG,* 132–33. See Derrida, *GT1,* 13. This becomes an interesting question, since for Derrida, gifts such as love, forgiveness, or "what one does not have" are possibilities. Their survival as gifts depends on their not being present, not being any "thing" at all, but Marion would counter that these are the sorts of (non)-things that are symbolized by gift-objects. Thus the widow's mites could be read as symbols of what she does not have. The difference between Marion and Derrida on this point might not be as clear as first thought.

as a result of a sense of obligation. The gift begins when the donor realizes that he or she owes something to someone:[68]

> The gift begins and, in fact, is completed, as soon as the donor envisages owing something to someone, thus when the donor admits that he should be a debtor, thus a recipient. The gift begins when the potential donor suspects that another gift has already preceded it, for which he owes something, to which he must respond. Not only does the gift reside in the decision to give taken by the potential donor, but the donor can only thus decide insofar as he recognizes that another gift has already obliged them. The gift is decided.[69]

The gift thus arises as a result of both the recognition of givability and the recognition of indebtedness. The upsurge of givability and the recognition of indebtedness always relate to an anterior gift, which prompts a new gift.

To what is the gift really reduced in this description? Is Marion's gift, as the lived experience of the giver, simply the upsurge of givability? Is it my decision to give? Is it my acknowledgment of debt? Is it the noematic gift, given to consciousness, as givable? If a gift is a response to indebtedness, how does it escape the cycle of exchange? It seems to me that there are at least two ways to read what Marion is saying, directly related to the ways in which he makes the various reductions. According to the first way, the new "definition" of gift at which Marion arrives would be as follows: a gift is a decision regarding givability that comes about in response to my recognition of being indebted. It would relate primarily to the exclusion of the transcendence of the gift-object. The gift would thus be the decision to view something as givable. The decision would arise out of an anterior debt, involving a choice to acknowledge that debt. The gift itself would be neither

[68] This notion of debt is, of course, completely opposite to what Derrida would consider appropriate.

[69] Marion, *E,* 86: "Le don commence et, en fait, s'achève, dès que le donateur envisage de devoir quelque chose à quelqu'un, donc lorsqu'il admet qu'il pourrait être débiteur, donc donataire. Le don commence quand le donateur potentiel soupçonne qu'un autre don l'a déjà précédé, auquel il doit quelque chose, auquel il se doit de répondre. Non seulement le don réside dans la décision de donner prise par le donateur potentiel, mais celui-ci ne peut ainsi décider qu'autant qu'il reconnaît qu'un autre don l'a déjà obligé. Le don se décide." *SPCG,* 133.

the gift-object nor that which the gift-object symbolizes, but simply the decision to view the object or symbol as gift. The decision would not be that which is exchanged, since a decision "is" nothing.[70] The decision would be mine insofar as I chose to recognize the claim of the anterior gift. Since the decision would be nothing other than a way of seeing something, it would escape all entry into an economy, even in being a response to an anterior gift. Yet such a reading of Marion seems generous. Perhaps the gift lies in the moment of decision, yet it is not the decision that is given, but the gift-object, be it real or ideal. And as soon as there is a response, it is hard to argue that there is no cause of this effect. How would Marion consider the anterior gift that gives rise to the obligation? It also seems that Marion's definition might work in terms of a human donor, but what of a divine donor? If the gift always and only arises in response to a debt, what kind of anterior debt would prompt a divine gift? Surely wherever there is indebtedness, there is no gift. Would it make any difference if the anterior gift were undecidable?

A second way of reading Marion would result in a "definition" with the following emphases: the gift is that which is witnessed in that trace of undecidable indebtedness that is given in the decision of response, that which is the only possible response to giftedness.[71] This reading would remove the gift from an economy insofar as it takes away the donor as cause. The gift itself would lie in what has always already been given. But is such a reading possible on the basis of the text? It seems unlikely. This is mainly because, at least in the Sketch, Marion does not specify that the indebtedness has an undecidable origin. Because of this factor, he is really unable to effectively remove the gift from the horizon of causality.

It is not difficult to see why some of these aspects of the donor's experience of the gift are not brought out in a reading of *Étant donné*. Nevertheless, the Sketch is a current text in the sense that its translated version was published after that book, and it could be argued that since many of its conclusions are not clearly repu-

---

[70] And remembering that according to Derrida, an aporia can only be negotiated by decision.

[71] This would be consonant with a reading of Marion that emerges from later material, where the gift gives itself in giving "receiving."

diated, it still has a bearing on Marion's position. In any case, having examined it, we are well prepared to continue with the second phase of the suspensions carried out in *Étant donné:* the suspension of the donor.

When the donor (*le donateur, la donatrice*) is suspended, what we have to consider is the experience of the recipient, who is cast in terms of an inability to respond to a particular giver. This is not quite to go so far as to say that the recipient cannot know if the gift is a gift (Derrida), but it is still to insert an element of risk in the receiving. Can an anonymous gift still be a gift? Marion illustrates that this can be so with some examples, the first of which is that of heritage. I receive a great deal from the State, to which I am obliged to respond by paying taxes. But in actual fact, it is not the State that provides these things, but others who, like me, contribute to the state. So when I make my response to the state in paying taxes, I am not responding to the individuals who make it possible for the state to give. Everyone gives, but at the same time, no one gives. Alternatively, where the donor is not anonymous in this dispersed sense but anonymous in that I do not know who he or she is, the economic cycle of the gift is broken.[72] When it is impossible to gain access to the donor, the recipient is in the position of having to recognize him- or herself as forever in debt. This is, in fact, how Marion goes on to speak about subjectivity. Indebtedness emerges once again with the recognition that I receive myself as a gift without a giver. The gift is always and already anterior, subject to *différance*.[73]

The section of the Sketch on the reduction of the gift brings to light the possible differences between the decisions to give and to receive. Marion notes that it is not only giving that is potentially arduous, but receiving as well. That is because the gift (whatever it "is") may be something unexpected, or not wanted, or even feared. To accept a gift means to renounce my independence, because it means that I will owe something because of it. Already, Marion's language suggests that he is still trapped within the causal horizon he hopes to escape. But he then adds the rider, along the lines that we have seen in *Étant donné:*

[72] Marion, *ED,* 136–39.
[73] Marion, *ED,* 139.

> Let us note well that it is not first or foremost about a recognition of debt towards the donor, such that we would be driven from [thinking] the gift according to givenness to [thinking] the gift according to an economy; because this recognition of dependence on a donating gratuity remains even if the donor stays unknown or is completely lacking (so towards absent parents, Nature, indeed the State etc.); it could even be that this recognition weighs all the more if it is not possible to attach it to any identifiable partner; because such a gratuity puts in question nothing less than the autarky of the self and its pretension of self-sufficiency.[74]

Allowing for the donor to remain unknown, Marion thus allows for the possibility that the anterior gift might somehow be immemorial in origin. Additionally, he considers how "the gift is decided" with regard to the recipient. Deciding to receive the gift means deciding to be obliged by the gift. It is the gift that wields its influence on the recipient, effectively provoking the recipient to decide in favor of it, prompting the yielding of self-determination to determination by the reception of the gift.[75] He concludes that "according to the regime of reduction, the lived experience of consciousness where the gift gives itself *consists in the decision of the gift* [emphasis added]—that of receiving the gift by the recipient, but especially that of persuading the recipient to the gift by the gift itself. The gift gives *itself* in giving to be received."[76]

---

[74] Marion, *E,* 88: "Notons bien qu'il ne s'agit pas d'abord ni surtout d'une reconnaissance de dette envers le donateur, telle qu'elle nous reconduirait du don selon la donation au don selon l'économie; car la reconnaissance de dépendre d'une gratuité donatrice demeure même si le donateur reste inconnu ou manque absolument (ainsi envers les parents absents, la nature, voire l'Etat, etc.); il se pourrait même que cette reconnaissance pèse d'autant plus qu'elle ne peut se fixer sur aucun partenaire identifiable; car une telle gratuité met en cause rien de moins que l'autarcie du soi et sa prétention d'auto-suffisance." *SPCG,* 136.

[75] Marion, *E,* 88: "La décision entre le donataire potentiel et le don ne s'exerce donc pas tant du premier sur le second, que du second sur le premier: le don, par son attrait et son prestige propres décide le donataire à se décider pour lui, c'est-à-dire le décide à sacrifier sa propre autarcie—l'autarcie de son propre—pour le recevoir." *SPCG,* 136.

[76] Marion, *E,* 88: "en régime de réduction, le vécu de conscience où se donne le don consiste dans la décision du don—celle de recevoir le don par le donataire, mais surtout celle de décider le donataire au don par le don lui-même. Le don *se* donne en donnant de le recevoir." My translation of this passage is awkward, and I add here what Conley and Poe arrive at: "in the regime of reduction, the experience of consciousness in which the gift gives itself consists in the deci-

What Marion has observed regarding the relationship between gift and recipient, he relates to the relationship between donor and gift. A gift is only possible where the "protagonists" recognize it in "a being, an object, indeed in the absence of being and object of an immediate relation between them."[77] In other words, it is about seeing the gift correctly, of having a particular sense for reading it. It is a phenomenology or hermeneutics that allows the gift to present itself, which means seeing the gift according to a donating horizon. This also means that neither donor nor recipient is an agent of the gift so much as acted upon by givenness.[78] The gift, as that which "is decided" (or decides *itself*), need not be read economically but can be appreciated simply as the given; it obtains its character as given only from the horizon of givenness. In this way Marion maintains that the gift is outside any economy, outside any causality, and outside any agency.

The third part of the parenthetical process suggested to us by Marion is the suspension of the gift itself. The reduced gift is one that may not be anything at all: it may be a promise, reconciliation, friendship, love or hate, life or my word. In this case, an object might represent the gift, but in an inversely proportional way. He uses the example of the conferring of power on a leader, which is represented in various insignia but not merely equal to them. The difficulty involved with a gift that is not anything at all is that it can be difficult to recognize. What determines such a gift as gift is an act of faith, a new hermeneutical stance, and what changes, when this risk of identifying something as givable is

sion of the gift—the decision to receive the gift by the recipient but especially the decision to decide the recipient of the gift by the gift itself. The gift *itself* gives by giving its reception." Marion's use of words relating to *décider* is frequently confusing. Where he uses *se décider* I have translated it by "to be decided." But he manifests a strong tendency toward personifying the gift. Where he uses *se décider à,* it has more of a personal sense ("to persuade, convince, decide"). It also seems, in examples such as this one as well as the one mentioned in the previous note, that he does wish to underline that sense. The gift itself influences the recipient. For that reason, *se décider* might also suggest "to decide itself," in the same way that *se donner* means "to be given," but also suggests "to give itself." *SPCG,* 136.

[77] Marion, *E,* 88: "un étant, un objet, voire dans l'absence d'étant et d'objet d'une relation immédiate entre eux." *SPCG,* 136.

[78] Marion, *E,* 89; *SPCG,* 136. Here it comes back to seeing, or to seeing correctly. In the corresponding passage in *ED,* 143–47, Marion opens us the element of risk or undecidability in interpretation.

The Toadstool Bookshop
Lorden's Plaza, Milford NH 03055
Phone (603) 673-1734
Special orders welcome, give us a call

H 3767 11/28/07 18:24

26656	1*RETHINKING GOD A 20.01	20.01
HERON	Total due:	20.01
	Cash	20.01

Thank You!
Sign up for our email newsletter at
www.toadbooks.com and we'll send you a
coupon worth 20% off your next purchase.

taken, is not the object itself, but its way of appearing, its phenomenality. This occurs for both donor and recipient.[79]

Marion indicates that he has achieved the description of the phenomenological gift, which is quite unlike the sociological or anthropological versions. It overcomes the deficiencies of these gifts insofar as they are implicated in causality and reciprocity. Further, it enables Marion to think the gift otherwise than according to transcendence, which, he claims, is the complication that most readily leads to his being accused of doing theology. But there is more. If one were to think theologically, he claims his phenomenological gift would be on the side of revealed, rather than rational, theology.[80] "Revealed theology could in return be defined as a thought of the gift without reciprocity, because without transcendent condition external to itself."[81] This is, of course, highly relevant to the question that motivates this book: how is it possible to speak of God as gift?

Marion's gift has been defined in a purely immanent way, with givenness characterized intrinsically, and he seeks to show further how the manner in which the gift gives itself is the same as the manner in which the phenomenon shows itself. This effectively means that all phenomenality will be able to be described as gift, a point that underscores his connection of the many cognates of *Gegebenheit.* It is a point that is not lost on Derrida, and one against which he will protest. But Marion maintains that he is able to achieve this without implicating phenomena-as-gifts in any metaphysical structure. His disconnection of any one of the three elements that would together constitute a gift economy enables him to sidestep the questions of exchange and causality. As a gift is given, so the phenomenon.[82] And according to this reading of phenomenology, it becomes possible to be open to any type of phenomenon that may give itself.

Rethinking the Given: Determinations

By delimiting the horizon according to which phenomena are given, Marion hopes to open a potentially unlimited "space" for

[79] Marion, *ED,* 147–61.
[80] Marion, *ED,* 161–64.
[81] Marion, *ED,* 163.
[82] Marion, *ED,* 164–66.

the non-objective to manifest itself. But what exactly is given in this manifestation, and how is it given? Marion devotes two sections of *Étant donné* to a discussion of this question, extending in particular his 1992 article "Le phénomène saturé."[83]

In *Étant donné* Marion maintains that givenness is equivalent to phenomenality.[84] He suggests that his method is a sort of empiricism, albeit one that does not limit itself to the sensible, and he specifies three requirements of an approach by way of givenness that will enable the given phenomenon to be described. Givenness must allow us to describe *intrinsically* the phenomenon as purely and strictly given, without reference to transcendence or to causality. Givenness must then determine the phenomenon as *irrevocably* given, so that the mode of phenomenality can be assessed. And givenness must *radically* determine the phenomenon *as* given, so that we consider the phenomenon precisely as and because it is integrally given.[85]

How are we to determine that the given has been given intrinsically? The constitution of the given is equivalent to the giving of its sense (*Sinngebung*), but this emphasis on immanence can take away both from the initiative of the given in giving itself and, as Marion points out, from the reality of its givenness as such. This Marion interprets in terms of the gift, which means that we enter immediately the somewhat murky waters of Marion's debate with Derrida and Greisch about the link between givenness, the given, and the gift. What is important here is that Marion wants to retain a characteristic of the gift—that it comes "from elsewhere" (following Aquinas)—as a characteristic of the given. Alerting us to the problematic implications of this insistence, in that it may draw us into the possibility of exchange and causality, Marion limits the "from elsewhere" characteristic to an aspect of the phenomenological mode of appearing so that he can exclude any metaphysical indication of causality. The given thereby does not need to

---

[83] Marion, *PS*.

[84] In a more recent article still, "L'évènement, le phénomène et le révélé," *Transversalités: Revue de L'Institut Catholique de Paris* 70 (April–June 1999): 4–25, 21, Marion more carefully distinguishes between the given and phenomenality, a distinction that can be read into *Étant donné* in the sense in which he means it here (it is in being received that the given is phenomenalized), but which is articulated more clearly in the later piece.

[85] Marion, *ED*, 169–73.

suggest an origin, a cause, or a giver, and it appears independently.

One of the essential traits of the given phenomenon is its "anamorphosis," its need to be put in perspective by its recipient.[86] Now Marion makes a very important move. Affirming that anything that is visible must appear, and so have a form, he distinguishes between unformed and informed form. The latter is what renders the phenomenon visible and enables it to be distinguished from other phenomena. Yet in contrasting the two forms, he asserts that only someone with the capacity to see will recognize the informed form, that which shows itself. Marion leaves open the possibility that there can "appear" what is unformed, while it may not be put in perspective until the recipient is capable of performing what might be described by others as a hermeneutical act.[87] One way of interpreting this move is to suggest that it prepares the ground for Marion to promote phenomena that cannot be understood (unformed form) but can be interpreted (informed form) by a person who is "able to see." The anamorphic phenomenon is further described by Marion as contingent and factical, which means that it can "arrive" or "happen" as a lived experience but without being expected or understood, or at least without being understood fully.[88] Facticity is a type of exposure: I become the objective of the object, not it for me; I experience the phenomenon as a fait accompli, always and already a fact.[89] The given is also described in terms of an "incident" (or "accident"), which reinforces its suddenness.[90] Once again, there is a distinction between an unformed and an informed appearance. A particle can appear to me without my being able to contextualize it; a painting can appear to me without form, but simply as the impact of color. Turning to a Levinasian example, the face of the Other can impose itself on me without my being able to

[86] An "anamorphosis" is a "distorted drawing appearing regular from one point" (*OED*): in other words, the anamorphic effect requires that the viewer find the perspective from which this regularity will emerge. While perspective may seem to be at the initiative of the viewer, Marion emphasizes that it imposes itself on the viewer from the given.

[87] Marion, *ED,* 174–95.

[88] Marion, *ED,* 195–99.

[89] Marion, *ED,* 211–12.

[90] Marion, *ED,* 213–21.

think it as substance. In Descartes, Marion finds a recognition that there are some "incidents" that remain unable to be thought, not because thought is deficient, but because what is given simply exceeds the capacity of thought.[91] What gives itself is neither an object nor a thing, but instead a "pressure" that takes place in an event beyond my control, an effect that is not subject to the requirement of a cause.[92] In this liberation of the effect or event from the cause, several important characteristics emerge. The event is irrepeatable: no two events are alike, and while every event has precedents, it can only be spoken of as an event if it exceeds these precedents.[93] In other words, every self-manifestation adds to the visibility of the phenomenality of the world. Additionally, every event sets off new possibilities—not metaphysical possibilities, but possibilities that cannot be foreseen. The event seems impossible, since it occurs outside essence, outside the principle of contradiction, without the notion of cause and suspending the principle of sufficient reason. Yet Marion argues that "possibility does not exercise itself firstly on essence in order to preview its effectivity, but, in an exactly inverse sense, by a proceeding towards form delivering an arrival, which provokes a fait accompli and finally liberates the incident 'outside essence.' "[94] The determination of the phenomenon by anamorphosis means that the phenomenon surges into visibility, and it is necessary to expose or even submit oneself to the phenomenon in order to receive it.[95]

All three of Marion's exigencies—that the given be given intrinsically, irrevocably, and radically—are observed in his analysis. It is given intrinsically because the phenomenon can be described without reference to a cause, a real essence, or a constituting I, since each of these conditions is bracketed. (With regard to the constituting I, Marion explains that the I does not go beyond its transcendental role as a screen for lived experiences.) The given

[91] Marion, *ED,* 223–24.

[92] Marion, *ED,* 225–36.

[93] Marion, *ED,* 240–41.

[94] Marion, *ED,* 243: "la possibilité ne s'exerce pas d'abord sur une essence pour prévoir une effectivité, mais, en sens exactement inverse, par une montée vers la forme délivrant un arrivage, qui provoque un fait accompli et libère enfin l'incident 'hors de l'essence.' "

[95] Marion, *ED,* 246.

is given irrevocably because as fait accompli and event, the phenomenon is irrepeatable, and because it is reduced.[96] The third requirement—radicality—is demonstrated insofar as all phenomena, and not just those of a limited region, are subject to the fold of givenness. This means that it is possible to describe any phenomenon as *l'étant donné*.[97]

Rethinking the Given: Degrees of Givenness

That all phenomena can be understood with reference to givenness allows us to question the variation in degrees of givenness. We note well that at this point Marion expresses a caution in linking phenomenology and religion, since he recognizes that what can be objectively defined may lose its religious specificity, while what is religiously defined may lose its objectivity. Importantly, his reading is that the religious phenomenon is impossible, or marks the point at which phenomenality is no longer possible.[98] Nevertheless, this view of the impossibility of the religious phenomenon rests on the assumption that a phenomenon is that which is possible. Marion prefers to ask about the terms of possibility, and to think about the religious phenomenon as a "privileged indication of the possibility of phenomenality."[99] This leads to a lengthy conversation with Kant, for whom possibility means that which accords with the formal conditions of experience. For Kant, possibility depends on phenomenality: not on the phenomenal object as such, but on its power to be known. Like Leibniz, Kant ties this power of knowability to the principle of sufficient reason.[100] In contrast, Husserlian phenomenology opposes the Kantian definition of phenomenality with a "principle of principles" that admits of phenomena without condition.[101] However, this principle is problematic where it seems to limit phenomena to

[96] Marion, *ED,* 246–47.

[97] Marion, *ED,* 248–49.

[98] Marion, *PS,* 79–80. *ED* largely repeats what is propounded in this seminal article.

[99] Marion, *PS,* 80; *ED,* 251ff.

[100] Marion, *PS,* 80–83; *ED,* 253–57.

[101] Marion, *PS,* 83–84; *ED,* 257–58. Marion quotes what he has elsewhere listed as the third principle of phenomenology.

the constituting intuition.[102] According to this principle, phenomena can therefore only appear according to a horizon.[103] It is these factors that seem to exclude the possibility of an "absolute" phenomenon. So Marion asks whether it is possible to envisage a phenomenon that is unconditioned, having no horizonal limits, or going beyond the horizon, and irreducible to an I, in that the I would be constituted instead of constituting.[104] It is here that he perceives an opening for the thinking of religious phenomena.[105]

The impossibility of unconditioned and irreducible phenomena is related to the determination of phenomena given in a weakness of intuition. So Marion asks about the possibility of phenomena that are instead saturated in intuition: "why not respond with the possibility of a phenomenon where intuition would give *more, indeed immeasurably more,* than the intention would ever have aimed at, or could have foreseen?"[106] Kant takes up the possibility of an intuition for which an adequate concept cannot be found when he speaks of aesthetic experience.[107] Where there is an excess of intuition, there is an excess of givenness.[108] "Intuition no longer exposes itself in the concept, but saturates it and renders it overexposed—invisible, not by default, but by an excess of light."[109] How could such a phenomenon be described? Marion

---

[102] Marion, *PS,* 84–86; *ED,* 262–64.

[103] Marion, *PS,* 86–88; *ED,* 259–62.

[104] Marion, *PS,* 88–89; *ED,* 264–65. Note Ricoeur once again, in terms of not being a prisoner to intentionality or representation, *ELDR,* 17–18.

[105] Marion, *PS,* 89–90.

[106] Marion, *PS,* 103: "pourquoi ne répondrait pas la possibilité d'un phénomène où l'intuition donnerait *plus, voire démesurément plus,* que l'intention n'aurait jamais visé, ni prévu?" *ED,* 275–77. Marion's footnote on page 276 of *ED* is instructive: "Nous proposons de parler de phénomène saturé et non pas saturant, comme on nous l'a parfois suggéré. En effet, c'est l'intuition qui sature tout concept ou signification, en sorte que ce phénomène se manifeste bien sur un mode saturé par intuition saturante. Plus, l'intuition qui le sature le sature uniquement au nom de la donation: le phénomène saturé l'est d'abord de donation. Certes, un tel phénomène sature-t-il ensuite et par conséquence le regard auquel il se donne à voir et connaître; on peut donc à la rigueur le dire aussi saturant. Pourtant la saturation qu'il exerce dans le champ de la connaissance résulte seulement de celle qu'il reçoit dans le champ de la donation; la donation détermine toujours la connaissance et non l'inverse."

[107] Marion, *PS,* 103; *ED,* 278.

[108] Marion, *PS,* 104.

[109] Marion, *PS,* 105: "l'intuition ne s'expose plus dans le concept, mais le sature et le rend surexposé—invisible, non point par défaut, mais bien par excès de lumière."

sketches an answer using the Kantian categories of quantity, quality, relation, and modality—except that the saturated phenomenon relates negatively to these categories since it exceeds them: not an object, the saturated phenomenon prefigures the possibility of a phenomenon in general.[110]

The saturated phenomenon exceeds the category of quantity because it defies the ability of intuition to apply successive syntheses to it. It cannot be aimed at, is thus unforeseeable, and cannot be measured according to what has preceded it.[111] It exceeds the category of quality because it defies the ability of intuition to bear it: it is blinding, giving reality without limitation or negation, an excess, glory, joy, an overflow.[112] The saturated phenomenon is absolute according to the category of relation because it defies the ability of intuition to bring it back to any analogy with experience.[113] Marion asserts that not all phenomena have to respect the unity of experience, giving as an example the "event," to which he has already referred in the determinations.[114] "Event, or unforeseeable phenomenon (from the past), not exhaustively comprehensible (from the present), not reproducible (from the future), in short absolute, unique, happening."[115] The saturated phenomena goes beyond any horizon, unable to be limited by it, saturating it, or in fact playing on several horizons at once.[116] And

[110] Marion, *PS*, 105–6; *ED*, 280–88.

[111] Marion, *PS*, 106–8.

[112] Marion, *PS*, 108–11. Marion observes, incidentally, that holiness blinds us to the One we cannot see without dying. *PS*, 110.

[113] Marion, *PS*, 112–18.

[114] Marion, *PS*, 112–13.

[115] Marion, *PS*, 113: "Événement, ou phénomène non prévisible (à partir du passé), non exhaustivement compréhensible (à partir du présent), non reproductible (à partir du futur), bref absolu, unique, advenant."

[116] Marion, *PS*, 116–18. See also Marion's discussion of Kant on this point in *ED* at 289–96. Marion likes neither the necessity of a horizon nor the necessity of time as that horizon, asking whether there are some phenomena that go beyond their horizons. Yet again he goes on to say that it is not about dispensing with a horizon altogether, since there can be no manifestation without a horizon, but about using horizon in another mode, freeing it from its anterior delimitations so that it does not forbid the appearance of an absolute phenomenon. Marion imagines two examples. In the first example, the phenomenon fits within the horizon but at the same time pushes it open, working against it. In the second example, the phenomenon goes beyond the limits of the horizon. It seems as if Marion is speaking about seeing the phenomenon according to different horizons that are in fact opposed, so that the phenome-

it exceeds the final category of modality because it is irregardable. Where Kant's use of modality relates to the accordance of objects of experience with the power to know, which inevitably relates to a transcendental I, Marion argues that with a saturated phenomenon, the I cannot constitute the object but is in fact constituted by it. This is the imposition of a "counter-experience" on experience.[117] "Confronted with the saturated phenomenon, the *I* cannot not see it, but it cannot look at it like an object, either."[118] What does the I see? It sees no-thing, no objectifiable given, but is simply dazzled by brilliance, by a paradox.[119] The paradox suspends the relation of the phenomenon to the I and inverts it, so that the I is constituted by the phenomenon as a *me,* a witness.[120] Importantly, Marion stresses that this constituting rather than constituted givenness does not necessarily have theological implications. It is also of interest in the light of the earlier discussion of Levinas that Marion here refers to the "trace" of the saturated phenomenon.[121] With his "description" of the saturated phenomenon, Marion goes beyond both Husserl and Kant. Yet he maintains that the possibility of a giving without reserve is very Husserlian. The saturated phenomenon is a possibility that goes beyond the very conditions of possibility, the possibility of the impossible.[122] It is readily exemplified in the Cartesian idea of the

---

non remains undefined. Then there is a third example, Marion says, a rare case in which there is no horizon and no combination of horizons that can contain the phenomenon. The ambiguity in Marion's writing on the question of whether or not there is a horizon is hard to resolve. A clearer position seems to emerge in Derrida and Marion, *OTG,* where Marion observes at p. 66: "I said to Levinas some years ago that in fact the last step for a real phenomenology would be to give up the concept of horizon. Levinas answered me immediately: 'Without horizon there is no phenomenology.' And I boldly assume he was wrong." This is precisely where he disagrees with Derrida about the nature of phenomenology.

[117] Marion, *PS,* 119–21. For his discussion of modality in *ED,* see pp. 296–303.

[118] Marion, *PS,* 121: "Affronté au phénomène saturé, le *Je* ne peut pas ne pas le voir, mais il ne peut pas non plus le regarder comme son objet."

[119] Marion, *PS,* 121.

[120] Marion, *PS,* 121. Marion elsewhere names this "me" "the interlocuted," or in *ED,* "the devoted one." In the latter case the religious imagery is striking, and one wonders why Marion has moved to this appellation if he simultaneously wants to distance himself from a univocal reading of the phenomenon.

[121] Marion, *PS,* 122.

[122] Marion, *PS,* 123–25; *ED,* 303–5.

Infinite, Kant's sublime, and Husserl's internal time consciousness.[123]

Saturated phenomena are paradoxical insofar as they cannot be anticipated by an intention while being given to intuition. Marion observes four types of paradoxical phenomena, according to the saturation and subversion of each of the four Kantian determinations of quantity, quality, relation, and modality.[124] The historical event saturates the category of quantity.[125] The idol potentially saturates the category of quality.[126] Flesh saturates the category of relation.[127] And the icon saturates the category of modality.[128] The icon offers nothing to see, but itself "regards." The I simply becomes a witness of the givenness. It is in this context that Marion raises the possibility of the saturated phenome-

---

[123] Marion, *PS,* 124–25; *ED,* 306–9. While Graham Ward considers it in the context of other authors, his analysis of the sublime and its theological implications is very pertinent here. "With Lyotard's (and Cixous's) examination of the 'present' or the 'event' we are brought again to the theology of the gift and the economy of mediated immediacy. The moment itself, for Lyotard, is without content. It is an encounter with nothingness . . . consequent upon a certain personal ascesis. . . . Karl Barth consistently emphasized that revelation was a mediated immediacy in which the hidden face of God was revealed." Graham Ward, *Theology and Contemporary Critical Theory* (London: Macmillan, 1996), 129. Marion, too, will make this link with the gift; like Ward, his gift will be situated in a type of economy.

[124] Marion, *ED,* 314–17.

[125] A historical event is something that cannot be limited to an instant, a place, or an empirical individual. Marion gives the example of Waterloo, where no one actually "saw" this battle as such. Its possible horizons are infinite in number. *ED,* 318–19.

[126] The idol stops the gaze (and returns it to the viewer like a mirror). Marion gives the example of the painting, which gives itself without concept. Nevertheless, the idol is different from other saturated phenomena because it provokes solipsism. *ED,* 319–21.

[127] As we find in Levinas, Merleau-Ponty, and Henry, flesh or bodiliness cannot be reduced to consciousness. Marion echoes Henry's work on auto-affection and the absolute experiences of agony, suffering, grief, desire, and orgasm such that they saturate the horizon. He further specifies bodily experience in two ways: first, it is unlike the idol but like the historical event, in that it is not about seeing; and second, it is unlike the historical event but like the idol, in that it provokes and demands solipsism. Further, it is my affections that make me identical to myself, that give me myself. *ED,* 321–33.

[128] The icon contains within it the characteristics of the three preceding phenomena: it encompasses many horizons, it demands revisitation, and it dislodges the transcendental I. Marion, *ED,* 324–25.

non of the Other, who always precedes me.[129] Now, it is evident that with his discussion of the icon, Marion has moved deliberately to include the possibility of religious phenomena. It is at this point that the debate with Janicaud and Derrida becomes very real, and also that echoes of Marion's previous work start to become dominant, for his writing on the icon is extensive. The point Marion initially wishes to illustrate is that although the four phenomena named are similar by virtue of their saturation, they vary in degrees of givenness. He then wishes to address the question of how far saturation can extend, a question he frames in terms of two conditions: phenomenality and possibility.[130] Once again pointing out his reservations in linking phenomenology with theology, he argues that the phenomenon that could best achieve these conditions would be the phenomenon of revelation.[131] This is primarily because a phenomenon of revelation would give itself as each of the types of saturated phenomenon listed, effectively becoming a fifth "super" type, the paradox of paradoxes: "it saturates phenomenality to the second degree, by saturation of saturation."[132] At the same time, the phenomenon of revelation would always remain just a possibility, which could be described without the assertion that it had occurred. In fact, that assertion would lie beyond the bounds of phenomenology. A phenomenon of revelation would define itself as the possibility of impossibility, where impossibility would not destroy possibility (as in the case of death), but where possibility would allow for impossibility.[133] Marion therefore describes his task as considering the possibility of revelation, refraining from the judgment about it that would rest in the realm of revealed theology. So, he underlines in response to Janicaud, phenomenology and theol-

---

[129] Marion, *ED,* 323–24.

[130] Marion, *ED,* 326–67.

[131] In *PS,* 127, Marion defines revelation phenomenologically as "une apparition purement de soi et à partir de soi."

[132] Marion, *ED,* 327: "elle sature la phénoménalité au second degré, par saturation de saturation."

[133] Marion, *ED,* 327–28. Cf. Ricoeur, *ELDR,* 20, where he observes that there can be no single, universal religious phenomenon, but only phenomena incarnated in particular religious traditions. This will be important given Janicaud's later response to Marion.

ogy must remain completely separate disciplines.[134] Nevertheless, he uses the manifestation of Jesus Christ as a paradigm of revelatory phenomena according to the four modes he has previously outlined.

With regard to quantity, Christ is an unanticipatable phenomenon. Marion explores this with regard both to the Incarnation and to texts that refer to the Second Coming. This meets the conditions of the event.[135] In relation to quality, the intuition that saturates Christ as phenomenon goes beyond what the phenomenological regard can bear. What cannot be borne is the recognition of Christ as such, exemplified in texts such as those referring to the Transfiguration and Jesus' command not to touch him after the Resurrection. This meets the conditions of the idol.[136] From the point of view of relation, Christ appears as an absolute phenomenon because he saturates every horizon. He is not of this world, a point that is reflected in the need for a plurality of titles for Christ, since no single title is adequate. This is a saturation of

[134] "La phénoménologie décrit des possibilités et ne considère jamais le phénomène de révélation que comme une possibilité de la phénoménalité, qu'elle formulerait ainsi: si Dieu se manifeste (ou se manifestait), il usera d'un paradoxe au second degré; la Révélation (de Dieu par lui-même, *théo*-logique), si elle a lieu, prendra la figure phénoménale du phénomène de révélation, du paradoxe des paradoxes, de la saturation au second degré. Certes, la Révélation (comme effectivité) ne se confond jamais avec la révélation (comme phénomène possible)—nous respecterons scrupuleusement cette différence conceptuelle par sa traduction graphique. Mais la phénoménologie, qui doit à la phénoménalité d'aller jusqu'à ce point, ne va pas au-delà et ne doit jamais prétendre décider du fait de la Révélation, ni de son historicité, ni de son effectivité, ni de son sens. Elle ne le doit pas, non seulement par souci de distinguer les savoirs et de délimiter leurs régions respectives, mais d'abord parce qu'elle n'en a aucunement les moyens: le fait (s'il en est un) de la Révélation excède l'empan de toute science, y compris de la phénoménologie; seule une théologie, et à condition de se laisser construire à partir de ce fait seul (K. Barth ou H. U. von Balthasar, plus sans doute que R. Bultmann ou K. Rahner) pourrait éventuellement y accèder. Même si elle en avait le désir (et, bien entendu, jamais ce ne fut le cas), la phénoménologie n'aurait pas la puissance de tourner à la théologie. Et il faut tout ignorer de la théologie, de ses procédures et de ses problematiques pour ne fût-ce qu'envisager cette invraisemblance." Marion, *ED,* 329 n.

[135] Marion, *ED,* 328–31.

[136] Marion, *ED,* 331. In his awareness that recognition of Christ as such cannot be borne, Marion seems to be in accord with the view that recognition comes only after the event, that is, immemorially. Elsewhere Marion describes the idol as that which reflects the gaze of the idolater.

the flesh.[137] And concerning modality, Marion maintains that Christ constitutes the one who adores him, rather than the other way around. Christ in this way operates iconically. Here we are given examples of Jesus' inversion of values, particularly in the story of the rich young man. From this story Marion observes two essential traits. One concerns the constituting regard of Jesus, which is given differently to each person. His election of persons does not objectify or reify them, but witnesses his love for them. The other trait concerns the redoubling of saturation. Obedience to the commandments, for the rich young man, is a first saturation, and the giving of everything to the poor a second type. Taken together, coming before the regard of Christ means not only doing good in obedience to the law but loving the poor.[138] This redoubled saturation meets the conditions of the icon. In Christ, Marion asserts, we have the saturated phenomenon par excellence. The phenomenon of revelation gives itself without reserve and without conditions. It is not subject to the need for evidence, for conceptualization, or for the opening of *Ereignis.*

Yet there remains the question of the integrity of the relation between Husserlian phenomenology and theology. Marion proposes that Husserl does not put the question of God in brackets: Husserl brackets only the *transcendence* of God, reducing God thought as ground.[139] From the theological side, is there a contradiction between the idea of the saturated phenomenon of revelation and the tradition of apophatism? What we see in the saturated phenomenon is more the dazzling than a particular spectacle. For example, the face of the Other manifests itself while the regard that looks at me remains invisible: from the point of view of objectivity, there is nothing to see, but not nothing. Marion submits that it is not a choice between apophatism and kataphatism, but between saturation and the poverty of intuition.[140]

This brings Marion back to a central question: if the privilege of intuition comes from its character of givenness, how is it possible to explain that givenness is often accomplished without intu-

[137] Marion, *ED,* 332–34.
[138] Marion, *ED,* 334–35.
[139] Marion, *ED,* 335–37.
[140] Marion, *ED,* 337–40.

ition? The choice between saturation and poor intuition is undecidable. Marion claims to refer to a pure given, both empty and saturated, and he suggests that there are three types of givens such as these. There is the case where givenness gives something inherently non-objectifiable, such as time, or life. These are given without intuition by default. Then there is the case where givenness gives something that is not, such as death. This is given without intuition by definition. The third type is the case where givenness gives something that is not only not entitative, but also not objectifiable, such as my word, peace, or meaning.[141] Here we simply cannot decide between excess and penury. This is givenness without intuition by excess, what Marion calls "the abandoned."[142]

After the Subject

In this chapter I have examined four of the five books of *Étant donné* with a view to seeing how Marion responds to the critics of *Réduction et donation* and how his phenomenological enterprise works overall. Evidently, there is a final book to consider, but the place for a complete review of that material, extraordinarily fruitful as it might be, is not here. Instead, I will sketch those areas of particular interest for the current project and refer the reader to the many discussions of subjectivity that take place elsewhere.[143] To maintain an emphasis on the priority of what gives itself to intuition, there has been a corresponding lack of emphasis on the role of that intuition in constituting the given as a phenomenon. But in the final book, Marion turns to contemplate how the self that constitutes is given, a feat of self-reflection that delivers only a minimum to comprehension. The one to whom that constituting self appears is given the names of "witness," "the assigned" or "attributary" ("*l'attributaire*"), and "the devoted one" ("*l'adonné*") by Marion, the last of which has complex and perhaps

[141] Marion is not unlike Derrida on this point. See Derrida, *VR*, 27.

[142] Marion, *ED*, 340–42.

[143] For example, *RED;* "The Final Appeal of the Subject," in Critchley and Dews, *DS*.

unusual connotations in a work that is explicitly non-theological in content.

Marion suggests that the aporias that characterize any investigation of the subject arise because it is the ego or *Dasein* that is being considered. He argues for a reversal, a substitution of these figures by the attributary who simply receives what is given, including itself. In receiving itself, the attributary is individualized by facticity, not liable to solipsism because submitted to otherness, passive rather than spontaneous because affected rather than cognitively masterful, and liberated from subsistence because unable to become an object. Marion's subject is a subject without subjectivity.[144] How is this subject constituted? In the giving of phenomena, the attributary is also given: first, as a screen for phenomena, the "me" who receives and transforms; and second, as the respondent to a call, in which the attributary itself is transformed into the devoted one.[145] Now, what is clearly of interest to us here is the origin of this call. Marion offers three perspectives. Repeating his argument about Heidegger from *Réduction et donation,* Marion reinforces that the origin of the call must remain undecidable. He then considers how the call reverses intentionality, along the lines of the Levinasian face. Finally, he makes a connection between the call and saturated phenomena, which, characterized by an excess of intuition, subverting and preceding any intention, and so behaving counter-intentionally, make a call not only possible but, he insists, inevitable.[146] The call is phenomenologically determined only by the four traits it manifests: convocation, surprise, interlocution, and facticity.[147] And since the call is always and already given, remains unknown in origin, and is only recognizable in the response made, it is like a gift.[148]

The call comes to us as a gift, but as a gift that is necessarily anonymous. It is this feature of anonymity that I wish to emphasize from Marion's discussion, although I am leaving many other aspects of his brilliant exposition of the subject without subjectivity to one side. The anonymity of the call is protected, he main-

[144] Marion, *ED,* 360–61.
[145] Marion, *ED,* 361–66.
[146] Marion, *ED,* 369.
[147] Marion, *ED,* 369–73.
[148] Marion, *ED,* 372–73, 396–97.

tains, because there is no specification of the type of saturated phenomenon (or paradox) involved. And in the case of revelation, since it involves not only one but all of the paradoxical types, it cannot be further specified. What is of great interest is the example Marion chooses: the divine name (YHWH). The name, it seems, is a paradox, which cannot provide access to the divine essence:

> The voice that reveals, reveals justly because it remains without a voice, more exactly without a name, but in *the Name.* The Name only gives in saying without any name, thus completely. Far from making us fear that such a call drives surreptitiously to name a transcendent *numen* and—badly—to turn to "theology," we have to conclude that to the contrary all phenomena of revelation (under the heading of possibility) and especially a Revelation (under the heading of effectivity) would implicate the radical anonymity of that which calls.[149]

It is not in calling that the caller is identified, but in the risked response of the devoted one.

We note in Marion's discussion of subjectivity not only the influence of Levinas but also that of Ricoeur, whose article in the 1992 collection is instructive.[150] There we find Ricoeur speaking of the (divine) Other as the source of the call: "Prayer is turned actively toward this Other by whom consciousness is affected at the level of feeling. In return, this Other who affects it is perceived as the source of the call to which prayer responds."[151] Later, with reference to the experience of the Jewish people, he also speaks of the Law as the word that is the origin of the call, but Scripture insofar as the legislator is absent.[152] Or again, with reference to the prophets who speak in the name of YHWH, he observes the coincidence of two voices: God speaks in the response of the one who listens, even though this means that the word is fragile.[153] Finally, Ricoeur sketches "the retreat of the Name." "The name of God is at once that which circles between

[149] Marion, *ED,* 410.

[150] Not only in *ELDR,* but in Paul Ricoeur, *Oneself As Another,* trans. Kathleen Blamey (Chicago: University of Chicago Press, 1992).

[151] Ricoeur, *ELDR,* 16; my translation.

[152] Ricoeur, *ELDR,* 31.

[153] Ricoeur, *ELDR,* 32–33.

genres and between scriptures, not belonging to any one, but intersignifying by all,—and also that which escapes from each and from all, in a sign of the non-achievement of all discourse about God."[154] The question that must be raised at this point in respect to both Marion and Ricoeur is, however, whether knowing a name is already knowing too much. This difficulty underlies the debate between Marion and Derrida on the gift, as it is recorded in *God, the Gift, and Postmodernism.* Can the saturated phenomenon give anything *as such,* even if its origin cannot be specified? Can the gift be known *as such,* even in the absence of a specific giver? Does Marion's phenomenology require him to have a certain faith? Having examined the complex phenomenological schema of *Étant donné,* we are now in a better position to consider these questions more closely.

---

[154] Ricoeur, *ELDR,* 35.

6
The Limits of Phenomenology

Responding to *Étant donné*

Étant donné represents an extraordinary achievement, situating Marion among the foremost thinkers of his generation. Its massive scope, high degree of coherent systematization, and striking and often singular readings of important players in the history of phenomenology mean that it has a significant place in contemporary philosophy. Because of that place, however, we are obliged to enter into debate with Marion concerning the legitimacy of those readings, particularly bearing in mind the questions about God, the gift, and phenomenology that motivate this inquiry.

It would be unusual, given the tone of *Le tournant théologique,* if Dominique Janicaud were not to respond to the responses made to him in *Étant donné.* This he does in *La phénoménologie éclatée.*[1] Here Janicaud raises two main objections: first, that Marion's use of a capital letter when he speaks of "Revelation" seems to suggest that he is not interested merely in the general possibility of revelatory phenomena, but in phenomena in which he has a theological stake; and second, that to isolate such phenomena as ultimate paradoxes would require that their theological truth claims be given consideration, a task that, he asserts, does not belong to phenomenology. Now, the answer to Janicaud's question of whether or not Marion is interested in revelation or in Revelation is, once again, yes and no. This equivocation is reflected in the text itself. At one point we have several references to Revelation (p. 10); at another point we have references to "le phénomène de révélation" (pp. 327ff.).[2] I will return to this in a moment.

---

[1] Dominique Janicaud, *La phénoménologie éclatée* (Combas: Éditions de l'éclat, 1998).

[2] And in the *Revue* article, *RQQ,* we have "révélation" (see p. 73).

Like Janicaud, Derrida also meets *Étant donné* with two questions. The first relates to Marion's association of *Gegebenheit* and gift, which fits in, as a problem, with earlier questioning about the semantic association of gift, given, and givenness. It is a problem also signaled, once again, by Jean Greisch: "The French language would allow us to reassemble under a single hat (that of the magician) that which the German language does not cease to separate."[3] Greisch, however, is more forgiving than Derrida, who observes:

> I am not convinced that between the use of *Gegebenheit* in phenomenology and the problem we are about to discuss, that is, the fit, there is a semantic continuity. I am not sure that when, of course, Husserl refers, extensively and constantly, to what is given to intuition, this given-ness, this *Gegebenheit* has an obvious and intelligible relationship to the gift, to being given as gift. What we are going to discuss, that is the gift, perhaps is not homogenous with *Gegebenheit.* That is one of the problems with the connection to phenomenology. I will come back to this later on. Now, the way, the mediation or the transition, you made between *Gegebenheit* in phenomenology and the *es gibt* in Heidegger is also problematic to me. The way Heidegger refers to the *Gabe* in the *es gibt* is distinct from intuitive *Gegebenheit.* When Husserl says *Gegebenheit,* and when phenomenologists in the broad sense say *Gegebenheit,* something is given, they refer simply to the passivity of intuition. Something is there. We have, we meet something. It is there, but it is not a gift.[4]

Marion's response (remembering that here we are in the context of a public debate, conducted in English) is more complex than previously. The first part is as follows: "I disagree with you on the point that givenness, *Gegebenheit,* would be restricted for Husserl to intuition. I would quote some texts and I would stick to that. For him, even significations are given, without intuition. He assumes openly a 'logical givenness.' " Derrida interjects: "I agree with you. The point was, what is the gift?"—in response to which Marion reverses his initial position on the equivocity between the gift and givenness:

---

[3] Jean Greisch, "Index sui et non dati," *Transversalités: Revue de L'Institut Catholique de Paris* 70 (April–June 1999): 27–54, 32; my translation. *Prestidigitateur* (someone who performs sleight of hand) has been translated as "magician" for the sake of sense in English.

[4] Derrida and Marion, *OTG,* 58.

> This is a good point, and I emphasize it, because Paul Ricoeur asked me the same question and raised the same objection which I myself would sum up as such: Between the givenness, if any, in the phenomenological meaning of the word, and the gift, there is nothing but pure equivocity. *I tried to demonstrate the contrary, because to assume this so-called equivocity as a starting point proves to impoverish both the question of the gift and that of givenness.* . . . I think of the gift as a kind of issue reaching to the most extreme limits, that should be described and be thought and neither explained nor comprehended, but simply thought—in a very radical way. I suggest that, in order to achieve description, if any is possible, of the gift, we can be led to open for the first time a new horizon, much wider than those of objectivity and being, the horizon of givenness.[5]

What we see here is Marion seeking to rely less on a semantic association between givenness and gift and instead seeking, through the question of the gift, to develop the horizon of givenness. This enables him to respond more strongly to Derrida's subsequent assertion that for Marion, "every *Gegebenheit* (is) gift," and by extension that "everything is a gift, a gift from God, from whomever." Marion stresses the reverse: "Every gift (is) *Gegebenheit.*" Yet Derrida brings the question back to the nature of phenomenology: "If you say the immanent structure of phenomenality is *Gegebenheit,* and if by *Gegebenheit* you refer to something given, to some common root, then every phenomenon is a gift. Even if you do not determine the giver as God, it is a gift. I am not sure that this is reconcilable or congruent with what I know under the name of phenomenology."[6] What exactly does Derrida mean by "some common root"? Does he mean to include the given with *Gegebenheit,* and thereby imply that the link between these two words is inappropriate? Or does he interpret the given by "common root" with the gift (a given is a gift, rather than a fact)? There is no clear answer here. Instead, we will progress further if we consider the second issue he raises in this last paragraph, which is what might legitimately go "under the name of phenomenology."

The real issue for Derrida is this:

---

[5] Derrida and Marion, *OTG,* 61; emphasis added.
[6] Derrida and Marion, *OTG,* 71.

> What I understand as phenomenology, the principle of all principles, which you have recalled here, implies finally intuition, that is, the fullness of the intuition, the presence of something. When there is a gap between intuition and intention, there is a crisis, there is a symbolic structure. But the principle of all principles is intuition. If you agree, as I think you agree, about the impossibility of equating the gift to a present, then you cannot define every phenomenon as gift. That is what puzzles me.[7]

What Marion and Derrida are really debating, albeit contextualized by the problem of the gift, is the nature and limits of phenomenology. For Derrida, as we have seen, phenomenology is about presence, and where it fails to bring into presence it fails as a methodology. For Marion, phenomenology is also about presence, but without that presence equating to the fullness of intuition. For Derrida givenness equals presence, whereas for Marion givenness may equal presence, but not in the sense of present to intuition. By way of an argument over semantics, the question once again becomes: "Can there be a given that does not deliver itself in presence to intuition?"—and only then can we ask: "Can there be a gift?"

While coming from a different angle, Derrida leads us in the end to the same point as Janicaud, whose critique I will now address. We saw earlier how Marion's thought of givenness could be situated in the theological trajectory of his previous works. Yet it was also evident that in *Réduction et donation* Marion was producing a work of phenomenology, not theology. In *Étant donné,* as I have indicated, Marion similarly argues that his task is strictly phenomenological. Nevertheless, in the latter work we find Marion examining phenomena of revelation/Revelation and arguing that this examination is within the realm of possibility for phenomenology. It seems feasible to understand, then, that Marion sees phenomenology as a sort of prolegomena for theology. I do not mean by this that he tries to deduce revealed theology from phenomenological method, an undertaking that he would find unquestionably abhorrent, although this possibility is suggested

[7] Derrida and Marion, *OTG,* 71.

by Vincent Holzer.[8] Instead, I am proposing that Marion seeks the enlargement of phenomenology to include the possibility, rather than the actuality, of something like theology, based on the point that revelatory phenomena cannot simply be excluded from the limits of phenomenological investigation. That being said, it cannot be ignored that to complete this enlargement, Marion has to give examples, and the examples he chooses are from Christian tradition. The problems Janicaud identifies reduce to this: if phenomenology is to include revelatory phenomena, it must presumably be able to point to examples of such phenomena, even if it is to illustrate the possibility, rather than the actuality, of revelation. But as soon as examples are identified, the question arises as to whether they are what it is they are claimed to be: *revelatory* phenomena. There is in the exemplification always a necessary shift from phenomena of revelation to phenomena (or better, the phenomenon) of Revelation. If Marion were to add examples of revelation from other religious traditions, there would be no less of a problem, for the issue is in the naming itself. A phenomenon of revelation must reveal something; it is therefore invested with the power to Reveal. If, on the other hand, and here I go beyond Janicaud, I were confronted with a saturated phenomenon such as Marion describes, I would have to be able to put to one side the question of whether or not it was a phenomenon of revelation in order to preserve its very quality of saturation. The disposition Marion seeks to assume here is that of the dispassionate observer, the phenomenologist of religion, perhaps, who is able to stand back and describe what religious traditions refer to by "phenomena of revelation."[9] Keeping this in mind, it seems what he achieves in *Étant donné* is legitimate. But Marion is not cataloging what others say is revelatory; on the contrary, he is asking us to contemplate that when someone bears witness to a revelatory phenomenon, it might actually be Revelatory. To describe something as revelatory involves a commitment in advance, not to the possi-

[8] Cf. the comments of Vincent Holzer in "Phénoménologie radicale et phénomène de révélation. Jean-Luc Marion, *Étant donné.* Essai d'une phénoménologie de la donation," *Transversalités: Revue de L'Institut Catholique de Paris* 70 (April–June 1999): 55–68, 66–68 [hereafter Holzer, *PRPR*].

[9] Bearing in mind the injunction of Paul Ricoeur in *ELDR,* 20.

bility of revelation, but to its actuality.[10] For this reason, Janicaud is correct to point out that Marion exceeds the limits of phenomenology.

It seems that we have reached an impasse, one that was suggested in the examination of *Réduction et donation* and which has now been confirmed by *Étant donné*. Phenomenology cannot deliver phenomena of revelation/Revelation *as such*, and therefore it seems that the conversation between phenomenology and theology cannot take place, at least not without doing violence to the neutral (as distinct from the natural) attitude of phenomenology. From a Derridean point of view, this is because revelatory phenomena would have to be delivered in presence, a requirement that would undo any possible revelatory quality they might have. Like the gift, a God handed over into intellectual custody would be no God at all. And from Janicaud's point of view, the impossibility of delivering phenomena of revelation stems from the requirement that phenomenology observe what appears to consciousness without involving a leap of faith. It could, of course, be argued in response that phenomenology always involves such a leap, for as Derrida has shown, there is no phenomenology without a tacit hermeneutics. Marion falls somewhere in between these positions. His desire is to reformulate phenomenology, but in accordance with its inherent Husserlian possibilities, where it can examine what is more than an object but less than an intuited presence. But on both counts, it is the hermeneutical dimension that can be called into question. If what gives itself is not an object and is not present, what does it mean? At the same time, it would be foolish to discount what Marion is trying to do, namely, to find a way of thinking what is greater than thought. This is the basis of the attractiveness of his work to theology.

In one sense, it is very difficult to prove that what Marion is doing is not phenomenology but working at the point of phenomenology's failure. I say that because in the debate with Derrida at Villanova, as well as in the fine print of *Étant donné*, definitions make all the difference. For example, where Marion uses the language of horizon it seems he is stuck in a metaphysics of presence. But then he redefines presence, and renounces the horizon, and

[10] Holzer, *PRPR*, 58.

is even prepared to go so far as to say that "as to the question of whether what I am doing, or what Derrida is doing, is within phenomenology or beyond, it does not seem to me very important."[11] In other words, it all depends on how the limits of phenomenology are described. The way to judge the success of Marion's work is instead to focus on its hermeneutical dimension. To what extent are those phenomena that, according to his schema, resist presence-to-intuition reinscribed in metaphysics by way of hermeneutics, or can they resist being solely tied to the particular hermeneutical approach that is Christianity?

The breakdown of classical phenomenology occurs at the point where what is given exceeds conscious thematization, and we see this in a negative way thanks to Janicaud, because he indicates that any decisive reading of what surpasses intelligibility requires a leap of faith. We observe the breakdown more positively in the work of Levinas, where keeping faith with phenomenology is less of an issue insofar as the failure is concomitant with living, as distinct from merely thinking. But with Levinas—and more especially the later Levinas, where a number of difficulties concerning the Other have been resolved—the leap of faith is recognized without our having to commit to it. This is what distinguishes him from Marion, at least to the extent that identifying a saturated phenomenon as *revelatory* in the sense in which Marion uses the word involves making a judgment about its origin. Yet it is not so much the making of a judgment that is the problem. The difficulty occurs when the judgment is passed off as pure description. Now, it seems to me that Marion's thinking of saturated phenomena provides him with an opportunity to describe the conditions surrounding what interrupts or exceeds consciousness, without his having to take the next step of committing to an interpretation of that interruption. Prescinding from the question of whether or not a phenomenon is revelatory, how are we to deal with it if it overruns consciousness either by excess (Marion) or by aridity (Derrida)? If it is possible to locate such "phenomena" in general, is it possible to approach phenomena from a religious tradition (a text, for example) and without presuming to describe them as revelatory, to investigate their potentiality for saturation?

---

[11] Derrida and Marion, *OTG,* 68. Marion renounces the horizon at 66.

It seems to me that this is a valid path to take. That being the case, let us examine how Marion reads such phenomena, using the example of the icon.

The Icon

Many sources in Marion's work provide access to his thinking of the icon. As early as *L'idole et la distance,* he is developing a theme that will become his trademark: icon versus idol. It appears constantly in articles and books up to and including *Étant donné.*[12] Since Marion himself uses the icon as an example of a saturated phenomenon in this last text, it provides an ideal study in the present context. Nevertheless, I will also draw from his theological works in illustrating how the icon functions, especially in relation to the idol.

In *L'idole et la distance,* the idol is characterized not as the personification of its god but as the image by means of which the worshiper is referred only to the human experience of divinity.[13] The icon, in contrast, is characterized as that which works as a kind of negative theophany.[14] Where Paul names Christ the "icon of the invisible God," Marion explains, God the Father does not lose invisibility so much as become visible in transcendence.[15]

---

[12] For example, *ID;* "La double idolatrie: Remarques sur la différence ontologique et la pensée de Dieu," *Heidegger et la question de Dieu,* ed. Richard Kearney and Joseph S. O'Leary (Paris: Grasset, 1980), 46–74; "La vanité d'être et le nom de Dieu," *Analogie et dialectique: Essais de théologie fondamentale,* ed. P. Gisel and Ph. Secretan (Geneva: Labor et Fides, 1982), 17–49; *Dieu sans l'être: Hors-texte* (1982; Paris: Quadrige/Presses Universitaires de France, 1991), trans. as *GWB;* "De la 'mort de dieu' aux noms divins: L'itinéraire théologique de la métaphysique," *Laval théologique et philosophique* 41, no. 1 (1985): 25–41, and *L'être et Dieu* (Paris: Cerf, 1986); *Prolégomènes à la charité,* 2nd ed. (Paris: Editions de la Différence, 1991) [hereafter Marion, *PC*]; *CV; ED.*

[13] Marion, *ID,* 19–22.

[14] Marion, *ID,* 24.

[15] Marion, *ID,* 23: "La profondeur du visage visible du Fils livre au regard l'invisibilité du Père comme telle. L'icône ne manifeste ni le visage humain, ni la nature divine que nul ne saurait envisager, mais, disaient les théologiens de l'icône, le rapport de l'une à l'autre dans l'hypostase, la personne." ("The depth of the visible face of the Son lets the invisibility of the Father be seen as such. The icon manifests neither the human face, nor the divine nature that no one would be able to envisage, but, theologians of the icon would say, the relationship of the one to the other in the hypostasis, the person.")

While the idol is about preserving the proximity of the divine, the icon manifests distance.[16] Concepts, too, can function idolatrously or iconically. Therefore Marion is able to understand the Nietzschean "death of God" in terms of the death only of an idolatrous concept of God.[17] Yet words can also refer, he maintains, to the unspeakable.[18] Where theology has been practiced as onto-theology, the conceptual idols of metaphysics are rightly condemned.[19] But where theology preserves "distance," where it allows for the divine to overflow what is merely human, it goes beyond idolatry.[20]

Marion's understanding of how idols and icons function is deepened in *God Without Being*. Here he perceives that the difference between them lies in their "manner of being for beings" rather than in their being two classes of beings. This is because frequently the same object can function as an idol or an icon. But either way it is a question of veneration, and an object is venerated when it is seen as a sign of the divine.[21] Artistic works are so venerated when "they no longer restrict their visibility to themselves . . . but, as such and by thus remaining absolutely immanent in themselves, . . . they signal indissolubly toward another, still undetermined term."[22] It is in this referring that the value of the

[16] Marion, *ID*, 23–24. Here Marion's thought reminds us of Balthasar.

[17] Marion, *ID*, 15–16, 45ff. This is affirmed once again in *GWB*, chapter 2.

[18] Marion, *ID*, 24: "le concept ne pourrait-il pas jouer, aussi et d'abord, comme une icône, au sens où, comme l'icône offre la figure de l'invisible, 'les mots ne sont pas la traduction d'autre chose qui était là avant eux' (L. Wittgenstein), mais la profération même de ce qui demeure au même instant à jamais indicible." ("could not the concept play, also and firstly, as an icon, in the sense where, as an icon offers the figure of the invisible, 'words are not the translation of anything else which was there before them' (L. Wittgenstein), but the very utterance of that which remains at the same time forever unspeakable.")

[19] Marion explores Western metaphysical idolatry in *GWB*, 16, where, he suggests, God is made idol as *causa sui* and as source of morality: "The concept consigns to a sign what at first the mind grasps with it (*concipere, capare*); but such a grasp is measured not so much by the amplitude of the divine as by the scope of a *capacitas*, which can fix the divine in a specific concept only at the moment when a conception of the divine fills it, hence appeases, stops, and freezes it. When a philosophical thought expresses a concept of what it then names 'God,' this concept functions exactly as an idol."

[20] Marion, *ID*, 24–42.

[21] Marion, *GWB*, 7–8.

[22] Marion, *GWB*, 8.

work resides; it is the mode of signaling that will determine the difference between the idol and the icon.[23]

An idol is not an illusion: it consists precisely in being seen, in becoming an object of knowledge. "The idol depends on the gaze that it satisfies, since if the gaze did not desire to satisfy itself in the idol, the idol would have no dignity for it."[24] Hence it is not in the fabrication of the idol that its venerability resides, but in its consideration by the gaze. The intention of the gaze aims at the divine, but it is stopped there. Prior to being arrested by the idol, the gaze sees nothing that will satisfy it. But in the face of the idol, what Marion calls "the first visible," the gaze allows itself to be filled, to be dazzled. At the same time, in the idol the gaze discovers its own limit. The idol acts as a mirror that reflects "the image of its aim and . . . the scope of that aim."[25] Yet the mirror effect remains secondary to the spectacle itself, and so remains invisible. In this way the emptiness of idolatry is never exposed to the idolater. The mirror function of the idol is an essential feature, since it indicates not only the extent of the aim of the gaze but also what the gaze cannot see for being blocked by the idol. The gaze cannot be critical, but rests in the idol, incapable of going beyond it.[26] "The invisible mirror thus marks, negatively, the shortcoming of the aim—literally, the *invisable*."[27] In the idol we see the divine, but only according to the measure of our own gaze.[28] Marion evaluates the idol in terms of this measure: "it represents nothing, but presents a certain low-water mark of the divine; it resembles what the human gaze has experienced of the divine."[29] The idol itself does not reproduce the god, but only fixes in stone what the gaze has seen of the god, "the point marked by the frozen gaze."[30] It is the emotion

---

[23] Marion, *GWB*, 8–9. "Variations in the mode of visibility indicate variations in the mode of apprehension of the divine itself." *GWB*, 9.

[24] Marion, *GWB*, 10.

[25] Marion, *GWB*, 11–12.

[26] Marion, *GWB*, 11–12. "The idol would not be disqualified thus, vis-à-vis a revelation, not at all because it would offer to the gaze an illegitimate spectacle, but first because it suggests to the gaze where to rest (itself)." *GWB*, 13.

[27] Marion, *GWB*, 13.

[28] Marion, *GWB*, 13–14.

[29] Marion, *GWB*, 14.

[30] Marion, *GWB*, 14.

of this initial fixing that is represented in the idol and which fixes others.[31]

"The icon does not result from a vision but provokes one."[32] Contrary to the idol, the icon allows the visible to become saturated by the invisible, without the invisible being reduced in any way to the visible.[33] The invisible is unenvisageable. It is represented in the visible only insofar as the visible constantly refers to what is other than itself. It retrains the gaze.[34] Yet how can the invisible become visible in the icon at all? Marion distinguishes between God's presence as substantial (referring to the Greek *ousia,* substance, which he associates with metaphysics) and God's presence as personal (using the Greek *hupostasis* or the Latin *persona*). "*Hupostasis* . . . does not imply any substantial presence; . . . the *persona* attested its presence only by that which itself most properly characterizes it, the aim of an intention . . . that a gaze sets in operation."[35] Marion defines the icon, like the idol, in terms of the gaze, but here he is concerned with the gaze of the invisible rather than the gaze of the human. "The icon regards us—it *concerns* us, in that it allows the intention of the invisible to occur visibly."[36] The icon shows us a face that opens on the infinite.[37] It does not act as a mirror, but overwhelms us. "In the idol, the gaze of man is frozen in its mirror; in the icon, the gaze of man is lost in the invisible gaze that visibly envisages him."[38] Invisi-

[31] "The idol consigns and conserves in its material the brilliance where the gaze froze, in the expectation that other eyes will acknowledge the brilliance of a first visible that freezes them in their material scope." Marion, *GWB,* 15.

[32] Marion, *GWB,* 17.

[33] "The visible [proceeds] from the invisible. . . . [T]he invisible bestow[s] the visible." Marion, *GWB,* 17.

[34] "The icon summons the gaze to surpass itself by never freezing on a visible, since the visible only presents itself here in view of the invisible." Marion, *GWB,* 18.

[35] Marion, *GWB,* 18–19.

[36] Marion, *GWB,* 19. This "being envisaged" is characteristic of Balthasar's theology. See Hans Urs von Balthasar, *The Glory of the Lord,* vol. 7, *Theology: The New Covenant,* trans. Brian McNeil, C.R.V. (San Francisco: Ignatius Press, 1989), 286–87 [hereafter Balthasar, *GL7*].

[37] "The icon alone offers an open face, because it opens in itself the visible onto the invisible, by offering its spectacle to be transgressed—not to be seen, but to be venerated." Marion, *GWB,* 19. It is possible to trace here something of Levinas's influence on Marion.

[38] Marion, *GWB,* 20.

bility is made visible in the face; the infinite gives itself in the icon.[39] Infinite intention, it is excessive, abyssal, overflowing the capacity of the human gaze. It seems that in the face of the icon, the infinite passes.[40] The intention from beyond the icon substitutes itself for the human intention. Further, the human face then also serves as a mirror to reflect divine glory.[41]

The concept can function as an icon as easily as an idol, but to function in this way requires that "the concept renounce comprehending the incomprehensible, to attempt to conceive it, hence also to receive it, in its own excessiveness."[42] Is it possible to have such a concept? "The only concept that can serve as an intelligible medium for the icon is one that lets itself be measured by the excessiveness of the invisible that enters into visibility through infinite depth."[43] Marion suggests that the Cartesian idea of the Infinite might act in this way.[44] The concept determines an inten-

[39] "The icon is defined by an origin without original: an origin itself infinite, which pours itself out or gives itself throughout the infinite depth of the icon." Marion, *GWB*, 20.

[40] Again we are reminded of Levinas: "the icon painted on wood does not come from the hand of a man but from the infinite depth that crosses it—or better, orients it following the intention of a gaze." Marion, *GWB*, 21.

[41] "The invisible summons us, 'face to face, person to person' (1 Cor. 13:12), through the painted visibility of its incarnation and the factual visibility of our flesh: no longer the visible idol as the invisible mirror of our gaze, but our face as the visible mirror of the invisible." Marion, *GWB*, 22.

[42] Marion, *GWB*, 22.

[43] Marion, *GWB*, 23.

[44] Note the influence of Levinas once again. In the Sorbonne interview, Marion speaks of the significance of the idea of the infinite and the role it plays in Levinas, revealing some interesting and highly pertinent thoughts on the horizon: "It would be possible to think God as the infinite, on the condition that it is a positive infinity and non-objective, that it not be spoken of as a representation—that is what Levinas says. Me, I will say that it is necessary that the infinite appears as a horizon more than a phenomenon, or rather—because a horizon limits, by definition—it is a non-horizon, it is that which is always beyond the horizon, that which is the greatest thing of which we can think (Anselm)—this is Anselm's definition, a non-definition. Thus the idea of the infinite is only possible as a non-definition of God. . . . [I]t is a concept of that which is indefinable. It is a precise concept of that which goes beyond all definition. It is that which is interesting in the concept of the infinite. Thus . . . for Levinas, the idea of the infinite is an intentionality which goes beyond all objects. It is an intentionality without objects, the infinite. And that is why he applies the infinite not to God but to the face in general, because the face in general is that which is infinite, and infinite in the sense that there is no object. . . . The infinite means that which is greater than we can think." Marion discusses both Anselm's

tion, not an essence. In the iconic concept, the distance between the visible and the invisible is assured.

In *La croisée du visible,* a collection of four essays, Marion focuses on the iconic function of art.[45] The first essay, "La croisée du visible et de l'invisible," moves from a consideration of art in general to the special and distinctive case of the icon, where it is necessary to go beyond both objectivity and perspective in favor of fostering a new relationship between the visible and the invisible. In the icon, the invisible is *in* the visible. The icon offers itself to the gaze without setting perspective in motion.[46] It shows its own gaze to the face of the faithful person who prays before it, so that two invisible regards cross. The icon accomplishes both the insertion of the invisible in the visible and the subversion of the visible by the invisible.[47] "The invisible exercises itself as the look itself, which looks invisibly at another invisible regard, by the intermediary of a painted visible . . . it results in a less classic phenomenological situation, where intentionality no longer accomplishes itself as an objectivity, indeed accomplishes the putting in question of its own status as an *I.*"[48]

---

definition and Descartes's idea of the infinite in his *Questions cartésiennes,* 2 vols. (Paris: Presses Universitaires de France, 1991, 1996) [hereafter Marion, *QCI* and *QCII*]. With regard to Levinas, see *QCII,* 45, 245. At the latter page Marion refers us to Levinas's short piece "Sur l'idée de l'infini en nous," which appears in *Entre nous: Essais sur le penser-à-l'autre* (1991; Paris: Livre de Poche, 1993), 227–30; this is now available as *Entre Nous: On Thinking-of-the-Other,* trans. Michael B. Smith and Barbara Harshav (New York: Columbia University Press, 1998). With regard to the idea of the infinite, see *QCII,* 245ff. and 275–79. With regard to Anselm and God as concept, see *QCI,* 221–58.

[45] Marion, *CV.*

[46] Marion, *CV,* 41: "l'économie de l'icône ne dépend pas de l'investissement de l'espace par l'invisible; l'invisible y tient en effet un rôle plus fondamental que celui d'organiser l'espace, en simple chorège du visible. L'invisible joue ailleurs et autrement." ("the economy [is it an accident that he uses this word?] of the icon does not depend on the investment of space by the invisible; the invisible holds there in effect a role more fundamental than that of organizing space, as a simple 'conductor' of the visible. The invisible plays elsewhere and otherwise.")

[47] Marion, *CV,* 42–43.

[48] Marion, *CV,* 45: "l'invisible s'exerce comme le regard lui-même, qui regarde invisiblement un autre regard invisible, par l'intermédiaire d'un visible peint . . . il en résulte une situation phénoménologique moins classique, où l'intentionnalité ne s'accomplit plus en une objectivité, voire accomplit la mise en cause de son propre statut de *Je.*"

"Ce que cela donne," the next essay, is concerned with how a painter is able to make something of the invisible visible in what Marion calls *l'invu* ("the unseen"). "*L'invu* is not seen, in the same way that the unheard of is not heard, the unknown is not known. . . . *L'invu* certainly belongs to the invisible, but does not merge with it, since it can transgress it precisely in becoming visible; . . . *l'invu,* only provisionally invisible, exerts all its demands of visibility in order to, sometimes by force, burst into the visible."[49] *L'invu* gives the painting a certain independence, a powerfulness that does not reside in visibility alone. It opens us up to desire for what cannot have been foreseen. The painting itself teaches us to see. And either it will act as an idol, giving us nothing more than our own projections (which results in a crisis of the visible), or it will witness to the unseen, to depth and to glory. In this way it will be a gift for vision.[50] Marion comments, and not without some significance: "To see is to receive, since to appear is to give oneself to be seen."[51] The given demands reception.[52]

The third essay, "L'aveugle à Siloé," addresses the question of the image versus the original.[53] The original may be consigned to invisibility, but this invisibility is not simply a denial of its reality.[54] The original is defined by its invisibility, by the fact that it cannot be reduced to an image. Among his examples, Marion refers to the case of the cube, which cannot be seen "as such." The distance between perception and knowledge requires active reconstitution of the cube as an object. The invisible remains invisible, but is confirmed by the increase of the visible.[55] Marion also gives

---

[49] Marion, *CV,* 51: "L'invu n'est pas vu, tout comme l'inouï n'est pas entendu, l'insu n'est pas su. . . . L'invu relève certes de l'invisible, mais ne se confond pas avec lui, puisqu'il peut le transgresser en devenant précisement visible; . . . l'invu, invisible seulement provisoire, exerce toute son exigence de visibilité pour, parfois de force, y faire irruption."

[50] Marion, *CV,* 57–81.

[51] Marion, *CV,* 80: "Voir, c'est recevoir, puisqu'apparaître c'est (se) donner à voir."

[52] Marion, *CV,* 81. We cannot but be reminded of Balthasar.

[53] Marion observes how images operate in contemporary society, and the way that perception becomes everything. Frequently, the image destroys the original. Marion, *CV,* 85–98.

[54] It is hard not to imagine this in somewhat Platonic fashion, although I am sure that this is not what Marion means.

[55] Marion, *CV,* 99–101.

the example of the irreducibility of the face. In the case of a lover, "that which someone wants to see does not coincide with that which the face gives to be seen to every other regard."[56] Once again, it is the weight of the other's regard that is glimpsed. "I do not see the visible face of the other, [as an] object still reducible to an image . . . but the invisible regard that swells up from the obscure pupils of the other; in short, I see the other of the visible face."[57] In love, therefore, I am no longer bound to the image.[58]

The two examples I have just quoted from Marion serve to support strongly his argument that invisibility and reality are not mutually exclusive. We are thus prepared for a denouement of the theological implications of the study. Christ as icon is a further—and, he will add, superlative—example of visibility referring us to invisibility:

> Christ offers an icon to the regard only in manifesting a face, that is to say a look, itself invisible. It is therefore a matter, in the first place, of a crossing of regards, as it is for lovers; I look, with my invisible look, at an invisible look that envisages me; in the icon, in effect, it is not so much me who sees a spectacle as much as an other regard that sustains mine, confronts it, and eventually, overwhelms it. But Christ does not only offer to my regard to see and to be seen by his [regard]; if he demands from me a love, it is not a love for him, but for his Father. . . . But since the Father remains invisible, how am I able to see the Father in seeing Christ? Would not Christ constitute only what can be seen of the Father in the place of the Father, that which holds visibly the place of the invisibility of the Father?[59]

---

[56] Marion, *CV,* 101: "ce qu'il veut voir ne coïncide pas avec ce que ce visage donne à voir à tout autre regard."

[57] Marion, *CV,* 102: "Je ne vois pas le visible visage de l'autre, objet encore réductible à une image . . . mais le regard invisible qui sourd des obscures pupilles de l'autre visage; bref, je vois l'autre du visible visage." This is a very useful reading of Levinas on the face.

[58] Marion, *CV,* 102.

[59] Marion, *CV,* 103: "Le Christ n'offre au regard une icône qu'en manifestant un visage, c'est-à-dire un regard, lui-même invisible. Il s'agit donc, en un premier temps, d'une croisée des regards, conforme au schème amoureux; je regarde, de mon regard invisible, un regard invisible qui m'envisage; dans l'icône, en effet, ce n'est pas tant moi qui vois un spectacle qu'un autre regard qui soutient le mien, l'affronte, et éventuellement, le terrasse. Mais le Christ ne propose pas seulement à mon regard de voir et d'être vu par le sien; s'il réclame de moi un amour, ce n'est pas un amour pour lui, mais pour son Père. . . . Mais

Christ does not offer an image of the invisible, but the face of the invisible itself. He is the visible image of the invisible as invisible, and yet "image" here is to be rethought as "icon," for the icon is the opposite of the image, or at least it is a different type of image.[60] With the icon, in addition to the two elements of spectator and object, there is added a third—the "prototype"—not a second visible, but a second look that pierces the first visible. In this case the image no longer operates as a mirror. The iconic image does not concern the visible or the aesthetic, but the crossing of the two regards. The one who prays before the icon is not drawn to an image but by the origin of the other regard. The iconic image thus breaks with the usual understanding of the image.[61] Those images that qualify as icons are those where the visible renounces itself.[62] It is this type of kenosis that characterizes Christ's ministry and which means that he functions iconically to manifest the glory of the Father.[63] So when Christ loses his human figure, he becomes the figure of the divine will. In a quasi-Levinasian move, Marion adds: "In the gestures of his body accomplishing not his will, but the will of God, the Christ indicates, not his face, *but the trace of God.*"[64] In Christ, then, we see not God's face *as* the face of Christ, but the trace of God passing *in* the face of Christ.

The final essay, "Le prototype et l'image," has to do with protecting the sanctity of the Holy even in its iconic manifestation. In other words, it is concerned with ensuring that icons do not revert to being idols.[65] Here Marion himself sets out the problem with which I have been concerned throughout this book, the problem

---

puisque le Père reste invisible, comment puis-je voir le Père en voyant le Christ? Le Christ ne constituerait-il pas seulement ce qui peut se voir du Père à la place du Père, ce qui tient visiblement lieu de l'invisibilité du Père?"

[60] Marion, *CV,* 104. The scriptural passage that most readily springs to mind—"He is the image of the invisible God" (Col. 1:15)—is thus reinterpreted by Marion.

[61] Marion, *CV,* 106–8.

[62] Marion, *CV,* 109.

[63] Marion, *CV,* 110, and also chapter 6 of the essay.

[64] Marion, *CV,* 110: "Dans les gestes du corps accomplissant non sa volonté, mais celle de Dieu, le Christ indique, non sa face, *mais la trace de Dieu*" (emphasis added).

[65] Marion, *CV,* 119.

of the manifestation of the divine according to the human horizon:

> But every spectacle only accedes to its visibility in submitting itself to the conditions of possibility of objects of visual experience, that is to say an intuition, intelligible or sensible; in one and the other case, the intuition is measured according to the dimensions of the mind receiving them and thus is defined by finitude. Phenomenology is in agreement on this observation with critical philosophy: no phenomenon can enter into the visibility of a spectacle, unless it is first submitted to the conditions of this very visibility: donation to a finite mind. Consequently, the most elementary piety will hold itself to this inevitable dilemma: either the Holy keeps itself as such, but refuses in this case [the entry into] any visible spectacle—and the holiness of God remains with neither image nor face; or the image that delivers the Holy to the visible only abandons itself to it as a victim to the outrage of the hangmen—and the image, bereft of any holiness, accomplishes an obscene blasphemy. Either the invisible, or imposture.[66]

The problem concerns the incompatibility of the image with holiness, since the image so readily lends itself to idolatry. Using the decisions of the Second Council of Nicaea as a basis, Marion tries to distinguish once again between the idol and the icon, noting that the icon will demand and merit veneration, and that it will both keep and manifest holiness.[67]

With regard to these conditions, Marion gives the example of the Cross as icon. Christ kills the image of himself, digging in himself a measureless abyss between his appearance and his glory.

---

[66] Marion, *CV,* 120: "Or tout spectacle n'accède à sa visibilité qu'en se soumettant aux conditions de possibilité des objets de l'expérience visuelle, c'est-à-dire à une intuition, intelligible ou sensible; dans l'un et l'autre cas, l'intuition se mesure elle-même aux dimensions de l'esprit qui la reçoit et se définit donc par la finitude. La phénoménologie s'accorde sur ce constat avec la philosophie critique: nul phénomène n'entre dans la visibilité d'un spectacle, s'il ne se soumet d'abord aux conditions de cette visibilité même: la donation à un esprit fini. Par conséquent, la plus élémentaire piété s'en tiendra à ce dilemme inévitable: ou bien le Saint se garde comme tel, mais il se refuse alors à tout spectacle visible—et la sainteté de Dieu reste sans image ni visage; ou bien l'image qui livre le Saint au visible ne le lui abandonne que comme une victime à l'outrage des bourreaux—et l'image, veuve de toute sainteté, accomplit un obscène blasphème. Ou bien l'invisible, ou bien l'imposture."

[67] Marion, *CV,* 121–23.

The Cross only gives a figure of Christ under the paradox that hides his glory. In fact, the Cross gives nothing to see: it is a scandal.[68] What is more, those who view the Cross will be able to interpret it differently.[69] The type of the Cross thus only carries the mark of the Holy where the Holy abandons itself fully to rejection and injury by being completely misunderstood. The icon repeats the crossing from the visible to the invisible that makes of the Cross the sign of the glory of the Holy One. It is the trace that facilitates this transition.[70] Since Christ in the Cross always refers us always to the Father, the Cross is able both to manifest holiness and to protect it. In other words, it is not the visible that is to be venerated, but always the invisible to which the visible refers. The icon is ordained to the Holy in never claiming the Holy for itself: "[it] does not represent, it presents, not in the sense of producing a new presence (as the painting), but in the sense of making a present of all holiness to the Holy."[71] The icon transgresses itself, as it were, in order to glorify what Marion, following Basil, calls the "prototype."[72] It draws the invisible and the visible together in the same way that Christ does in the hypostatic union.[73] The distance between the invisible Father and the Son visible in the icon is bridged by virtue of their trinitarian communion, where the movement of the Spirit is the love that links Father and Son. This movement is both what draws us beyond the icon and what prevents it from becoming a static or idolatrous representation.[74] The icon demands a new way of seeing—veneration—that contests objectification.[75] It receives veneration but does not appropriate it, referring all glory to the Father, and having as its role

[68] Marion, *CV,* 127–29.

[69] Marion, *CV,* 129.

[70] Marion, *CV,* 130–33.

[71] Marion, *CV,* 137: "L'icône ne représente pas, elle présente, non au sens de produire une nouvelle présence (comme la peinture), mais au sens de faire présent de toute sainteté au Saint." What does he mean here by "making present"? My thanks to Joseph S. O'Leary for his assistance with the translation of this problematic passage.

[72] Marion, *CV,* 139.

[73] Marion, *CV,* 148.

[74] Marion, *CV,* 148–50.

[75] Such veneration occurs in the context of my "being seen," rather than seeing.

only to allow for the crossing of gazes, which Marion defines as both love and communion.[76]

In the phenomenological context of *Étant donné,* Marion situates the icon in his series of four saturated phenomena, of which revelation/Revelation is the fifth, culminative super-type. We can perhaps then assume that the icon of its own does not need to be equated with a revelatory phenomenon. Once again, we are reminded that the icon offers nothing to see, but itself regards its onlooker: "The look that the Other poses and makes weigh on me thus neither gives itself to be looked at, nor even to be seen—this invisible look only gives itself to be endured."[77] However, we learn something more in this context, that the icon contains within itself the characteristics of the three preceding saturated phenomena (the event, the idol, and the flesh). These characteristics are the encompassing of many horizons at once, the demand for revisitation, and the dislodging of the priority of the transcendental I.[78]

Having drawn from several of Marion's major theological and phenomenological works in order to note his observations concerning the icon, it may be helpful here to summarize his understanding, grouping the many characteristics described. On the one hand, the icon refers us to the invisible or unspeakable by way of the visible, provoking a vision and retraining the gaze. But on the other hand, it does not reduce the invisible to visibility, and does not represent distance, but manifests it. In fact, it renounces its visibility, abandoning visibility to misinterpretation. Further, the icon refers not to an essence but to an intention. It subjects the worshiper to a gaze from beyond, so that in the encounter with the icon there is a crossing of regards. Infinite intention substitutes for the finite, overwhelming the finite, putting the worshiper in question and playing on several horizons at once. Whether or not it is experienced as a phenomenon of saturation, an icon does not, in theory, refer to itself but to what is beyond it. Yet to what, therefore, does it refer?

There is little doubt that an icon is generally understood in a

[76] Marion, *CV,* 152–53.
[77] Marion, *ED,* 324.
[78] Marion, *ED,* 324–25.

religious context, and therefore its consideration seems, at least initially, to violate Janicaud's imperative that we not take a theological turn. But Janicaud's argument is less convincing where it is not assured that we are speaking about revelation as such. More important is the lesson we can apply here from Derrida, which is that if there were to be a God, then God's entry into human experience would be subject to that same difference and deferral of meaning that disrupts all experience. In other words, the theological turn of the consideration of the icon is only an issue where it corners the market, as it were, leaving us with no other choice. Does the icon present us with only one meaning? It seems to me that it offers a number of possibilities: the icon may refer to nothing beyond itself; it may refer to an illusion projected by the viewer; it may refer to a Christian (or some other) God; or it may refer to the vision of its painter. With regard to this last possibility, Marion's exposition of *l'invu,* the unseen, in a work of art provides us with a perfectly non-theological option. At the first level, then, the icon cannot be forced into making a reference to the Christian God, even if that is its subject matter. And we see this operative in Marion's description of the functioning of the icon of the Cross: it is necessarily open to "misinterpretation." But there is a second dimension to our questioning: if the icon refers a worshiper to God, what does the icon offer of this God? At this point the quality of saturation is of relevance, for, Marion will suggest, the icon opens onto God in such a way that intuition is ruptured by excess. The icon does not refer to any *thing,* but to what cannot be thought *as such.* It seems that in this gap—or using Marion's word, this "distance"—*différance* is operative to the extent that any desire to obtain God on the part of the worshiper is annulled.[79] For what is found in the gap is not God but "too much," a too much that invites the risk of faith but refuses the certainty of knowledge. Yet while Marion insists that the icon does not refer to any essence, he allows that it refers to an intention. It is this "counter-intention," addressed to the "me" who responds to the call of saturation, that threatens his reading.

John Milbank observes the acute constitutional difficulties entailed in the phenomenological manifestation of the other to the

[79] It is of interest that Marion speaks, in *ED* of "*la donation différée,*" at p. 82.

same. He addresses quite a detailed objection to Marion (and Levinas) in an essay appearing in *The Word Made Strange,* "Only Theology Overcomes Metaphysics," where he states:

> The radicality of a non-apparent phenomenon equivalent to an irreducible excess of intuition over intention is maintained, because the "I" itself first *is* as called, or is subject only as "interlocuted," as given "me" before it is an I. The problem here, indicated by Philip Blond, is that, as with the late "theological" Husserl of the unpublished archives, and with Levinas, the calling "other" can after all only be identified as a subjective caller, or as a giver, *by way of* a projection of one's own ego upon the other, an ego that would be once again an initial "I," constituted first as the ground of intentional representation of objects.[80]

It is possible to recognize here a similarity to Derrida's critique of Levinas and the face, where recognition of the face as Other depends on a projection of the self.[81]

There are in fact two problems: the problem of the recognition of otherness as otherness, and the problem of the identification or knowing of otherness. Milbank's (and Blond's) argument runs: the excess works as excess only because it precedes the I, yet the caller who is manifest in that excess can only be known by an I who is capable of recognizing a caller in relation to itself. The only other alternative is that the call remains anonymous, devoid of identification in a specific caller, and Milbank explains that Marion's desire that God be manifest in the call undermines this option.[82] If the call remains anonymous, there is no guaranteeing that it is not the *Es gibt,* the *il y a* or the *Ereignis;* no guaranteeing that it is the call of the Good.[83] Elsewhere, Marion goes to great lengths to establish that it is Love which calls to love, but he is unable to overcome the problem of constitution without resort-

---

[80] John Milbank, "Only Theology Overcomes Metaphysics," *The Word Made Strange* (Oxford: Blackwell, 1997), 36–52, 38 [hereafter Milbank, *OTOM*]. Evidently this is before the release of *Étant donné,* although I suspect his criticisms would not be answered in a way he would like in any case.

[81] See also Graham Ward, "The Theological Project of Jean-Luc Marion," in Blond, *PSP.*

[82] Milbank, *OTOM,* 39.

[83] Milbank, *OTOM,* 39, 43. Interestingly enough, this criticism is addressed to Derrida, concerning his reading of the desire for the "*tout autre,*" by Richard Kearney in "Desire of God," in Caputo and Scanlon, *GGP,* 112–45, 126.

ing to an "act of ethical or even religious faith."[84] Marion's problematic reading of the icon as saturated phenomenon, where the excess gives itself as a call or as an intention, is expressed by Milbank in terms of the gift: "Marion oscillates between (1) the absolute anonymity of the gift; (2) the gift as a 'natural' manifestation of a giver = God; (3) recognition of this manifestation only through an act of will."[85]

Milbank's critique of counter-intentionality is a useful one, although some of the problems he identifies can be overcome by preserving two levels of undecidability. At the first level, I cannot be sure of the icon's reference. At the second level, even if I hope it refers to God, what I am given is not knowledge but an excess, which itself is undecidable, although this is not a word that Marion uses with sufficient regularity to overcome all our doubts. It may also be helpful to make use of the "double dissymmetry" argument that Blanchot applies to Levinas in order to overcome the constitutional problems Milbank suggests. Additionally, it must be recognized that the "otherness" in the Levinasian face of the Other is not based on the manifestation of the face (recognized as a face in relation to my own), but on the manifestation of a trace in that face, for which I can never take account, and which has always and already withdrawn into immemoriality. It is not possible, on the basis of the saturated given (even of the call, which is given only as a trace), to identify positively a giver or a source of givenness.[86] Nevertheless, it is a sobering thought that the undecidability of the excess risks an encounter with "the Devil," so to speak, as much as an encounter with God.

In all of this we see that for Marion to gain access to the excess of the saturated phenomenon requires him to undertake a hermeneutics. To risk God rather than the Devil involves "seeing" the icon in a particular way. Seeing makes use of the light; phenomenology is a science of the light. Perhaps that is why Marion refers to phenomena of revelation/Revelation as blinding in their

---

[84] Milbank, *OTOM,* 39. See Marion, *GWB* and *PC.*

[85] Milbank, *OTOM,* 39.

[86] Milbank is too dismissive of the faith that affirms what cannot be known *as such.* His alternative (a theology of analogy, which "evacuates" philosophy) is no less dependent, surely, on a decision of the will (faith) to affirm that it is God who speaks or acts or is revealed.

excess, dazzling, overwhelming, whereas Derrida's undecidable gap is a black hole. It is not hard to trace the influence of theologian Hans Urs von Balthasar in Marion's preference for seeing correctly. In the first volume of the seven that constitute *The Glory of the Lord,* Balthasar writes: "The Word of God became flesh, Jesus Christ, God and man—and so we are led unreservedly to affirm that here we have a true form placed before the sight of man. Whatever else might be said about God's hiddenness . . . the fundamental thing is that here we have before us a genuine, 'legible' form, and not merely a sign or an assemblage of signs."[87] Jesus is the form of God made visible. The implications of this statement are reinforced where Balthasar affirms that "the God whom we know now and for eternity is Emmanuel, God with us and for us, the God who shows and bestows himself: because he shows and bestows *himself,* we can know this God not only 'economically' from the outside, but may also possess him 'theologically' from within and just as he is."[88] Because of Jesus, God is not only seen but also known, revealed not only in deeds but in the Word. However, this seeing and knowing only becomes possible when the believer is conformed to that Word: "the human beholder can be brought to such perception only by the grace of God, that is, by a participation in this same depth that makes him proportionate to the wholly new dimension of a form-phenomenon which comprises within itself both God and world."[89] God's revelation in Christ is a phenomenon that can be seen by those who, allowing themselves to be determined by the phenomenon instead of determining it for themselves, learn to see it for what it is. God "shows" Godself to those who have eyes to see, gives Godself "to be recognized," is unveiled in an "epiphany."[90] Further, God in Christ "is not appearance as the limitation . . . of an infinite non-form . . . but the appearance of an infinitely determined

[87] Hans Urs von Balthasar, *The Glory of the Lord: A Theological Aesthetics,* vol. 1, *Seeing the Form,* trans. Erasmo Leiva-Merikakis, 2nd ed. (San Francisco: Ignatius Press, 1982), 153 [hereafter Balthasar, *GL1*].

[88] Balthasar, *GL1,* 154.

[89] Balthasar, *GL1,* 154.

[90] Hans Urs von Balthasar, *Mysterium Paschale,* trans. Aidan Nichols, O.P. (Grand Rapids, Mich.: Eerdmans, 1990), 206 [hereafter Balthasar, *MP*]; *GL1,* 131; *GL7,* 275ff.

super-form."[91] The examples from Balthasar's work could easily be multiplied, but the point is this: the object of theology is here being described as a phenomenon. The nature of that phenomenon is not entirely clear, but it has a form and a content that, under certain circumstances, can be seen and known.

But there is a second and very important emphasis in Balthasar's theology to be noted. We read in *Mysterium Paschale:* "In bringing to their climax, in the Resurrection of the Son, all these lines of meaning, the Father *shows* to the world his risen and glorified Son. 'God shows Jesus *as* his Son.' This showing is a gift, an act of benevolence, as the Lucan formula makes clear."[92] In *The Glory of the Lord,* Balthasar says: "The revelation may be termed epiphany, or receive some other name, but it is the perfect self-gift of the 'goodness and loving-kindness of God our Saviour' (Tit. 3.4): this alone is the content of the audible and visible Word, to which man replies with the gift of himself in loving faith."[93] Or again: "Idealist thinking lacked the personal categories of Scripture, which prevent God's knowledge from becoming human knowledge by a total omission of God's gift of himself in revelation. . . . Insofar as God's revelation appears as his free favour, which merits the name *gratia* not only by its exterior gratuitousness but by its interior quality . . . the content of this self-revelation of God bears the name of *doxa* (majestic glory, *kâbôd*)."[94] Balthasar is interested not only in God's self-revelation as phenomenon, but also in this same phenomenon of self-revelation as gift.

Balthasar exercises a most powerful theological influence on Marion, not least in his preference for using the language of gift to describe the encounter between the divine and the human. Marion frequently acknowledges his debt in this regard and expresses a profound admiration for Balthasar's work.[95] And in the examples given above we begin to see the deep correspondence between them, a correspondence that underlies the theology of gift and seemingly makes it possible. The giving is intrinsically

[91] Balthasar, *GL1,* 432.
[92] Balthasar, *MP,* 206.
[93] Balthasar, *GL7,* 278:
[94] Balthasar, *GL1,* 140.
[95] For example, Marion, *ID,* 13.

linked with the showing; the gift becomes gift in the revealing. The theology of gift is sustained by a structure of givenness where the phenomenon shows itself as and for itself. It is in the thinking of this structure, as we have seen, that Marion tries to open the dialogue between theology and philosophy, for such a structure also lies at the basis of phenomenology. So, for example, Marion is able to ask:

> Are the phenomena of revelation still phenomena in full right? If yes, do they belong to objective phenomenality, either ontic, or of another type—that of the event, of the paradox, of the saturated phenomenon, etc.? Should one enlarge the path until now known or admitted of phenomenality? Should one admit non-visible phenomena, and in that case are they so provisionally, partially or definitively? All these questions, though they can only be formulated in the way of revealed theology, belong nevertheless also and by full right to phenomenology—since revelation itself claims to deploy a particular figure of phenomenality.[96]

We have come almost full circle. It is fruitless to insist, against Marion's specific instruction, that he has made of his phenomenology or "post-phenomenology" a theology. But we can and do observe that his theology requires a light that thought alone cannot provide. In seeking to establish the credentials of phenomenology in terms of opening a theological conversation, we have observed not only the limits of phenomenology but also the limits of thought itself. That being the case, the difficulty of the question with which we began this inquiry is once again shown to be most pressing. How are we to think God as gift? How are we to think God at all?

It remains to respond to the figure of the gift as it is outlined by Marion in the Sketch and *Étant donné*, and to ask whether or

[96] Marion, *LAPP*, 49: "les phénomènes de révélation sont-ils encore phénomènes de plein droit? Si oui, appartiennent-ils à la phénoménalité objective, ou ontique, ou bien d'un autre type—ceux de l'événement, du paradoxe, du phénomène saturé, etc? Doit-on élargir le champ jusqu'ici connu ou admis de la phénoménalité? Doit-on admettre des phénomènes non visibles, et dans ce cas le sont-ils provisoirement, partiellement ou définitivement? Toutes ces questions, bien qu'elles ne puissent se formuler que dans le champ de la théologie révélée, appartiennent pourtant aussi et de plein droit à la phénoménologie—puisque la révélation prétend elle-même déployer une figure particulière de la phénoménalité."

not it is possible to approach God in this way. A response from a theologian will provide a crucial perspective at this point. John Milbank, whose exchangist views were introduced earlier in response to Derrida's gift analysis, also comments on Marion's attempt to rethink the gift: "Jean-Luc Marion has rightly argued that to receive the *other* in receiving his gift demands that the *distance* of the other remains in place—to try to possess the other and his gifts, to receive them as exactly due rewards, or as things we do not need *to go on* receiving, would be simply to obliterate them."[97] Yet while initially approving of Marion's "distance," Milbank observes in it several problems, which reduce to a thinking that must be so unspecific as to give, in Milbank's terms, "nothing." "Hence Marion's gift is *only* of the subjective other, *only* of distance and not of the transference and content-filled 'in-between' which alone *makes* that distance: 'what distance gives is the gap itself.' To be given *only* what is held at a distance is to be given . . . nothing."[98] Milbank maintains that the thinking of the icon is really a thinking of the idol (and so gives nothing); and that the move Marion poses from "vanity" (the supreme *ennui* with being and beings) to God fails because it gives nothing specific.[99]

> Therefore, if it is true, as Marion stresses, that a gift abides only in distance, it is equally true that if a gift is to pass, and not rather to be endlessly expected, the giver abides only in the specific form, measure and character of this distance. And such specificity there must always be, for even in the case of our infinite distance from God, we ourselves exist in some specific measure of such distance, albeit never completed, never fully apprehended.[100]

What Milbank seeks is not "only giving, the pure gesture," but a giving that manifests a content.[101] But as I have already indicated, such specificity runs its own risks.

In Milbank's judgment, Marion is at least correct where he recognizes that no one could ever assume to give back to God.[102] And

---

[97] Milbank, *CGG,* 132–33.
[98] Milbank, *CGG,* 133.
[99] Milbank, *CGG,* 133–34.
[100] Milbank, *CGG,* 134.
[101] Milbank, *CGG,* 134.
[102] The reason here being that "counter-gift cannot possibly be predicated of God, since there is nothing extra to God that *could* return to him." Milbank, *CGG,* 134.

yet Milbank also wishes to assert that exchange must characterize the relationship, or further, that it inaugurates and sustains the relationship.[103] "Divine giving occurs *inexorably,* and this means that a return is inevitably made, for since the creature's very being resides in its reception of itself as a gift, the gift is, in itself, the gift of a return."[104] The non-acceptance of the divine gift leads, he suggests, to the discontinuation of the gift. The gift occurs as exchange partly because it must inevitably be received. And it has already been received on our behalf, according to Milbank, by Mary.[105] Marion fails, in Milbank's view, because he cannot see the necessary reciprocity in the gift, persisting in his idea of an "extra-ontological discourse."[106] In the subsequent discussion of Marion's relationship to Heidegger and the failure of "post-modern" thought, what is most significant for our purposes is Milbank's analysis of the two threads that sustain Marion's work, which I quote at length since it sums up a particular approach to Marion and, through him, Derrida:

> If, in the first place, Marion accepts Heidegger's completion of ontology, and therefore, in order to speak theologically is compelled to *exceed* ontological discourse, he also, in the second place, derives the very space of this exceeding *from* Heidegger's ontology itself. This space has already been detailed in my account of Derrida: Heidegger's ontology is itself internally exceeded by gift, since time and Being outside the mode of presence are, in Heidegger's terms, *no longer* Being. They turn into that which "gives" Being, although this "that" is really identical with "nothing." Marion then converts the donating *nihil* into a phenomenologically apprehended "call" from a gift now standing at a *distance* from Being, with which it is no longer "enfolded." In a second move, which appeals to revelation, he "identifies" the call as divine love, and ontological emergence *ex nihilio* [*sic*] as creation *ex nihilio* [*sic*]. But surely this raises the suspicion that the space of the gift, *as* an extra-ontological space, is only required within the logic of a strictly immanentist

[103] Milbank, *CGG,* 134–35.

[104] Milbank, *CGG,* 135.

[105] Milbank, *CGG,* 136. With a Rahnerian slant I would think it more accurate to say by Christ in himself, that is, by Christ as the apex of human evolution and as the absolute Word of God. See Karl Rahner, *Foundations of Christian Faith,* trans. William V. Dych (1976; New York: Crossroad, 1992), 176–227.

[106] Milbank, *CGG,* 136–37.

> construal of the ontological difference, which as I have argued, expresses a philosophical option, not the termination of philosophy. An unattainable "beyond being" is demanded by an atheism which tries to think onto-emergence out of nothing, not the revealed word of the Bible.
>
> This suspicion, nevertheless, is relatively trivial. What is of much more moment is that the nihilistic account of the unilateral gift, as professed by Derrida, thinks through this unilateral character in the only possibly consistent fashion, as compared with Marion's theological variant.[107]

Milbank's complaint touches on many themes, but of most interest is his belief that Marion's gift gives "nothing." If nothing else, this should confirm for the skeptic that Marion's work, from a theological point of view, does not deliver theology in the desired or required specificity. But Milbank's comments also betray a fear that if thought has met its match with God, it is nihilism or atheism that triumphs, and I am not convinced that this need be the case. It is telling that Milbank concludes of Derrida's gift: "But this gift cannot *be* given, since subject and object exhaust the whole of ontological reality."[108] What kind of reality are we talking about? If we come up against the limits of thought, is it because thought should be able to contain "everything"? With Marion, we are led to thought's excess, an excess that he readily reads in terms of the Gospel, while admitting that he has no phenomenological justification for doing so. With Derrida we are led to thought's interruption, which opens not onto a plenitude but onto a desert. Yet in both cases it could be argued that we are not far from that theological tradition known as mysticism.

If Milbank is disappointed that Marion's gift gives too little to deserve the name, I am inclined to argue that it still gives too much. Marion is correct to identify causality as a major problem for the gift, but causality is a problem only because presence is a problem. The difficulties of causality can only be overcome where presence—of the giver, the recipient, or the gift—is overcome. This is evident in a number of ways: in the reduction itself, in the

---

[107] The discussion occurs at Milbank, *CGG,* 137–44. It is valuable but I cannot enter further into it here. The quotation is from 142–43.

[108] Milbank, *CGG,* 130.

suspension of one or the other of the "poles" of giver or recipient, and in the allowance for the invisibility of the gift.

Marion sees the phenomenological reduction as the only way forward with the gift, meaning that the reduction of all transcendence will give the gift outside all causality.[109] Yet the mark of transcendence must remain determinative of the gift. As Marion says earlier of the given, the gift must be "from elsewhere." It seems to me that it must therefore be *irreducible* to my consciousness, and for this reason, what is important is not so much the reduction of transcendence but the maintenance of undecidability in that very reduction.

In his discussion of the "poles" of the gift, Marion emphasizes that it is sufficient for one pole to be active if the gift is going to work. What he is effectively doing is maintaining that it is sufficient for one pole to see the gift as gift for it to be gift. And yet that seeing would in Derrida's terms annul the gift. Certainly, the lack of coincidence between one pole's seeing the gift as gift and the other pole's seeing the gift as gift is important. But while time is crucial in Derrida's analysis, so is undecidability, which relates to the gift itself. Marion tries to assert this undecidability by positing a donor who does not know to whom he or she gives and a recipient who may not choose to receive, but it needs to be asserted at a deeper level. The donor must not know *whether or not* he or she gives, and the recipient must not know *whether or not* it is a gift that he or she receives. In other words, the gift must remain unrecognizable as a gift if it is to accomplish its work as a gift. This insight is reinforced by Caputo's lucid commentary in his "Apostles of the Impossible."[110] While Marion keeps hinting that the gift "decides itself," here trying to prop up the autonomy of the gift against the efforts of the constituting donor and recipient, in fact he cannot maintain this. The aporia of the gift is only resolved in the decision of either donor or recipient to read what Marion rightly identifies as donability and receivability on a given. The gift does not decide; it is I who choose to see in something inherently undecidable that it is gift. Marion observes at one point that the gift is an act of faith, and this confirms my reading.

---

[109] Marion, *ED,* 121–22.
[110] Caputo, *AI,* 210–11.

Ultimately, his attempt to withdraw the gift from the realm of causality cannot work in the way he intends. That is not because he suspends the donor and the recipient, but because he eventually needs to reinstate them in some fashion if he is going to determine a given as a gift. It is not the complete loss of the donor and the recipient that counts, but their intrinsic undecidability. And that undecidability will have to be the hallmark of any given if it is ever to deliver the unknowable gift.

In redefining the gift as what is lost, rather than what is gratuitous, Marion offers an interesting twist. This definition works well in relation to the suspension of the donor and the recipient and in relation to promoting the lack of return (by conversion) of the gift, but it involves certain ambiguities. To redefine the gift does not solve the problem of the gift, for such a redefinition is not widespread. When most people speak of a gift, they do not mean something they have simply lost, but something they intended to dispose of. And yet this could easily be recouched in terms of "intending to lose" or "opening oneself up to the possibility of losing," and here lies the merit of Marion's proposal. Giving, in the deepest sense of the word, refers to loss, and gratuity (the freedom of giving) is here understood as not intending to be compensated for the loss.

Marion seems to imply that Derrida has misread the gift, or read it "commonly," as a causal relation. Yet Marion really only wants to achieve, surely, the same result Derrida reaches in his recognition that where a gift is something given by someone to someone else, it undoes itself. So his criticism of Derrida here falls flat. Derrida does not read the gift commonly, but as it functions and fails to function; he looks, like Marion, for another option. Further, Marion's dismissal of Derrida's thinking of the gift as the condition of possibility for the given in general is based on a misconception. Marion accuses Derrida of trying to establish a ground for the gift, which he construes as metaphysical. But if we read on we discover that Derrida's thinking of the gift as condition of possibility is also a thinking of it as condition of impossibility.

The discussion of indebtedness is problematic. It is possible to see in Marion's analysis here an attempt to tie the gift in with Levinasian responsibility. And it is not that I disagree with his understanding of the constitution of the subject as a response to the Other, but that the notion of indebtedness seems to fly in the face of the very possibility of gift. How can a gift be free if it is always a response to debt? Marion speaks of an always anterior (immemorial) debt to which we must respond in giving. If, by chance, he wanted to suggest that we are always indebted to God and that therefore we must give, he would run the risk of entering into Pelagian waters, and that in spite of the biblical reminder that we love God because God loved us first.[111] There is only one way of thinking this question that makes any sense. To read responsibility as a response to a gift (of self, of life, of a world), it must be protected from identification, for otherwise the gift will be undone. That in responding I receive myself as a gift must always be undecidable—it could be a given or a gift, and therefore I need posit no donor. If I see it as a gift, rather than a given, there can be no response out of indebtedness, but only a response of giving if that response forms the gift itself. In other words, if I give, it can only be because I have been gifted with the capacity to give, not because I feel that I must give back. The saying from 1 John can thus be read, not that we love God because God first loved us and we have so been obliged, but that we love God because God in loving enables us to love. And even if just the capacity to give is the gift, it must not be returned. Levinas's conversion of desire here becomes very important. Goodness does not return to the Infinite but is lavished upon the undesirable Other. Therefore my giving must always remain undecidable. I must never know whether or not I truly give, for otherwise I could rest rewarded by self-congratulation.

[111] 1 John 4:19.

7

Rethinking the Gift I

IN ACCORDANCE with both Christian tradition and his vision of phenomenology, Marion answers the question of how God might enter into human thought in terms of the gift. For Marion there is an essential coherence, if not a correlation, between what takes place at the outer limits of thought and what theology identifies as the inbreaking of God in human life. Derrida, on the other hand, is less convinced of the capacity of phenomenology to work at these outer limits, and is suspicious of what a theological hermeneutics promises to deliver. Nevertheless, as we find Marion more and more insistent that he speaks in the name of phenomenology and not of God, we find Derrida absorbed more and more by God as a question. And while Derrida insists that the gift is impossible, he also maintains that it is not thereby unthinkable.[1] It is, instead, a figure of *the* impossible, a figure that might also bear the name of God. Strangely enough, then, both writers might be said to approach God by way of the gift. Marion's approach has been examined in some detail; in this chapter and the one that follows it will be necessary to consider how Derrida thinks the impossible.

DERRIDA AND THREE THOUGHTS OF THE GIFT

The two works of Derrida that deal most thoroughly with the question of the gift are *Given Time: 1. Counterfeit Money* and *The*

---

[1] Derrida, *GT1,* 7, 10. Thomas A. Carlson describes this difference very well: "The gift, Derrida suggests, is not simply impossible, but rather *the* impossible. I take this distinction to mark, among other things, the difference between that 'about which one [simply] cannot speak' and, by contrast, 'that about which one cannot speak, *but which one can no longer silence.*' In other words, 'the impossible' articulates this double bind: it engenders thought, speech, and desire that remain oriented around what, precisely, thought, speech, and desire can never attain. Indeed, the impossible might well engender thought, speech, and desire

Gift of Death. Derrida's thinking of the impossibility of the gift proceeds with reference to time and to the potential that lies in the idea that there might be gift where no gift *appears as such,* where no gift presents itself, since this seems to be at the heart of the problem. This thinking will be considered according to a distinction Derrida himself draws, although it will be imposed here more strongly to produce two readings of Derrida on the gift. The second of the two readings will then again be divided to produce a third possible reading. At one point in *Given Time,* Derrida differentiates two approaches to the gift, and these approaches will form the bases of the two readings that will be made. He distinguishes the gift as that which is given from the gift as the condition of possibility for the given. "There would be, *on the one hand,* the gift that gives something determinate . . . and, *on the other hand,* the gift that gives not a given but the condition of a present given in general, that gives therefore the element of the given in general."[2]

When Derrida says of the gift that it is the condition of a "present given," he seems to understand this gift as the condition of all thought.[3] It is the condition of possibility (or transcendental) for anything at all, including the condition of possibility for subjectivity. However, there are two important qualifications to be made here. First, since Derrida generally speaks not only of conditions of possibility but also conditions of *im*possibility, it would perhaps be more accurate for us to refer to this giving condition that enables *or* disables as a "quasi-transcendental."[4] This qualification places a certain distance between Derrida and Kant. Such a distance is reinforced by a second qualification, to be made with regard to the subject. The Kantian use of "transcendental" refers

---

to the very extent that it announces itself and yet remains inaccessible." *Indiscretion: Finitude and the Naming of God* (Chicago: University of Chicago Press, 1999), 226.

[2] Derrida, *GT1,* 54.

[3] See also Derrida's discussion at *GT1,* 126–28, regarding nature and donation.

[4] "A transcendental condition is a sufficient and enabling condition; a quasi-transcendental condition is insufficient and equi-disabling, seeing that the effect that makes it possible is also made unstable." Caputo, *PTJD,* 12. The difference is suggested quite nicely by Derrida in the current context of discussion in *GT1* where he says, "The transcendental question or rather the question *on* the transcendental gets complicated, it even goes a little mad." *GT1,* 54.

us to the power of a constituting subject, and it is problematic because Derrida will call those very constitutive powers into question. The Derridean use of "transcendental" does not primarily relate to a subject, and where so it only relates to a "subject" who is never self-present and at best constituted, and certainly very different from that of Kant.[5]

To return to the two readings that are currently being contemplated, there is in Derrida this distinction between what could be called "the Gift" (as quasi-transcendental, even if not originary) and "gifts in general" (any actual gift).[6] "The Gift" is the condition of donation and thus determines any other possibility of gift. The way of proceeding from this point will therefore be first in terms of an attempt to discern this Gift, to ask: "What Gift makes giving possible (or impossible)?" Nevertheless, although the two initial readings to be suggested will be based on Derrida's own distinction, it would be artificial to imply that he himself always adheres to that distinction in speaking of the gift. This is borne out by the fact that it is not until well after his consideration of the conditions of the gift (largely in the first chapter of *Given Time*) that he mentions the possibility of such a distinction (at p. 54). In other words, the space between the two readings itself is inhabited by *différance.* Much of what is said with regard to the Gift may also apply to the gift. For example, they both arise in a "moment of madness."[7] That is why the second path to be followed, that of discerning the possibility or impossibility of gifts in

[5] The discussion by Simon Critchley in his "Prolegomena to Any Post-Deconstructive Subjectivity," in Critchley and Dews, *DS,* 13–45, is helpful in grappling with this difference.

[6] See Derrida, *D,* 131. Derrida quotes Mauss, who seems to observe the Gift/gift distinction to refer to the ambivalence of the word—the gift is at once good (Gift) and bad (gift). I have adopted the distinction for a different reason, namely, to indicate the difference between the Gift as transcendental and the gift as anything else. It is also to be noted that Derrida does not seek an "originary" gift (see his comments related to Heidegger on p. 162), although he does enter into discussion elsewhere about originary donation with reference to nature (Derrida, *GT1,* 128). Yet we see the problem of seeking "the originary" as nature, the father, mother, or anything or anyone else at p. 66. Perhaps "older" is a more suitable description than "originary" (cf. *GT1,* 95).

[7] See Derrida, *GT1,* 47; Derrida, *GD,* 65; and Søren Kierkegaard, *Fear and Trembling,* trans. Alastair Hannay (Harmondsworth, Middlesex: Penguin, 1985), 103, for example.

general, will bear some relation to the first but will also draw from other material in *Given Time,* and then from *The Gift of Death.*

The Time of the Gift

Playing on the double meaning of the word "present," Derrida explores the relationship between time and the impossibility of the Gift.[8] On the one hand, and according to the common understanding, only what is in time can be given.[9] And yet, on the other hand, "wherever time predominates or conditions experience in general, wherever *time as circle* . . . is predominant, the gift is impossible. A gift could be possible, there could be a gift only at the instant an effraction of the circle will have taken place, at the instant all circulation will have been interrupted and *on the condition* of this instant."[10] At this point two readings become possible, and we turn to follow the first.

For there to be Gift, there would need to be an interruption to the economy of exchange, an interruption to the cycle of the present.[11] It would only be in not returning, that is, in not being present, that the Gift could operate aneconomically.[12] But it is not only the present as present that would need to be interrupted. Derrida includes all the temporal ecstases, the past because it can

[8] "The relation of the gift to the 'present,' in all the senses of this term, also to the presence of the present, will form one of the essential knots in the interlace of this discourse." Derrida, *GT1,* 9–10. "If he recognizes it *as* gift, if the gift *appears to him as such,* if the present is present to him *as present,* this simple recognition suffices to annul the gift. Why? Because it gives back, in the place, let us say, of the thing itself, a symbolic equivalent" (11).

[9] Derrida, *GT1,* 3.

[10] Derrida, *GT1,* 9.

[11] "There is gift, if there is any, only in what interrupts the system as well as the symbol in a partition without return and without division [*répartition*], without being-with-self of the gift-counter-gift." Derrida, *GT1,* 13.

[12] "Time, the 'present' of the gift is no longer thinkable as a now, that is as a present bound up in the temporal synthesis." Derrida, *GT1,* 9. "It cannot be gift as gift except by not being present as gift" (14). "In any case the gift does not *exist* and does not *present* itself. If it presents itself, it no longer presents itself" (15). The gift would operate aneconomically, or at least outside a restricted economy.

be remembered, and the future because it can be anticipated.[13] This means that for there to be Gift, it would have to be given outside the circle of time, and yet still maintain some relationship to the circle in order to have any signification. And this is the heart of the problem. In Derrida's words:

> Now the gift, *if there is any,* would no doubt be related to economy. One cannot treat the gift, this goes without saying, without treating this relation to economy, even to the money economy. But is not the gift, if there is any, also that which interrupts economy? That which, in suspending economic calculation, no longer gives rise to exchange? That which opens the circle so as to defy reciprocity or symmetry, the common measure, and so as to turn aside the return in view of the no-return? If there is a gift, the *given* of the gift (*that which* one gives, *that which* is given, the gift as given thing or as act of donation) must not come back to the giving (let us not already say to the subject, to the donor). It must not circulate, it must not be exchanged, it must not in any case be exhausted, as a gift, by the process of exchange, by the movement of circulation of the circle in the form of return to the point of departure. If the figure of the circle is essential to economics, the gift must remain *aneconomic.* Not that it remains foreign to the circle, but it must *keep* a relation of foreignness to the circle, a relation without relation of familiar foreignness. It is perhaps in this sense that the gift is the impossible.[14]

For there to be Gift, it must interrupt time and interrupt economy. Once again, the "relationless relation" is invoked. The "given" must not come back to the "giving" if there is to "be" Gift. Derrida highlights his avoidance of saying that it must not come back to the subject: the Gift could never be passed between subjects.[15] But he also wishes to say more than that. Not coming back to the "giving," which is prior to the specification of a subject or donor, is not coming back to the origin. *Il n'y a plus d'origine,* there is no longer an origin.

---

[13] "The temporalization of time (memory, present, anticipation; retention, protention, imminence of the future; 'ecstases,' and so forth) always sets in motion the process of a destruction of the gift: through keeping, restitution, reproduction, the anticipatory expectation or apprehension that grasps or comprehends in advance." Derrida, *GT1,* 14.

[14] Derrida, *GT1,* 7.

[15] "If there is gift, it cannot take place between two subjects exchanging objects, things, or symbols." Derrida, *GT1,* 24.

In another part of the text, Derrida reemphasizes the exteriority of the Gift to the circle:

> The overrunning of the circle by the gift, if there is any, does not lead to a simple, ineffable exteriority that would be transcendent and without relation. It is this exteriority that sets the circle going, it is this exteriority that puts the economy in motion. It is this exteriority that *engages* in the circle and makes it turn. If one must *render an account* (to science, to reason, to philosophy, to the economy of meaning) of the circle effects in which a gift gets annulled, this account-rendering requires that one take into account that which, while not simply belonging to the circle, engages in it and sets off its motion. What is the gift as the first mover of the circle? And how does it contract itself into a circular contract? And from what place? Since when? From whom?[16]

Given Derrida's general approach to binary oppositions such as presence and absence, being and non-being, or speech and writing, for example, it appears unusual for him to use a word such as "exteriority." For exteriority implies an opposition to interiority, and such an opposition would always be "contaminated" by undecidability. What does exteriority mean in this context? It does not mean, Derrida insists, "a simple, ineffable exteriority that would be transcendent and without relation." In other words, it seems that he does not wish to posit a reality external to the circle, a *cause* such as God, for example. (At the same time, why does he then speak of the gift as "first mover" of the circle? Why use language that has resonated so forcefully in the context of "onto-theology"?)[17] It seems that Derrida is speaking of a breach, an interruption to the economy of the circle by something that is related to it but which is perhaps not anything as such within the circle. There are two possibilities. One is that the breach is instigated by an external force. The other is that the

---

[16] Derrida, *GT1,* 30.

[17] In *The Truth in Painting,* Derrida speaks of having "set in train a divided Prime Mover," which perhaps tells us that any origin will always be divided disseminatively and thus never original. With regard to the gift as first mover, it seems to me that since the gift "is" impossible it reaches the same point as the divided origin, that is, that it cannot be original. See Jacques Derrida, *The Truth in Painting,* trans. Geoffrey Bennington and Ian McLeod (Chicago: University of Chicago Press, 1987), 2 [hereafter Derrida, *TP*].

exteriority that is not anything as such within the circle is not anything as such at all. The latter option makes a certain amount of sense given Derrida's comments on the "trait" in *The Truth in Painting:* "One space remains to be broached in order to give place to the truth in painting. Neither inside nor outside, it spaces itself without letting itself be framed but it does not stand outside the frame. It works the frame, makes it work, lets it work, gives it work to do (let, make, and give will be my most misunderstood words in this book)."[18] Of further note in the extract from *Given Time* just quoted is that Derrida uses the phrase "render an account." Here we find the very point of interface—the very uncomfortable point of interface—between economy and its interruption. For the account rendered seeks to take account of the unaccountable, and so it cannot take account, but falls endlessly between the cracks.

Derrida's thinking of the time of the Gift is related to a radical forgetting. The Gift cannot be present, cannot be anticipated, and cannot be remembered; but even further, it cannot even lie forgotten in the unconscious.[19] Such is the character of the Gift that it cannot be an event within the realm of consciousness at all. This is why the forgetting must be so radical. For the Gift to be Gift, having a relationship with consciousness (the circle, time) while not occurring within it, it would have to be radically anterior to it, and, Derrida will say, even constitutive of it. Both subject and object "are arrested effects of the gift."[20] The Gift would have passed before a distinction could be drawn between subjectivity and objectivity.[21] It would be immemorial, an event of a past that

---

[18] Derrida, *TP,* 11–12.

[19] "For there to be gift, not only must the donor or donee not perceive or receive the gift as such, have no consciousness of it, no memory, no recognition; he or she must also forget it right away and moreover this forgetting must be so radical that it exceeds even the psychoanalytic categoriality of forgetting. This forgetting of the gift must even no longer be forgetting in the sense of repression." Derrida, *GT1,* 16.

[20] Derrida, *GT1,* 24.

[21] Cf. Derrida's comments in *Points* with regard to the "who" in "being-thrown": "Starting at 'birth,' and possibly even prior to it, being-thrown re-appropriates itself or rather ex-propriates itself in forms that are not yet those of the *subject* or the *project.* The question 'who' then becomes: 'Who (is) thrown?' 'Who becomes—"who" from out of the destinerrance of the being-thrown?' That it is still a matter here of the trace, but also of iterability (cf. my *Limited Inc.*)

was never present. All we could know of the Gift would be the trace of its having already passed, the trace of its total erasure, a trace that would somehow nevertheless mark consciousness:

> And yet we say "forgetting" and not nothing. Even though it must leave nothing behind it, even though it must efface everything, including the traces of repression, this forgetting, this *forgetting of the gift* cannot be a simple non-experience, a simple non-appearance, a self-effacement that is carried off with what it effaces. For there to be a gift-event (we say event and not act), something must come about or happen, in an instant, in an instant that no doubt does not belong to the economy of time, in a time without time, in such a way that the forgetting forgets, that it forgets *itself,* but also in such a way that this forgetting, without being something present, presentable, determinable, sensible or meaningful, is not nothing.
>
> Far from giving us to think the possibility of the gift, on the contrary, it is on the basis of what takes shape in the name *gift* that one could *hope* thus to think forgetting. For there to be forgetting in this sense, there must be gift.[22]

There would be no point in talking about giving if it were so completely forgotten that it became, in Derrida's words, "a simple non-experience" or "a simple non-appearance." Giving may not be able to be "processed" as experience, but unless it touches experience in some way it literally does not even rate a mention.[23] Somehow there is signification, even if it does not coincide with the event, even if it is marked only in the forgetting, even if the signification is of forgetting and not of the Gift. The trace of the Gift is the forgetting of the forgotten; the possibility of forgetting and the hope of thinking the forgetting come from the Gift itself.

The conditions of the Gift are, therefore, as follows. The Gift

---

means that this ex-appropriation cannot be absolutely stabilized in the form of the subject. The subject assumes presence, that is to say sub-stance, stasis, stance. Not to be able to stabilize itself *absolutely* would mean to be able *only* to be stabilizing itself: relative stabilization of what remains *unstable,* or rather *non-stable.* Ex-appropriation no longer closes itself; it never totalizes itself." Derrida, *Po,* 270.

[22] Derrida, *GT1,* 17.

[23] What does Derrida mean by *l'expérience?* In *Points* he speaks of experience as a traversal (373). He seems to favor a sense of *Erfahrung* rather than *Erlebnis,* and after all, for Derrida the latter is complicated by Husserl's emphasis on the "living present." Yet at the same time, there is a sense that experience is not primarily theoretical. Experience, too, has an aporetic structure. See Hart, *EP.*

cannot be present, cannot be anticipated, and cannot be remembered. It is an event, but it cannot be an event within the realm of consciousness, even though it will somehow bear a relationship to consciousness that is constitutive of it. The Gift cannot take place between subjects. It will always and already have been, that is, it will be immemorial; and it will be known only by the erased trace of its having passed. In other words, the Gift can only be known by way of a trace: it can have no decidable origin, cannot exist as such, and can have no decidable destination. What Gift could fulfil these conditions? To be consistent with his critique, if Derrida were ever to identify the Gift outright he would already in a certain sense have undermined it. But it is possible to guess at what he might choose.

The Gift As Condition of Possibility and Impossibility

In *Given Time,* a number of passages point to what we might name as Gift. Derrida speaks of absolute forgetting. He suggests that "the thought of this radical forgetting as thought of the gift should accord with a certain experience of the *trace* as *cinder* or *ashes* in the sense in which we have tried to approach it elsewhere."[24] There are three linked elements here: the thought of

[24] Derrida, *GT1,* 17. In the footnote, Derrida refers us to one such "elsewhere," *Feu la cendre,* "and the other texts intersecting with it at the point where, precisely, a certain 'il y a là' [there is there] intersects with the giving of the gift." This text explores the cinder as the trace: "—but that is just what he calls the trace, this effacement. I have the impression now that the best paradigm for the trace, for him, is not, as some have believed, and he as well, perhaps, the trail of the hunt, the fraying, the furrow in the sand, the wake in the sea, the love of the step for its imprint, but the cinder (what remains without remaining from the holocaust, from the all-burning, from the incineration the incense [*sic*])." Jacques Derrida, *Cinders,* trans. Ned Lukacher (Lincoln: University of Nebraska Press, 1991), 43. But at the same time, it is an exploration of the trace or the cinder as the gift. " 'What puts itself in play in this holocaust of play itself?' / This perhaps: the gift, the sacrifice, the putting into play or the setting on fire of everything" (46). Once again, the gift is related to time and to the immemorial: "Before, if one could count here with time, before everything, before every determinable being [*étant*], there is, there was, there will have been the irruptive event of the gift [*don*]. An event that no more has any relation with what is currently designated under this word. Thus giving can no longer be thought starting from Being [*être*] but 'the contrary,' it could be said, if this logical inversion here were pertinent when the question is not yet logic but the

radical forgetting, the thought of the Gift, and the experience of the trace or cinder or ashes. The thought of radical forgetting is understood as a thinking of the Gift that *accords with* (is equal to, the same as?) an experience of the trace. Perhaps one could say that the thought of radical forgetting is the thinking of the Gift as a trace. This might mean that the Gift is experienced by way of the trace, or that the Gift "is" a trace. It might be possible to say that the Gift is given according to the trace, or that it works undecidably in the same way that the trace does.

Another hint emerges in the context of an analysis of Marcel Mauss. Derrida describes how time, as a term, becomes significant in Mauss's evaluation of a gift economy: "For those who participate in the experience of gift and countergift, the requirement of restitution 'at term,' at the delayed 'due date,' the requirement of the circulatory differance *is inscribed in the thing itself* that is given or exchanged."[25] Momentarily, Derrida becomes diverted by this *différance.* The gift object of which he speaks remains within the economy, within the range of calculation, but the "force" of the gift is not only in its demand for restitution but also in its exercising of delay. *Différance:* the effect of difference and deferral.[26] Hence "differance, which (is) nothing, is (in) the thing itself. It is (given) in the thing itself. It (is) the thing itself. It, differance, the thing (itself). It, without anything other. Itself, nothing."[27]

A further observation might be made from the perspective of Derrida's discussion of language and giving. Derrida posits the possibility of linguistic dissemination. He notes that "this hypoth-

---

origin of logic. In *Zeit und Sein,* the gift of the *es gibt* gives itself to be thought before the *Sein* in the *es gibt Sein* and displaces all that is determined under the name Ereignis, a word translated by event" (46, 48). Derrida is most suggestive of the self-effacement of the trace at 57: "If you no longer recall it, it is because the incineration follows its course and the consummation proceeds from itself, the cinder itself. Trace destined, like everything, to disappear from itself, as much in order to lose the way as to rekindle a memory. The cinder is exact: because without a trace it precisely traces more than an other, and as the other trace(s)." For many other passages on the gift we could also refer to Jacques Derrida, *Glas,* trans. John P. Leavey, Jr., and Richard Rand (Lincoln: University of Nebraska Press, 1986), especially at 242–47.

[25] Derrida, *GT1,* 40.

[26] Derrida, *SP,* 129–30.

[27] Derrida, *GT1,* 40.

esis of a dissemination without return would prevent the locution from circling back to its meaning. It thus also concerns—whence this paradoxical fold—the without-return of the gift."[28] Dissemination as without-return concerns the without-return of the Gift. Why dissemination? Because of *différance*—the difference and deferral that make absolute identity impossible, that make a complete return impossible. Dissemination is the effect of scattering in multiple contexts that marks each context with *différance,* with a difference and a deferral of meaning. Derrida draws this connection between language and giving elsewhere.[29]

In writing on the gift, Mauss is involved in a certain giving, and here we are provided with another clue. "The theoretical and supposedly constative dimension of an essay of the gift is *a priori* a piece, only a part, a part and a party, a *moment* of a performative, prescriptive, and normative operation that gives or takes, indebts itself, gives and takes, refuses to give or accepts to give—or does both at the same time according to a necessity that we will come back to." What is this necessity to which Derrida will return? Will it not be a *structural* necessity, one that marks the non-return of all returns, one that inhabits and corrupts all that is "a piece, only a part, a part and a party, a *moment* of a performative, prescriptive, and normative operation that gives or takes, indebts itself, gives and takes, refuses to give or accepts to give—or does both at the same time."[30] In other words, it seems that Derrida is referring to the structural effect of *différance* that is operative in Mauss's writing.

It will be sufficient to note a few of the other passages to which we might refer. There is the discussion on Baudelaire's "Serpent" where Derrida observes that "the gift, if there is any, will always be *without* border."[31] A little later, as part of the same discussion, Derrida talks about Baudelaire's giving up the text to a dissemination without return. "The structure of trace and legacy of this text . . . surpasses the phantasm of return and marks the death of the signatory or the non-return of the legacy, the non-benefit, therefore a certain condition of the gift—in the writing itself."

[28] Derrida, *GT1,* 48.
[29] Derrida, *GT1,* 80.
[30] Derrida, *GT1,* 62.
[31] Derrida, *GT1,* 91.

He continues: "That is why there is a problematic of the gift only on the basis of a consistent problematic of the trace and the text."[32] Derrida speaks of the undecidability of the Gift in terms of writing: the "scene" of writing is the "scene" of the Gift; the death of the donor agency "is only thinkable on the basis of, setting out from the gift"; and the addressee, too, remains uncertain.[33] The Gift and the narrative find themselves intrinsically intertwined. "The gift, if there is any, requires and at the same time excludes the possibility of narrative. The gift is on condition of the narrative, but simultaneously on the condition of possibility and impossibility of the narrative."[34] What is it that is "the condition of possibility and impossibility of the narrative"? What is the condition of the gift that is inscribed "in the writing itself"? What is the "consistent problematic of the trace and the text"? It "is" nothing. It (is) *différance.*

That to which Derrida consistently refers as providing the conditions of possibility and impossibility for writing, and so ultimately for giving, is *différance.* We might tentatively say that the Gift "is" *différance,* except that *différance* is not anything.[35] But then, neither is the Gift. I return, in order to facilitate comparison, to the conditions of the Gift that have previously been outlined. The Gift cannot be present, cannot be anticipated, and cannot be remembered. It is an event, but it cannot be an event within the realm of consciousness, even though it will somehow bear a relationship to consciousness that is constitutive of it. The Gift cannot take place between subjects. It will always have already been, that is, it will be immemorial; and it will be known only by the erased trace of its having passed. In other words, the Gift can only be known by way of a trace: it can have no decidable origin, cannot exist as such, and can have no decidable destination. Does *différance* meet this description? Derrida describes *différance* as "strategic," and one of his commentators, Gasché, describes it as an "infrastructural" device.[36] In other words, while *différance* is

[32] Derrida, *GT1,* 100.

[33] Derrida, *GT1,* 102.

[34] Derrida, *GT1,* 103. See also 122.

[35] "Différance *is not,* does not exist, and is not any sort of being-present (*on*)." Derrida, *SP,* 134. See Derrida, *GT1,* 127–28 n.

[36] Derrida, *SP,* 131; Gasché, *IDJD,* 4ff.

operative in any text, it is not of the same order as the text. It can be named, observed as a trace through its effects, but *différance* is never present, since *différance* "is" not. Since it cannot be present, it can neither be anticipated in presence nor remembered in presence. It is thus not an object that can be grasped by consciousness. Is it nevertheless possible to say that *différance* is constitutive of consciousness? Perhaps so, in the sense that since consciousness is never coincidental with itself, it is always inhabited by a species of *différance*. But it would not be possible to posit *différance* as the cause of consciousness. And *différance* itself refers us to no giver: its origin is undecidable, and its passing immemorial. With *différance* we would have a Given that would not attract any of the problematic elements of the gift. For there would be no giver (*différance* "is" without origin); no gift as such (*différance* "is" not anything); and no recipient (since it would be a given without destination). But there would have been (*il y aurait eu*) Gift. The Gift would have been given without being anything at all. The Gift that enables or disables donation would have been given. Such an understanding of the Gift would not be undone by its impossibility, but in fact enabled by it.

What questions remain in the wake of this understanding of the Gift? I have at this point basically two. In the first place, does the disengagement of the conditions of *possibility* of the gift (someone gives something freely to someone else), even if that enables a meeting with its conditions of *im*possibility (there can be no giver, no gift as such, and no recipient), annul the Gift we have just described? If the Gift is perfectly impossible but not at the same time really possible, even if its possibility is less impossible than simply undecidable, "is" there really Gift? In other words, do we find ourselves lost in that "transcendental illusion" that is the first of the double risks of the gift to which Caputo seems to point?[37] The Gift for which Derrida allows appears to rest on the making of no distinction between "the given" and "the gift." For surely the latter implies, at the very least, a donor, whereas the former enables us to escape the implication of origin through the subtlety of language. When we speak of a "given," the question of the donor slips away into the night. But are givens

[37] Caputo, *PTJD*, 170.

and gifts the same? They are connected, certainly, in etymology, yet they carry different implications. I submit that the only way through this particular difficulty is by way of undecidability. Whatever is "given" may also be "gift," but whether or not it is so is an undecidable question. And if we take the risk of naming it gift, then we can do so only according to this reading of Derrida's criteria: that the donor rests undecidable, the gift undecidable, and the destination undecidable. In that way, the conditions of both possibility *and* impossibility are met. My other question is a related one. Does a reading of the Gift as *différance* preclude any possibility of belief that God is Giver? It seems to me that this need not be so, but it will modify any way of speaking about God's dealings with the world. If there were to be revelation, it would be revelation characterized by *différance,* not because God has become a kind of Cartesian evil genie out to trick us, but because no human experience can remain unaffected by *différance,* and because the relationless relation cannot be understood otherwise.

8
Rethinking the Gift II

We turn now to the second way in which Derrida addresses the gift—as that which is given, rather than the condition for the given, although as it has already been pointed out, such a clear distinction is not always to be found in Derrida's writing. Both readings of gift stem from a "moment's madness," from "an effraction of the circle," or from "the instant all circulation will have been interrupted."[1] Similarly, the conditions of possibility and impossibility for the gift will here remain the same, although they will be applied in their abbreviated form and will take into account an element of futurity. This second way, it will be recalled, can be further subdivided into two types. The first of these subspecies I have entitled "A Moment of Madness" because it is a consideration of the possibility of "any other gift" from the perspective of human giving. The second of the subspecies I have headed "Giving in Secret" because while it too is a consideration of the possibility of any other gift, it is an attempt to deal with gifts whose origin is more truly undecidable: life, death, the world, and the call.[2]

One Impossible Gift: A Moment of Madness

Turning to the first variety—the gift made in madness, or perhaps even the gift of madness—it is useful to bear in mind Caputo's "double risk," that of "illusion and of hypocrisy: on the one end, the risk of entertaining a transcendental illusion; on the other end, the risk of 'entering the destructive circle,' of getting ground up in the wheels of giving-in-order-to-get-back, the hypocrisy of

[1] Derrida, *GT1,* 34ff., 9.
[2] With regard to Derrida on "the secret," see chapter 1 of Derrida, *GD.*

taking under the guise of giving."[3] Derrida himself talks of responding both to the gift and to reason, "both to the injunction or the order of the gift ('give' [*donne*])" *and* to "the injunction or order of meaning (presence, science, knowledge)."[4] In trying to speak of the gift or in trying to give we risk losing it in either of two ways: by holding on to its impossibility and losing its possibility, or by holding on to its possibility and losing its impossibility. Since we can afford to lose neither of these characteristics of the gift, and since they appear to be mutually exclusive, there is every reason to conclude that the gift incites a kind of madness, that the gift only belongs in a kind of madness, that the gift "is" madness.

Yet who would rather stay sane than enter into this madness? For despite the fact that each and every human gift bears the wounds of its loss, undoes itself in one way or another, human beings continue to give, and continue to believe that the impossible gift is possible. For this reason, in this lack of reasoning, it is possible to trace in the madness of the gift the figure of desire, of expectation, of anticipation, of faith. The pure gift (the gift that meets all its conditions of possibility and impossibility) is always the gift that is to come, the gift that is hoped for.[5] The pure gift is of an order that is asymptotic; always *à-venir,* always to come but never coming to closure:

> The possibilization of the impossible possible must remain at one and the same time as undecidable—and therefore as decisive—as the future itself. What would a future be if the decision were able to be programmed, and if the risk [*l'aléa*], the uncertainty, the unstable certainty, the inassurance of the "perhaps" were not suspended on it at the opening of what comes flush with the event, within it and with an open heart?[6]

The deal is never done. The pure gift is of a future that is never here, now. Throwing oneself into the madness of the gift is throwing oneself into the groundlessness of what has not been realized,

[3] Caputo, *PTJD,* 170. "The way to negotiate this double risk is with the delicacy of a double gesture. Everything comes down to seeing that the gift is a *quasi*-transcendental, slightly messianic engagement (*gage*) which both plays the economic game and outplays it."

[4] Derrida, *GT1,* 30.

[5] "Faith is the assurance of things hoped for, the conviction of things not seen." Heb. 11:1.

[6] Derrida, *PF,* 29.

and what cannot be realized. It is a participation in a particular kind of messianism where the messiah is always to be anticipated but never actually arrives.[7]

That being the case, is it feasible to speak at all of this gift that is at the point where illusion and hypocrisy collide, where there can only be desire? Yes and no. Insofar as yes, no. (What we try to save, we invariably lose.) But insofar as no, perhaps yes. (For what we loose, we lose, and in the losing in loosing might be giving.) Such is the movement of desire, which is not in the grasping but in the being grasped. Such is the moment of madness to which I might surrender. And in an attempt to render an account of that for which we cannot take account, I propose to examine some of Derrida's writing thematically. What are the sorts of gifts that "one" might try to give? What are the gifts that might emerge from the collision of illusion and hypocrisy? Can I make a gift of writing? Might it be possible to imagine love as a gift born of madness? What of hospitality and justice, of responsibility and forgiveness?

The Text

One of the questions addressed analytically by Derrida in the latter part of *Given Time,* and performatively in the essay "At This Very Moment in This Work Here I Am," is whether or not a text can be given.[8] In *Given Time,* we note Derrida's observation: "This text—apparently finite, this bit of corpus titled 'Counterfeit Money'—is for us a *given.* It is there before us who read it and who therefore begin by receiving it. If it has the structure of the

[7] A messianism without a messiah, which Derrida himself explores. In relation to the structure of messianism, and its use by Walter Benjamin, see Jacques Derrida, *Spectres of Marx: The State of the Debt, the Work of Mourning, and the New International,* trans. Peggy Kamuf (New York: Routledge, 1994), 55, and the corresponding note at 181. Derrida discusses it further at 167–69. He also speaks of this in *VR,* 20–25, which is taken up at length by Caputo in *DN* at 156–80, and in "Foi et Savoir," *La Religion,* ed. Jacques Derrida and Gianni Vattimo (Paris: Editions du Seuil, 1996), 9–86 [hereafter Derrida, *FS*], in English as "Faith and Knowledge," *Religion,* trans. Samuel Weber (Stanford: Stanford University Press, 1998), 1–78 [hereafter Derrida, *FK*]. See also Levinas in "Jacques Derrida: Wholly Otherwise," in his *PN,* 57: "A project impossible of accomplishment, ever deferred, a *messianic future* as that missing present."

[8] Derrida, *ATVM.*

given, it is not only because we are first of all in a receptive position with regard to it but because it has been given to us."[9] The Baudelaire text is a given: is it therefore a gift? Does it meet the conditions of possibility and impossibility of the gift, that it be known only via a trace: that it can have no decidable origin, cannot exist as such, and can have no decidable destination? This seems impossible, since surely we can identify the author of the text by its signatory, we have the text as an object in our hands, and we can identify the intended recipient by the dedication.

If the author is known, then it would appear that the giver of the given or gift is also known, and this would seemingly interfere with the necessary undecidability of the origin of the gift. Yet is this so? Why has it been insisted so strongly that the origin of the gift is undecidable? Only because undecidability offers some protection against return, and hence against the annihilation of the gift in its certain recognition. In the case of a text, however, Derrida suggests that the author dies once the text is "delivered." Once the text is released, both its content and its destination inevitably become uncertain: it is given in a "dissemination without return." Derrida explains:

> Whatever return it could have made toward Baudelaire or whatever return he might have counted on, the structure of trace and legacy of this text—as of anything that can be in general—surpasses the phantasm of return and marks the death of the signatory or the non-return of the legacy, the non-benefit, therefore a certain condition of the gift—in the writing itself.[10]

The text cannot return to Baudelaire, not only because he is literally dead, but because he will never have been present to the text as it disseminates. Working in all sorts of contexts that were unimaginable to the author, the text does not mediate the presence of the author or of his ideas, but only the play of presence and absence. The text will always exceed what Baudelaire intends. What I might receive from Baudelaire is simply not the same as what he has given, and therefore no exchange has taken place.

Derrida uses this line of argument to suggest additionally that what I might receive in the gift is not the result of any generosity.

[9] Derrida, *GT1,* 91.
[10] Derrida, *GT1,* 100.

"But whereas only a problematic of the trace or dissemination can pose the question of the gift, and forgiveness, this does not imply that writing is *generous* or that the writing subject is a *giving subject*."[11] There "is" gift in the excess that is not intended by the author but which is structurally a part of the text. Similarly, since the destination of the gift cannot be ultimately specified, it cannot be a gift given to someone in particular. The gift will go where it will. There can be no calculated return, hence the identification of the author does not necessarily destroy the gift of the text.[12] Baudelaire cannot even know whether or not he gives. "The problem remains intact, the problem of knowing whether one *gives* tokens and whether one gives when one gives tokens or signs or simulacra."[13]

In considering the question of the author, I have anticipated consideration of the two subsequent questions. The second question, relating to the gift object that is the text I have before me as I write, can be addressed by a thinking of the specific content of the gift. What is the content of the gift? It is the text. But what is the content of the text? Can it be specified? No, because all the contexts of the text could never be specified, and *différance* works in the text in such a way that one could never account for all its meanings. Derrida addresses these issues in *Given Time* by asking about the title of the text. This is a question about the text's borders, or frame. If the text could be held within an area, it would become a specific object with a particular signification. But it quickly becomes apparent that the borders of the text are more

[11] Derrida, *GT1*, 101. On the question of generosity, it is important to observe a further distinction that Derrida draws: "Would a gift that proceeds from a natural power, from an originary aptitude for giving, be a gift? Simultaneously, we come around to dissociating the gift from generosity in a paradox the full rigor of which must be assumed. If it is not to follow a program, even a program inscribed in the *phusis*, a gift must not be generous. Generosity must not be its motive or its essential character. One may give *with* generosity but not *out of* generosity, not so as to obey this originary or natural drive called generosity, the need or desire to give, regardless of the translations or symptoms one may decipher in it." *GT1*, 162.

[12] See Jacques Derrida, "Télépathie," *Psyché: Inventions de l'autre* (Paris: Galilée, 1987), 237–70, 238 [hereafter Derrida, *T*]. See also Jacques Derrida, *The Post-Card: From Socrates to Freud and Beyond*, trans. Alan Bass (Chicago: University of Chicago Press, 1987).

[13] Derrida, *GT1*, 90.

fluid than might be first thought. The title itself cannot establish the parameters of what will take place in the text. "Its place and its structure as a title leave a great indetermination and a great possibility for simulacra that open the field precisely to *counterfeit money*."[14] Derrida goes on to suggest that "the title, 'Counterfeit Money' is already divided, betrayed, displaced," having two referents, one of which is "counterfeit money itself," and the other "the narrative that has counterfeit money as its referent or narrated content." But further, "this first division then engenders many other dehiscences, virtually to infinity."[15] In other words, even in the title of the text, the possibilities for meaning are multiplied beyond measure. With this in mind, what Derrida subsequently says about the borders of the gift, and the collapsing of the borders of the text, makes more sense:

> The gift, if there is any, will always be *without* border. What does "without" mean here? A gift that does not run over its borders, a gift that would let itself be contained in a determination and limited by the indivisibility of an identifiable *trait* would not be a gift. As soon as it delimits itself, a gift is prey to calculation and measure. The gift, if there is any, should overrun the border, to be sure, towards the measureless and excessive; but it should also suspend its relation to the border and even its transgressive relation to the separable line or trait of a border.[16]

[14] Derrida, *GT1,* 85. "If this title is so bifid and abyssal as to say all that (the content of the narrative, the narrative itself as fiction, as counterfeit money, the *I* of the narrator as false signature, and so forth), one must still add a supplement of 'counterfeit money.' And what is that? The title says, in effect: 'since I say so many things at once, since I appear to title this even as I title that at the same time, since I feign reference and since, insofar as it is fictive, my reference is not an authentic, legitimate reference, well then I, as title (but it does not say it . . .) am counterfeit money.' It (I) entitles itself and 'autonames' itself but without saying so, without saying *I* (otherwise it would not do it, it would have to say it). Counterfeit money is the title of the title, the (titleless) title of the title. The title is the title of the text. But does it give its title by saying: *I* am counterfeit money? No, since counterfeit money is only counterfeit on the condition of not giving its title." *GT1,* 86–87.

[15] Derrida, *GT1,* 85.

[16] Derrida, *GT1,* 91. With regard to the "without," and the giving, see *TP,* where Derrida is speaking of the beauty of the cut tulip: "The system is entire and yet is visibly lacking its end [*bout*], a bit [*bout*] which is not a piece like any other, a bit which cannot be totalized along with the others, which does not escape from the system any more than it adds itself on to it, and which alone can in any case, by its mere absence or rather by the trace of its absence (the

The defining moment of a gift is its undoing. Its givenness depends on an incalculable excess: not the excess generously offered by the donor/author, but the excess inscribed in the gift itself, which forbids or defies measure. What cannot be measured has no borders, or rather, it does not "occur" within the space or time (ironically, the dimension) of borders. What cannot be measured cannot become an object like other objects. Hence, and in a very particular way, it does not enter the realm of what is, of presence, of the economy. The text may well be a thing that seems to be present, but it endlessly eludes presence. "But insofar as it tells the story of a gift, this corpus is going to say 'in' itself, 'of' itself the exceeding that frames it and that exceeds its frame."[17]

The last question concerns the recipient of the text, and clearly I, along with many hundreds or thousands or even millions of others, have received it. Derrida does not deny that the text can be received, and received as *given*.[18] Surely the existence of a re-

---

trace—itself outside the thing and absent—of the absence of nothing), give me what one should hesitate to go on calling the *experience* of the beautiful. The mere absence of the goal would not give it to me, nor would its presence. But the trace of its absence (of nothing), inasmuch as it forms its *trait* in the totality in the guise of the *sans*, of the without-end, the trace of the *sans* which does not give itself to any perception and yet whose invisibility marks a full totality to which it does not belong and which has nothing to do with it as totality, the trace of the *sans* is the origin of beauty. It alone can be said to be beautiful on the basis of this trait. From this point of view beauty is never seen, neither in the totality nor outside it: the *sans* is not visible, sensible, perceptible, it does not exist. And yet *there is some of it* and it is beautiful. It *gives* [*ça* donne] the beautiful." *TP*, 90. See also 98ff., where Derrida speaks of framing and also of relationless relation. The latter remarks, in particular, are extremely useful to the unfolding of the current work: "*It has to be* thus interrupted: by having to be, purely, absolutely, removing all adherence to what it cuts itself off from, it liberates beauty (free, wandering, and vague). By having to be interrupted, the *sans*-text and the *sans*-theme relate to the end in the mode of nonrelation. Absolute nonrelation. And by having to be so, this absolute nonrelation must also, if possible, be inscribed in the structure of the artifact. The *sans* of the *sans*-theme and the *sans*-text must be marked, without being either present or absent, in the thing to which it does not belong and which is no longer quite a thing, which one can no longer name, which is not, once charged with the mark, a material support or a form of what is to be found neither here nor there, and which one might indicate, given a certain displacement, by the name of text or trace." *TP*, 98–99.

[17] Derrida, *GT1*, 102.

[18] Refer to the quote from Derrida, *GT1*, 99, which is given above.

cipient annuls the gift! But how can I be sure that the text was a gift to me? If we believe the dedication that prefaces "Counterfeit Money," the intended recipient of the text was one Arsène Houssaye. Baudelaire almost certainly did not conceive that the text would reach such a different destination.[19] Derrida remarks: "By giving it to be remarked, the dedication situates, then, the *dative* or *donor* movement that displaces the text. There is nothing in a text that is not dedicated, nothing that is not destined, and the destination of this dative is not reducible to the explicit dedication."[20] When Baudelaire dedicates or gives his text, he gives it *up,* because he cannot know its destination. So there may be recipients, but they will not receive the gift as a gift from Baudelaire. It may be given, but whether it is received as a gift will be a completely different question, one whose answer will be interminably undecidable.[21] It seems, then, that according to the basic gift criteria (donor without donor; gift without present; recipient without recipient, and all happening in a freedom that is really more freewheeling than the exercise of someone's will), the gift of a text would always be a possibility. But it remains to be seen whether or not this can be deliberately accomplished. For that reason, I will briefly refer to Derrida's essay "At This Very Moment in This Text Here I Am."

This essay originally formed part of a collection entitled *Textes pour Emmanuel Levinas,* which was designed to commemorate Levinas's work. However, the possibility of paying homage to Levinas became complicated by the fact that Levinas's project is characterized by an ethical structure. Giving thanks to Levinas threatened to become a violation of the ethical structure he himself

---

[19] See Derrida, *T.*

[20] Derrida, *GT1,* 87.

[21] "The gift inscribes another signature, one that joyfully gives itself up for lost, that surrenders its 'proper name,' that drops its defenses and its desire for reappropriation. After all, an 'edition' is supposed to be a 'gift,' a giving out, *e-dare, editio,* with a 'dedication,' a textual event of giving away that cannot be contained to some particular friend of the author's. When a text is published and dedicated, from that very moment, it is delivered over to the structure of the trace." Caputo, *DN,* 193. "But a text should be a gift, and a signature should make a gift of itself, give itself to the other without return, sent out without expectation of pay-back, that solicits and invites countless new and unexpected countersignatures." *DN,* 196.

imposed, a violation of the gift.[22] In "At This Very Moment," Derrida is struggling constantly with the difficulty of writing for Levinas without becoming bound in the system of exchange. How can Derrida give to Levinas without giving *back*? Only by giving in such a way that the gift does not return to Levinas but disseminates to the Other can Derrida escape the annulment of the gift:

> The gift *is not.* One cannot ask "what is the gift?"; yet it is only on that *condition* that there will have been, by this name or another, a gift.
>
> Hence, suppose that beyond all restitution, in radical ingratitude (but notice, not just any ingratitude, not in the ingratitude that still belongs to the circle of acknowledgment and reciprocity), I desire (it desires in me, but the it [*le ça*] is not a neutral non-me), I desire to try to give to E.L. This or that? Such and such a thing? A discourse, a thought, a writing? No, that would still give rise to exchange, commerce, economic reappropriation. No, to give him the very giving of giving, a giving which might no longer even be an object or a present said, because every present remains within the economic sphere of the same. . . . That "giving" must be neither a thing nor an act, it must somehow be someone (male or female) not *me:* nor him ("he"). Strange, isn't it, this excess that overflows language at every instant and yet requires it?[23]

Derrida's writing of a gift whose fault will convert its delivery from the Same to the Other is achieved through painstaking, sometimes painful attention to the *différantial* possibilities of the text. Levinas's name, for example, does not appear as such therein. Instead, there are references to *il* (he); to E.L.; to *el* (which in Hebrew refers to God); and to *elle* (she). The uncertainty of the reference not only confuses the identity of the one to whom the text is directed, but allows for a critique of Levinas's work to be made. For the voices of sexual difference are those that are most often silenced in Levinas's writing, despite the fact that his work

---

[22] "The logical and ethical necessity that haunts Derrida's essay is that by writing a text *for* Emmanuel Levinas, by paying homage to his work and recalling how his work works, one would return the work to its author, thereby betraying the ethical structure that Levinas's work tries to set to work." Critchley, *EDDL,* 110–11. This problem is also recognized by Derrida in *VM.*

[23] Derrida, *ATVM,* 15.

is an attempt to value alterity.[24] So the movement from "he," who might be Levinas, to E.L., where he seems to come a little closer, is undone when E.L. becomes *el,* and ultimately *elle.* And the gift to Levinas becomes in part a critique of Levinas. Further, the voice of the author himself becomes confused in the course of the essay. The "I" of the beginning, which we identify with Derrida, suddenly becomes part of a dialogue between "I"s, whose identities are unknown. And at one point, we hear a woman speak. "At This Very Moment" is a text given to Levinas during his lifetime, and we ascribe its authorship to his friend and admirer, Jacques Derrida. But it is a gift that, because of its structural tendency to conversion, does not pass between Derrida and Levinas, and so does not return Levinas's own gift. For in the text itself, both author and addressee become undecidable. And what we might consider a gift (unreserved praise of Levinas) is undone by the questions that are raised about Levinas's work. In these ways, the giving, the gift, and the recipient are unsettled, left open, left hanging. That is how he or she or Derrida gives a gift.

Two elements are striking in this whole process. One is the element of desire.[25] It was earlier noted that the moment of madness is the moment of the mutual exclusion of hypocrisy and illusion, and that because this is an impossible moment, the order of the pure gift is never to be realized, but only ever desired. The pure gift is of an order that is asymptotic, always *à-venir.* Derrida's gift springs from a desire to give to Levinas, but his gift can only be achieved by playing along its fault lines, because it traverses the interface between gift and economy. The other element of great interest is that of conversion. For the gift to be given to Levinas, it must not be given to Levinas, but to the Other. In other words, a gift does not return if the response to it is diverted. This idea holds tremendous theological possibilities, for it gives a space for giving that is really free. What if my response to God's giving (if

[24] See, for example, the critique offered by Luce Irigaray in "The Fecundity of the Caress," *Face to Face with Levinas,* ed. Richard Cohen (New York: SUNY Press, 1986), 231–56.

[25] On the gift as desire, see Jean-Luc Nancy, *The Sense of the World,* trans. Jeffrey S. Librett (Minneapolis: University of Minnesota Press, 1997), 50–53.

that it was God who gave remained undecidable) never returned to God, because it was converted into a gift to the Other?

Love and Hospitality

We turn now to reflect, in a preliminary way, on the possibility of the gift of love, as well as other gifts that fall into a similar category.[26] There is a degree of ambiguity in love mirroring that of the gift. For the model of love that I suspect many people hold to be ideal is one where the attitude of love does not depend on conditions, and hence is given freely. But effectively, such a purity in love is rare. For Derrida, love involves a degree of narcissism, although for him such narcissism is not so much a sign of the inevitable failure of love to meet its ideal, but the condition that makes relationships possible:

> I believe that without a movement of narcissistic reappropriation, the relation to the other would be absolutely destroyed, it would be destroyed in advance. The relation to the other—even if it remains asymmetrical, open, without possible reappropriation—must trace a movement of reappropriation in the image of oneself for love to be possible, for example. Love is narcissistic.[27]

Why would the relationship be destroyed in advance without "a movement of narcissistic reappropriation"? It seems that the I must come back to itself in recollection (it must be able to say "I") if it is to be in relationship at all. That is part of the deal when dealing with an economy.

At the same time, Derrida also observes the quality of separation that characterizes relationships. The beloved always remains transcendent, but Derrida sees in this "not an obstacle but the condition of love."[28] So with love there is an economic aspect that is necessary because it makes me I, and so enables me to enter into relationship with what is not-I. But there is also an aneco-

[26] There are, of course, the different varieties of love that could be considered. For the sake of space I will not attempt such an analysis. Derrida makes some interesting observations on the gift of friendship in *GT1,* 139, and *PF.*

[27] Derrida, *Po,* 199. In other words, it is narcissistic not essentially, but insofar as relationships between people require some assurance of identity on the part of each person.

[28] Derrida, *VR,* 14.

nomic aspect, because the Other is never reducible to the I. Love is therefore a fine example of the gift that emerges in the moment of madness occurring in the collision of illusion and hypocrisy. Perhaps love does involve degrees of narcissism. But there may be moments when one seeks to love with less narcissism, when one desires to love without return; and even if pure love, like a pure gift, is only ever to come, the aporetic moment might or might not be the beginning of the gift.[29] We will never know for sure.

How does love relate to the gift criteria? How can we speak of a giving without a donor when it comes to love, where it seems that the lover can be identified? We could say that the occasion when love is a gift is always to come, and is something for which we must always hope, although it is also something that we have to practice *as if* it were possible. In so loving, we will never know if we truly give. We will never be able to account for the moment's madness. Or we could say that, on a particular reading of immemoriality, two people can never be present to one another. The Other is simply not accessible to me because the Other remains transcendent and has always and already eluded me.[30] How then can we speak of love as a gift that is not a present? The answer has already been suggested, that pure love is a gift that is always to come. And how can we speak of the recipient of the gift of love, when it seems that the receiving of any gift must remain undecidable? In this case, the identity of the donor will not be protected by undecidability. However, the donor's giving will be so protected. For I will never know whether they have loved to the extent that they have given themselves up to love entirely. Even if

[29] "All this is a way of saying that, as there is no clean distinction between the gift and economy, that there is also no clean distinction between narcissism and non-narcissism, but only certain degrees, gradations, or economies of narcissism, more or less open and widened narcissisms, that self-love is capable of different forms, some of which are not so selfish. We are all more or less narcissistic, for that is what the agent/subject *is*. . . . If the agent stopped loving its own good, it would stop loving the good of the other, since the good of the other is the good for which the agent acts and by seeking the good of the other the agent is doing what it loves to do. Jesus said to love your neighbour *as* you love yourself, because if you stopped loving yourself you would stop loving God, your neighbour, and mammon too; you would stop loving, period." Caputo, *DN*, 148.

[30] Levinas suggests a variation of this position when he says that the Other always inhabits a future I cannot reach. See Levinas, *TA*, 68–69.

the other were to die in love for me, the loving in dying could only be read as a trace of love, and I would need to accept the gift purely out of faith.

The theme of the possibility and impossibility of hospitality was introduced in chapter 1. It will be recalled that hospitality is aporetic in two ways: because it involves an obligation yet is a gift, and because it involves the limits and exclusions implied in ownership and yet implies a generosity that has no bounds. Thus hospitality, very much like love, finds itself at the impossible intersection of the aneconomic and the economic, at the point where illusion and hypocrisy collide. And again, like love, hospitality will only begin where we practice it *as if* it were possible.[31] Hospitality is in fact the impossible performance of love.[32] In the experience of the aporia, there is no way of *knowing* whether or not there is gift: the decision to love and to welcome is the only way "through" the impasse.

Justice and the Law; Responsibility and Ethics

In the discussion of love and hospitality, it will have become apparent that there is a pattern with regard to the type of giving with which Derrida concerns himself. The gift is aporetic in structure, but additionally, particular gifts lead to their own aporias. This is no less true when we consider the gift of justice, which cannot be reduced to the application of the law, or the gift of responsibility, which cannot be reduced to the application of principles of ethics. In an effort to avoid further duplication, I will restrict my discussion here to a brief consideration of responsibility and secrecy, as it is observed by Derrida in *The Gift of Death.*

---

[31] See Caputo, *DN,* 111: "Like everything else in deconstruction, the possibility of hospitality is sustained by its impossibility; hospitality really starts to get under way only when we 'experience' (which means to travel or go through) this paralysis (the inability to move). Hospitality *is* impossible, what Derrida calls *the* impossible (the im-possibility of hostil-pitality), which is not the same as a simple logical contradiction. Hospitality really starts to happen when I push against this limit, this threshold and limit, its own self-limitation, to become a gift *beyond hospitality.* That requires that the host must, in a moment of madness, tear up the understanding between him and the guest, act with 'excess,' make an absolute gift of his property, which is of course impossible. But it is the only way a guest can go away feeling as if he was really made at home." On Derrida and the *comme si* (as if), see Dufourmantelle and Derrida, *DL'H,* 111.

[32] See Derrida's comments on Levinas in *Ad,* at 78–79.

According to Derrida's usual way of working, *The Gift of Death* is an engagement with other writings, and in chapter 3, "Whom to Give To," he is reading Kierkegaard's *Fear and Trembling*. Kierkegaard (or Johannes *de silentio*) is here considering the story of Abraham's sacrifice of Isaac. At God's command, Abraham undertakes to sacrifice his only son, the son granted to him in his old age, the one whom he loves dearly. Abraham enters into a secret given by the one who passes in secret, the *mysterium tremendum,* who cannot be seen or known in the present. Abraham can only make his sacrifice by keeping it secret, by not speaking, or by speaking so as not to speak, by assuming his responsibility alone. Derrida observes that responsibility is here tied to singularity.[33] This is contrary to our normal expectation that being responsible involves, as Derrida suggests, "acting and signing *in one's name,*" or "the necessity of accounting for one's words and actions in front of others, of justifying and owning up to them."[34] Being responsible usually means standing behind a decision and making what surrounds that decision fully transparent. Being responsible usually takes place in a community and according to the standards of a community. Language is one of the most obvious ways in which human beings are social, and the means by which we account for ourselves. It is the place where reason comes to the fore, where we explain, justify, argue, prove, condemn, liberate, or conquer. By entering into discourse, we enter into the realm of generality. But Abraham does not enter into discourse, and so he remains singular. Abraham bears a secret that cannot undo itself in the public domain, or at least one that would find itself undone in being made public. Abraham cannot account for what he is going to do.

This brings us to what I consider the one of the most interesting ideas to emerge from Kierkegaard's text: the sacrifice of ethics to responsibility. Derrida describes this paradox as follows:

> According to Kierkegaard, *ethical* exigency is regulated by generality; and it therefore defines a responsibility that consists of *speaking,* that is, of involving oneself sufficiently in the generality to justify

[33] As is the secret. See Jacques Derrida, "Remarks on Deconstruction and Pragmatism," Mouffe, *DP,* 77–88, 80.
[34] Derrida, *GD,* 58; 60.

> oneself, to give an account of one's decision and to answer for one's actions. On the other hand, what does Abraham teach us, in his approach to sacrifice? That far from ensuring responsibility, the generality of ethics incites to irresponsibility. It impels me to speak, to reply, to account for something, and thus to dissolve my singularity in the medium of the concept.[35]

In trying to behave ethically, we have to take into account the needs of the group. An ethical decision is one that promotes the good of all. There is no such thing as an individualized ethics, since that would result in mere relativism. Behaving ethically means entering into discourse and generality, or as Derrida suggests, "the medium of the concept." By the standards of ethics, Abraham would be considered a murderer, or could at least be charged with intention to cause grievous bodily harm.[36] Under any reasonable test, Abraham should not be permitted to proceed with the killing of his son. And given that he belongs to and would have been shaped by the community that would so judge, Abraham undoubtedly sympathizes with this view. Yet Abraham has a responsibility to God in faith, such that obeying the ethical exigency would force him to behave irresponsibly. Responsibility is thus aporetic. It appears that we have to seem to be irresponsible to be responsible, to be unethical in order to accord absolute value to one relationship and one demand or duty. There is, Derrida tells us, "an insoluble and paradoxical contradiction between responsibility *in general* and *absolute* responsibility."[37]

So we are brought again to a moment of madness. Derrida insists that "the paradox cannot be grasped in time and through mediation, that is to say in language and through reason."[38] When he speaks, then, of an "atemporal temporality," he is referring to an instant that is utterly removed from the present. When we act out of responsibility, it is impossible for us to comprehend or to grasp what happens in that moment. For Abraham, this instant of madness is at the point of absolute contradiction. "Abraham must assume absolute responsibility for sacrificing his son by sacrificing ethics, but in order for there to be a sacrifice, the ethi-

[35] Derrida, *GD*, 60–61.
[36] Derrida, *GD*, 65.
[37] Derrida, *GD*, 61.
[38] Derrida, *GD*, 65.

cal must retain all its value; the love for his son must remain intact, and the order of human duty must continue to insist on its rights."[39] Abraham's gift to God, his responsibility, his *response* to God, comes at the price of an ethics that remains valid. Yet the story of Abraham places us in an interesting situation with regard to the gift criteria. For in the story, surely we have observed the gift in action: "But the angel of the LORD called to him from heaven, and said, 'Abraham, Abraham!' And he said, 'Here I am.' He said, 'Do not lay a hand on the boy or do anything to him; for *now I know that you fear God, since you have not withheld your son, your only son, from me*' " (Gen. 22:11–12).[40] It would seem that the gift has been delivered, and yet, what was the gift? Who gave, and to whom did that one give?[41]

Forgiveness

What of the gift of forgiveness? Derrida often links giving with forgiving: "Whence comes the law that obligates one to give even as one renders an account of the gift? In other words to *answer* still for a gift that calls one beyond all responsibility? And that forbids one to forgive whoever *does not know how to give?*"; "only a problem of the trace or dissemination can pose the question of the gift, and forgiveness"; "the gift, forgiveness—if there is any"; "there is here a scene of gift and forgiveness, of a gift that seems to give nothing and of a forgiveness that is finally withheld"; "he will not be forgiven because he has not given what was expected of him."[42] The link between giving and forgiving is borne out elsewhere. The Latin verb *dono,* for example, means both "to give as a present" and "to pardon, forgive, remit."

In *Given Time,* Derrida has occasion to reflect on forgiveness where Baudelaire's narrator tries to evaluate the situation in which he has found himself. The narrator's friend, it will be re-

[39] Derrida, *GD,* 66.

[40] Emphasis added.

[41] In the same way that Jacob knows not whether he wrestles with a man or with God in Genesis 32:24ff. ("Me? or me that fought him? O which one? is it each one? That night, that year / Of now done darkness I wretch lay wrestling with [my God!] my God." Gerard Manley Hopkins, "Carrion Comfort," *Poems and Prose* [Harmondsworth, Middlesex: Penguin, 1953], 60–61, 61.)

[42] Derrida, *GT1,* 31, 101, 101, 115, 163.

called, has passed what he claims is a counterfeit coin to a beggar on the street. The narrator tries to make sense of this action, and he comes to the conclusion that his friend has tried to "win paradise economically." That being his judgment, he refuses to forgive his friend the fraud.[43] Derrida's reading of the refusal of forgiveness focuses not on the intention of the friend, but on the moment of the narrator's judgment. "It is at the moment he looks his friend in the eyes, in the white of the eyes, that the narrator sees, *believes* he sees the truth of what the other had wanted to do, his 'aim.' But perhaps this moment marks the very blindness out of which arises the speculative discourse of the narrator."[44] The lack of forgiveness arises from a judgment that is not, that *cannot be,* complete. For the Other cannot be reduced to the Same: the motives of the Other may never be clear to me. And I do not have the right to pass judgment. That being the case, I can do none other than forgive.[45] In this sense, giving means letting go. It is not just "letting be" (*Gelassenheit*), but letting go of all demand for the rendering of accounts. Giving forgiveness is the maddest moment of all. It is the giving up of the right to pursue, the right to condemn, and even the right to remember. Forgiving really must be forgetting: forgiving is the forgetting where there is no longer anything forgotten.[46] In the case of forgiveness, the asymp-

---

[43] Derrida, *GT1,* 31–33.

[44] Derrida, *GT1,* 163.

[45] Caputo observes: "Not only must we not be on the take when we give, we must also give away whatever we take, whatever we have on the other. We must give away what we think the other owes us, even if we get something on the other seven times a day, or seven times seven. We must; it's a responsibility, a responsibility without duty, a duty without debt, a debt that does not cut off possibilities. If we would give ourselves to the gift, we would also give ourselves to forgiving." *PTJD,* 181.

[46] "We know that absolution must come from an Other or the Other, and we know too that it erases a content, a list of omissions and/or commissions. A true absolution, however, also removes the obligation to make a return for what has been freely given: forgiveness, grace. Absolution requires us to think a gift outside or beyond the circuit of exchange, a scandalous thought because it is, at heart, a thought of faith, maybe *the* thought of faith, the thought that only faith can give. At any rate, an absolved language would be one that accepts what is offered to it and understands this strictly as a gift, with no return involved. Yet for this to happen the gift must somehow remove itself in advance from the circuit of exchange, for how could one who receives a gift absolve himself or herself from such a responsibility? To have a sense of absolved language is to have a thought of God, even if 'God' here does not refer to a supreme being or

totic quality of the gift protects it from being seized in certitude by either donor or recipient. The pattern is confirmed that where no gift *appears as such,* each of the other elements of the gift withdraws in undecidability.

While there are other places that we could glimpse gifts of madness (e.g., in Levinas's reflections on work, or in Caputo's commentary on Derrida that includes a reflection on giving "more" and "giving what I do not have"), the examples mentioned above should indicate sufficiently how Derrida treats the gift.[47] The gift is, always, an experience of the aporia, unable to be resolved satisfactorily but opening onto a break in the horizon. In aporetic experience the horizon cannot but be suspended: the gift is in this way a rupture of the economy that nevertheless relates (without relation) to economy.

Another Impossible Gift: Giving in Secret

It has been observed that giving can only be attempted in a moment's madness, and that in giving the gift seems to retreat into the future. Is the same true of other givens that we might be tempted to describe as gifts, whose origin remains completely hidden? It is common to speak of "the gift of life," and to speak of the world, which in actual fact "is" not any "thing," as a gift. We are referred by Derrida to that which we may not previously have thought to be a gift: death. Further, might it be possible to read in Derrida's works that the very sense of being called is a gift, a secret gift? And if it is possible to think the call and the secret, might it be possible to think, from such a position, God as gift? In what follows, I will attempt to address these questions in an introductory manner.

---

to being itself. Even so, as I have suggested, what Derrida calls 'God' cannot be a wholly private affair, while at the same time there can be no guarantee that anyone else will fully grasp how 'God' functions for him in his idiom." Kevin Hart, "Jacques Derrida: The God Effect," in Blond, *PSP,* 259–80, 261 [hereafter Hart, *JDGE*].

[47] See Caputo, *PTJD.* See also Levinas, *TI,* 168–74, and Robert Bernasconi's excellent article, "What Goes Around Comes Around: Derrida and Levinas on the Economy of the Gift and the Gift of Genealogy," in Schrift, *LG,* 256–73. Bernasconi argues that Derrida's understanding of the gift is highly influenced by Levinas.

Life and the World

While, to my knowledge, Derrida does not advert to the question of life or the world directly in his writing on the gift, the possibility of reading life and the world as gifts is raised by Marion.[48] Would this make sense in a Derridean "framework"? One of the contexts in which life is referred to as a gift is where the actions or sacrifice of one person for another promotes the life of the latter. For example, in the case of organ donation, the recipient of the new organ has been given a second chance at life, usually at the expense of the death of the donor. Another example where life is referred to as a gift is in the case where some type of applied medical technology allows either for the conception of a child or for the prolongation of a life. In a different sense, it is of course also possible to speak of one's parents as those who "gave me life." And in a religious context, it is equally common to hold the origins of life as sacred: life is a gift from the Creator. The belief that life is a gift (from God; of a benevolent force; or even of nature or the universe) underlies the controversy surrounding public debate on issues such as abortion or euthanasia.

According to Derrida's conditions, is it feasible to say that life is a gift? In the case of organ donation, at least where the donor remains alive, Derrida observes that the unconditionality of the gift of an organ "is not what it is or claims to be: unconditional," although he does not explore organ donation any further.[49] It would seem, however, that the *life* itself that is promoted by organ donation, or advanced medical technology, might fulfil the criteria. The recipient of the organ would find life *given,* but it would not be the donor's life that was in any sense "passed on." The donor has given the possibility for or conditions of life, but not life itself. Expressed in another way, the donor has "given life" without there being anything at all that was given. This might be one of the ways in which we could say that parents give life to their children. For the parents (or even the IVF team) create the conditions under which life could begin, but the life that they thus give is no "thing" that they can pass on. In spite of the ad-

[48] Marion raises these questions in *ED.* Derrida does, nevertheless, speak of the gift of nature. See Derrida, *GT1,* 126ff.

[49] Derrida, *GT1,* 17–18 n.

vances in scientific research, the possibilities of gene manipulation, cloning, fertility enhancement, conception outside the uterus, or the regeneration of prehistoric bacteria, life *as such* can be promoted but never really created *ex nihilo*. It may be that the parents or the scientists make life possible, but it is not as clear that they thus make life. The origins of life remain undecidable. Life is observable by its effects, whether they be the multiplication of cells or the maintenance of a heartbeat, but life itself is nothing that can be objectified. When someone dies, life is gone, but whether or not the loss of that life is reducible to the sum total of physical deficiencies is still in question.

The giving of life to me is always immemorial: there is no possibility that I can have witnessed its origin, and it has already been given when I can advert to it. And if my life is a gift, then I cannot know with any certainty who has given it. It seems that at the very least, life is a "given." But whether or not it is a gift will always involve some kind of faith. That is not necessarily religious faith, but a faith in the gift. In a similar way, the world is always a given, but whether or not it is a gift remains questionable. In contrast with the earth, the world is not anything as such. Heidegger's powerful analysis of "being-in-the-world" illustrates this point. A human being is always and already "enworlded," but to be enworlded does not mean to be on a planet or surrounded by things so much as enmeshed in a network of relations.[50] It is simply not possible to imagine *not* being enworlded, or to find a standpoint from which it would be achievable to observe "the world." We are deprived of its origins; we are deprived of its existence (since it is not anything as such, but a type of context); and we are deprived of certain knowledge of what it means for us.

Death and Sacrifice

It seems strange to think of death as a gift, for death in Western culture has mainly negative connotations, and despite the ambivalence within the word "gift" that was earlier pointed out, it is difficult to use this word to describe something that is usually

[50] Heidegger, *BT*, at 138, for example.

considered a loss rather than a gain. However, the many discussions on death that precede Derrida's reflections lead us to a perspective on death as what cannot be experienced, since it is never present.[51] Derrida speaks of "the gift of death" in a number of senses.

In *The Gift of Death,* Derrida reflects on Abraham's sacrifice of Isaac as a gift of death. "This is the moment when Abraham gives the sign of absolute sacrifice, namely, by putting to death or giving death to his own, putting to death his absolute love for what is dearest, his only son."[52] Whether or not sacrifice can be such a gift is a great question. Sacrifice attracts the same economic criticism that plagues the gift: if I make a sacrifice it might be in order to avoid some punishment or to gain some reward. Derrida refers to this "economy of sacrifice," but he also speaks of Abraham's sacrifice of economy. "Abraham has consented to suffer death or worse, and that without calculating, without investing, beyond any perspective of recouping the loss; hence, it seems, beyond recompense or retribution, beyond economy, without any hope of remuneration [*salaire*]."[53] In the moment when Abraham is utterly prepared to make the sacrifice, he has already made the sacrifice, apparently without the hope that God will intervene to ameliorate the situation. At the same time, however, God *does* intervene, and this intervention, according to Derrida, reinscribes "sacrifice within an economy by means of what thenceforth comes to resemble a reward."[54] Does God's action annul the sacrifice as sacrifice, or as absolute gift? It seems to me that this is another of Derrida's moments of madness. We will never know whether or not Abraham was secretly hoping that God would not allow him to go through with the murder. All we are given in the story is the assurance that Abraham is prepared to do it, and this preparedness is vouched for by the words of the angel of the Lord. So we may assume that Abraham's sacrifice is in one sense complete. That he is then rewarded does not thereby take away from the gift that is made in absolute self-expenditure, but it brings it back into the

---

[51] See, for example, Heidegger, *BT,* 279ff., and Levinas's response in *TI,* 233–36.

[52] Derrida, *GD,* 95.

[53] Derrida, *GD,* 95.

[54] Derrida, *GD,* 96.

circle of reckoning, from which Abraham could only momentarily escape. If there is gift, then it is only in the moment of madness, and never in the circle as such.

Another way of reading this sacrifice would be in the light of Jesus' teaching, and Derrida offers us scope for such a reading in the following chapter. He refers to the saying that when giving alms, the right hand should not know what the left hand is doing.[55] According to Derrida, the economics inscribed in the Gospels "integrates absolute loss." The vengeance that is rightfully exacted under Mosaic law (an eye for an eye) is suspended with the commandment to turn the other cheek. "Does this commandment reconstitute the parity of the pair rather than breaking it up, as we just suggested? No, it doesn't, it interrupts the parity and symmetry, for instead of *paying back* the slap on the cheek . . . one is to *offer* the other cheek."[56]

Once again, in Abraham's sacrifice we are referred to love. Derrida defines sacrifice as "the putting to death of the unique, irreplaceable, and most precious." It refers, he says, to "the impossibility of substitution."[57] This theme is developed in the discussion of love and hate. Apparent opposites are destabilized. Sacrifice is not the hate of enemies, but the hate of loved ones. Love must become hate to be love. "Hate cannot be hate, it can only be the sacrifice of love to love."[58] Derrida (and Kierkegaard) cite Luke 14:26 in support of this reading. We cannot be disciples of Jesus without hating what is closest to us. Perhaps we could also refer to the other inversion that characterizes Jesus' ministry, which is the command to love our enemies (Matt. 5:43–48). We must love what we hate and hate what we love. Yet it may be more appropriate to speak in both cases of a subversion rather than an inversion. Jesus does not simply invert values or beliefs, but actu-

[55] "If this spiritualization of the 'interior' light institutes a new economy (an economy of sacrifice: you will receive good wages if you rise above earthly gain, you will get a better salary if you give up your earthly salary, one salary is waged against another), then it is by breaking with, dissociating from, or rendering dissymmetrical whatever is paired with the sensible body, in the same way that it means breaking with exchange as a simple form of reciprocity." Derrida, *GD,* 101.

[56] Derrida, *GD,* 102.

[57] Derrida, *GD,* 58.

[58] Derrida, *GD,* 64.

ally reorients both them and their opposites. For example, when Jesus washes the feet of the disciples he does not simply substitute the role of master for the role of servant, but redefines leadership in terms of an outpouring of love.

So the first way in which Derrida uses "the gift of death" is in the sense of sacrifice, a sacrifice of what is most important, and even a sacrifice of oppositions. The second way also involves a type of sacrifice, but it is a sacrifice not of love but of knowledge. Death is something that cannot be experienced, at least in the terms that make it viable to speak of experience at all. Death arrives, but not in the sense that it "happens" to me.[59] For this reason, death remains always in the future, and it is a useful tool for Derrida to use when he tries to speak about that which cannot be present.

Reading Kierkegaard (and so not necessarily making a statement of personal faith), Derrida dwells for some time on the "experience" of God as one of fear and trembling. It is the "experience" of the *mysterium tremendum,* known only in the trembling that is the trace of its passing. Trembling is a response to a shock, the origin of which we cannot see. But trembling is also the anticipation of the unpredictable repetition of that shock. As Derrida suggests, "We tremble in that strange repetition that ties an irrefutable past (a shock has been felt, a traumatism has already affected us) to a future that cannot be anticipated."[60] Trembling forms the trace of a double secret, a secret that is kept intact via the two dimensions that deprive us of experience. The past dimension is immemorial—that is, the secret has always already passed by the time we respond to it in trembling. The future dimension remains always just beyond the horizon—that is, the secret can only be anticipated to the extent that it remains utterly unforeseeable. Nevertheless, we are told that the secret is the *mysterium tremendum.* That which makes us tremble is "the gift of infinite love, the dissymmetry that exists between the divine regard that sees me, and myself, who doesn't see what is looking at me; it is the gift and endurance of death

[59] In French the word *arriver* can be used to mean both "to arrive" and "to happen."
[60] Derrida, *GD,* 54.

that exists in the irreplaceable, the disproportion between the infinite gift and my finitude, responsibility as culpability, sin, salvation, repentance, and sacrifice."[61] This material evidently opens onto the questions of the secret, of the call, and of God, but a discussion of these questions will be momentarily deferred. What does Derrida mean by a "gift and endurance of death"? Perhaps it is that if there were to be an "experience" of God, it could only be an experience that defied knowledge, a gift or endurance of a death. In the same way that death excludes our consciousness of it, God's passing would be so foreign as to be irreducible.

Another, related way in which we might understand "the gift of death" is as the putting of oneself to death. This can be thought of as a movement of faith. Elsewhere, Derrida describes faith as a surrendering to the witness of the wholly other.[62] Faith is a surrender to witness rather than to knowledge as such. Further, we can consider the gift of death from the point of view of responsibility. It was mentioned earlier that Abraham's response and responsibility to God comes at the price of an ethics that nevertheless remains intact. Abraham demonstrates his complete obedience to God; he responds in responsibility to the Absolute Other. But in responding to the Absolute Other, he has necessarily suspended his duty to all the other others. He has suspended his duty of protection toward his son, he has suspended his duty of trust toward his wife, and he has suspended his duty to behave ethically in society. Entering into relationship with and fulfilling my duties with regard to one other, or in this case the Absolute Other, means that my duties to every other other are somehow compromised. The one starving person whom I am able to feed stands beside all those others whom I am not able to feed. And in a certain sense, because I have chosen to feed this one, I have chosen not to feed the others. I have given them death. "As soon as I enter into relationship with the other, I know that I can respond only by sacrificing ethics, that is, by sacrificing whatever obliges me to also respond, in the same way, in the same instant, to all the others. I offer a gift of death, I betray, I don't need to raise my knife over my son on Mount Moriah for that."[63] Death

[61] Derrida, *GD,* 55–56.
[62] Derrida, *FS,* 46; *FK,* 33.
[63] Derrida, *GD,* 68.

can be thought of as that which is dealt to us (perhaps causally, but without origin) or as something (no-thing) I deal to others. In either case, since death is another variant of the moment of madness, it meets the criteria of the gift.

The Call, the Secret, and Perhaps God

It will be remembered that "the call" is an insistent theme in the writing of Heidegger (the call of Being), Levinas (the call of the Other), and Marion (the call beyond Being). But how does Derrida think the call? Is the call a call that is made in secret? And is it possible, with certain provisos in place, to think nevertheless a secret call of God, or to think God as a secret, a gift in secret? I must immediately make the observation, however, that Derrida only infrequently makes of the call a theme to be explored *as such.* In fact, there is in Derrida, as in Levinas, far more attention devoted to response rather than call. But there are a number of places where it will at least be evident that the question of call, especially insofar as it demands a response, is one of Derrida's preoccupations.

"Whence comes the law that obligates one to give even as one renders an account of the gift? In other words, to *answer* [*répondre*] still for a gift that calls one beyond all responsibility?"[64] This short passage from *Given Time* registers in several keys at once. It refers us to Kant, to the categorical imperative that orders us to our one duty, and which elsewhere Derrida will expose in its impossibility.[65] It then refers us to the call as a call to an impossible responsibility (the responsibility "beyond all responsibility"). And it refers us to the call of the gift, to the gift as call, without specifying the gift any further, and with such an association reinforcing the idea that what is demanded in the call is impossible.

If we turn to "Passions," we find that the call is related to the invitation, and both call and invitation are related to the response. "What we are glimpsing of the invitation (but of the call in general, as well) governs by the same 'token' the logic of the

[64] Derrida, *GT1,* 31.

[65] See Jacques Derrida, "Passions," trans. David Wood, in *On the Name,* ed. Thomas Dutoit (Stanford: Stanford University Press, 1995), 3–31, at 7–8 [hereafter Derrida, *Pass*]; and Derrida, *GD,* 77.

response, both of the response to the invitation and the response by itself."[66] Yet responsibility and invitation are aporetic in structure, provoking an interruption to any logic. And in that aporia, where it is impossible to move, "it is not only religious sociality whose identity is thus menaced, it is philosophical sociality, insofar as it presupposes the order (preferably circular) of the appeal [or the call: *appel*—Tr.], of the question and the response."[67] What does Derrida mean by the presupposition of a "preferably circular" order? It seems to me that those discourses which are governed by the form of question and response, of knowledge (a circular order, an economy), are interrupted insofar as question and response will always lead to the aporia. The presupposition of the order of the appeal is overrun by the appeal.

Further on in the same essay, we learn that there is a call associated with the secret: "When it is the call [*appel*] of this secret, however, which points back to the other or to something else, when it is this itself which keeps our passion aroused, and holds us to the other, then the secret impassions us."[68] Yet the secret calls without speaking. "And the secret will remain secret, mute, impassive as the *khôra*. . . . It remains silent, not to keep a word in reserve or withdrawn, but because it remains foreign to speech." At the same time, "no discussion would either begin or continue without it.[69] The secret, that there "is" no secret (the secret "being" that we cannot ever *know* for sure), is what drives us, what drives literature, what drives thought, what impassions us and calls us forward.[70] Recalling from *Given Time* that the gift "must *keep* a relation of foreignness to the circle," and that it is also "the first mover of the circle," it seems that gift, secret, and call bear in common this quality of impassioning, of energizing, of enabling.[71] Each is immemorial and quasi-transcendental. Equally, gift, secret, and call thus also disable any possibility of an adequate response. Responding *as such* is impossible, for to respond to (by identifying) gift, secret, or call is to annul any one of them.

---

[66] Derrida, *Pass,* 15.
[67] Derrida, *Pass,* 23.
[68] Derrida, *Pass,* 29.
[69] Derrida, *Pass,* 27.
[70] Derrida, *Pass,* 29–30. See also Caputo's discussion in *PTJD,* 101–12.
[71] Derrida, *GT1,* 7, 30.

Derrida needs no caller, since the call of which he speaks needs no embodiment. And yet there is another turn within his work that unsettles this conclusion and opens ever so quietly onto a theological possibility.

In *Politics of Friendship,* Derrida explores the call of and to friendship, which once again is linked with impossible responsibility.[72] But here we are dealing with a slightly different question. For friendship implies a mutuality, a shared space. Under the guise of the call we have returned to the issue that plagues the relationship between Levinas and Derrida, which is the question of otherness, of the otherness of the Other and of the encounter with the Other.[73] Derrida asks: "How are we to distinguish between ourselves, between each of us who compose[s] this as yet so undetermined 'we'?" In other words, he is asking about the proximity (using Levinas's terms) of relationship prior to its articulation in knowledge, prior to its political manifestation. "Even before the question of responsibility was posed, the question of 'speaking in one's own name,' . . . we are caught up, one and another, in a sort of heteronomic and dissymmetrical curving of social space—more precisely, a curving of the relation to the other: prior to all organized *socius.*"[74] It is possible to observe in this idea a link with Maurice Blanchot's "double dissymmetry" of the relation to the Other.[75] Unlike in Levinas (and Marion), where the absolute asymmetry that orders the relationless relation is problematic, here we have a proximity that can sustain an immemorial call to responsibility.

Within the curved space of the relation to the Other, there is already responsibility.[76] That is why the call to friendship, which

[72] Derrida, *PF,* especially in the essay "In Human Language, Fraternity."

[73] I will continue to use "Other," rather than the "other" of the translations of both Derrida and Blanchot, in order to keep the clarity of the Levinasian distinction.

[74] Derrida, *PF,* 231.

[75] Blanchot, *IC,* 73.

[76] "What is unfolding itself at this instant—and we are finding it a somewhat disturbing experience—is perhaps only the silent deployment of that strange violence that has always insinuated itself into the origin of the most innocent experiences of friendship and justice. We have begun to respond. We are already caught up, we are caught out, in a certain responsibility, and the most ineluctable responsibility—as if it were possible to think a responsibility without freedom." Derrida, *PF,* 231.

is always futural rather than present, is nevertheless a call that can only be made on the basis of a past.[77] Speaking of the call in Heidegger, Derrida observes the strange "voice of the friend."[78] The call of the friend is prior to friendship, marking the very possibility (and impossibility) of friendship:

> It is perhaps in a region thus withdrawn from metaphysical subjectivity that for Heidegger "the voice of the friend" rings out. The issue is perhaps what we were calling above a minimal "community"—but also incommensurable to all others, speaking the same language or praying, or weeping, for translation against the horizon of a sole language, if only to manifest a disagreement: friendship prior to friendships. One would have to add: "prior to" enmity.
>
> This promise before friendships would be linked to the "yes, yes," this promise of memory that we have attempted to analyze elsewhere. The double affirmation must remain essentially risky, threatened, open. Above all, it cannot allow itself to be defined or posited, it cannot be reduced to a determined position.[79]

The call of friendship is a call to responsibility, but a responsibility that cannot be specified in advance.[80] It is a call to responsibility that comes from the Other.[81] Moreover, this call is irreducible to knowledge, even and perhaps especially to the knowledge that is made present in phenomenology. In what is a very important passage with regard to Derrida and phenomenology, he remarks:

> In the course of this experience, the other appears *as such*—that is to say, the other appears as a being whose appearance appears with-

[77] "(Let us note in passing that the logic of this call—'You-my-friends-be-my-friends-and-although-you-are-not-yet-my-friends-you-are-already,-since-that-is-what-I-am-calling-you')." Derrida, *PF,* 235.

[78] Derrida, *PF,* 241.

[79] Derrida, *PF,* 244.

[80] "But if *presently* there is no friend, let us act so that henceforth there will be friends of this 'sovereign master friendship.' This is what I call you to; answer my call, this is our responsibility. Friendship is never a present given, it belongs to the experience of expectation, promise, or engagement. Its discourse is that of prayer, it inaugurates, but reports nothing, it is not satisfied with what is, it moves out to this place where a responsibility opens up a future." Derrida, *PF,* 236.

[81] "It is assigned to us by the other, from the place of the other, well before any hope of reappropriation allows us the assumption of this responsibility." Derrida, *PF,* 232.

> out appearing, without being submitted to the phenomenological law of the originary and intuitive given that governs all other appearances, all other phenomenality *as such*. The altogether other, and *every other (one) is every (bit) other*, comes here to upset the order of phenomenology. And good *sense*. That which comes before autonomy must also *exceed* it—that is, succeed it, survive and indefinitely overwhelm it.[82]

This sequence is rich with possibilities, not least because, as an *experience* of relationless relation, it offers another opening on the question of God. That is not to say that the relation with the human other (where "the other appears as a being whose appearance appears without appearing") is the same as the relation with God, but it might be suggested that it points in the direction of the relation with God, who, certainly, also exceeds the capacity of phenomenology. The passage bears a family resemblance to certain passages in *The Gift of Death*, and surely that is not in the least coincidental.

Two types of secrecy are pursued in *The Gift of Death*. There is the secret that Abraham bears, that is, the secret that he knows and cannot divulge if he is to be responsible. And then there is the secret that is his very "experience" of God. Derrida speaks of the experience of God as the experience of *mysterium tremendum*, the secret known only in the trembling that is the trace of its passing. This is the secret that can never be known, that "is" not anything. And not "being" anything, it bears a relationship to that secret that I have already canvassed as that which drives all passion and all thought. The two secrets of non-knowledge can of course be distinguished by the fact that the one is a quasi-transcendental, while the other is not only transcendental, but possibly also transcendent and possibly the Transcendent. Nevertheless, each is named only as secret, and therefore there is an undecidability that protects any possible reference.

This leads me to ask whether, within that undecidability and because of the protection there afforded, there is elsewhere in Derrida room for a thinking of God as secret, for a thinking of a secret call of God, a secret giving of God. If there is such room, it is likely to be found in the context of Derrida's writing specifically

---

[82] Derrida, *PF*, 232.

on negative theology and religion. Three texts spring immediately to mind: "How to Avoid Speaking: Denials"; "Post-Scriptum: Aporias, Ways, and Voices," which was later adapted and published as "Sauf le nom"; and "Foi et Savoir."[83] For reasons already noted, it is generally recognized that Derrida is critical of negative theology.[84] Nevertheless, he is not dismissive of it, suggesting that "I trust no text that is not in some way contaminated with negative theology, and even among those texts that apparently do not have, want, or believe they have any relation with theology in general."[85] The texts above reflect different approaches. In "How to Avoid Speaking" Derrida is responding to the assertion that deconstruction is simply another form of negative theology, and so we find there that he reads negative theology largely in terms of its failure. Yet in "Sauf le nom" it seems that there is room for its rehabilitation.

In "How to Avoid Speaking" there is an initial attempt to suggest the parameters of negative theology, using for a Christian perspective the *Mystical Theology* of Denys (Dionysius) the Areopagite. Derrida tells us that

> "negative theology" has come to designate a certain typical attitude toward language, and within it, in the act of definition or attri-

[83] Derrida's "How to Avoid Speaking" is an important text, not least because it is one of the places where he adverts to Marion's work, most frequently in the notes. "Post-Scriptum: Aporias, Ways, and Voices" appears in the same collection at 283–323, although references will be made to Derrida, *SLN*.

[84] See Toby Foshay's "Introduction: Denegation and Resentment" in *Derrida and Negative Theology*, 1–24, especially at 3 and 5. See also Hart, *TS*, for example at 193.

[85] Derrida, *SLN*, 69. Regarding the relationship between deconstruction and theology, Hart observes: "Let us shift focus for a moment and see how deconstruction stands with respect to theology. At first the picture seems clear enough. Since God is 'the name and the element of that which makes possible an absolutely pure and absolutely self-present self-knowledge' any God talk, any theology, would be thoroughly shaken by *différance*. Not only is the sign complicit with metaphysics but also it is 'essentially theological.' All talk of a center is 'theological,' and *différance* 'blocks every relationship to theology.' for all that, deconstruction is neither proposing a 'return to finitude' nor calling for 'God's death.' And a closer inspection of Derrida's texts reveals that he is concerned solely with the metaphysics in theology, and would be sympathetic to those theologies, if any, that do not 'appropriate the resources of Greek conceptuality.' There is at least one, it seems, a contemporary deconstructive theology." Kevin Hart, introduction to an excerpt from "How to Avoid Speaking," *The Postmodern*

> bution, an attitude toward semantic or conceptual determination. Suppose, by a provisional hypothesis, that negative theology consists of considering that every predicative language is inadequate to the essence, in truth to the hyperessentiality (the being beyond Being) of God; consequently, only a negative ("apophatic") attribution can claim to approach God, and to prepare us for a silent intuition of God.[86]

Derrida notes that the rhetoric of negative theology can readily be imitated, but he points out that its context is quite specific, framed as it is by prayer and by the address to the other.[87]

We find within this definition—or at least this "provisional hypothesis"—the chief element of Derrida's concern. According to Derrida, while negative theology emphasizes the inadequacy of all predication, it nevertheless aims at a conceptual object that is still a type of being. In referring to God as "hyperessential," Derrida argues, Christian theology simply posits God as a preeminent being, even if this being is beyond the realm of being.[88] This seems to undermine the very negation that is characteristic of the genre.[89] In trying not to say anything, negative theology already

---

God: A Theological Reader, ed. Graham Ward (Oxford: Blackwell, 1997), 161–62 [hereafter Hart, *IHAS*].

[86] Derrida, *HAS,* 74.

[87] Derrida distinguishes between prayer and the encomium, and in a lengthy footnote he explains a connection here (and a fundamental disagreement) with the work of Marion in *ID.* Derrida's point is that the encomium, while performative, maintains some elements of attribution. *HAS,* 111. See also Hart, *IHAS,* 164: "Yet, as Derrida points out, there is no pure prayer, no 'address to the other as other,' for it is supplemented by an encomium. The God beyond being is determined in advance to be the Christian God. . . . Were it uttered in complete silence, the prayer still could not erase the possibility of its inscription and all that follows from this. And so, Derrida concludes, one cannot approach God, as negative theology promises, by passing from language to silence. Even silence is marked by the effects of *différance.*"

[88] " 'Negative theology' seems to reserve, beyond all positive predication, beyond all negation, even beyond Being, some hyperessentiality, a being beyond Being." Derrida, *HAS,* 77. See also the notes at 131–33, especially insofar as they concern a reading of Marion.

[89] And which is suggested by Derrida as follows: "By a more or less tenable analogy, one would thus recognize some traits, the family resemblance of negative theology, in every discourse that seems to return in a regular and insistent manner to this rhetoric of negative determination, endlessly multiplying the defenses and the apophatic warnings: this, which is called *X* (for example, text, writing, the trace, differance, the hymen, the supplement, the pharmakon, the parergon etc.) 'is' neither this nor that, neither sensible nor intelligible, neither

says far too much, effectively operating as a type of positive theology.[90] Since "hyperessentiality" is part of the language of the *Mystical Theology,* it seems that Derrida's criticism will be difficult to overcome. Those who respond on the issue tend to do so by questioning the meaning of hyperessentiality. Kevin Hart suggests that "hyper" has a negative rather than positive meaning, that it suggests transgression or violation. In other words, hyperessentiality is used to indicate a rupture of essentiality rather than a surplus. According to Hart, who borrows the phrase from Levinas, the God of Pseudo-Dionysius (is) "otherwise than being."[91]

To return to Derrida, there are other difficulties that he locates in regard to negative theology. There is its association with mystical prayer, which on his reading carries with it the promise of God's presence in the eventual union of the soul with God.[92] Then there is his insistence that what sharply divides *différance* from negative theology is that the latter springs from a cause and is oriented to a *telos.*[93] With regard to union, it must be underlined that in Christian mysticism the integrity and uniqueness of both human and divine persons is upheld to the end. In contrast to some other traditions, the Christian tradition maintains that the human soul never fuses with the divinity in the mystical experience. Whatever union means, it does not mean dissolution. Re-

---

positive nor negative, neither inside nor outside, neither superior nor inferior, neither active nor passive, neither present nor absent, not even neutral, not even subject to dialectic with a third moment, without any possible sublation ('Aufhebung'). Despite appearances, then, this *X* is neither a concept nor even a name; it does *lend itself* to a series of names, but calls for another syntax, and exceeds even the order and the structure of predicative discourse. It 'is' not and does not say what 'is.' It is written completely otherwise." Derrida, *HAS,* 74.

[90] See Derrida, *HAS,* 81. Hart disputes this, saying that "negative theology performs the deconstruction of positive theology." Hart, *TS,* 202.

[91] "To say that God is *hyperousious* is to deny that God is a being of any kind, even the highest or original being. As Jones remarks, Pseudo-Dionysius denies that God is a being and denies that God is be-ing (*on*). The divinity, he says, is 'beyond be-ing beyond beingly before all' or—to borrow Levinas' concise formulation—*otherwise than being.* Given this, Derrida is wrong to say that negative theology reserves a supreme being beyond the categories of being. Just as 'sign' must be crossed out in the deconstruction of metaphysics, so too must 'God' in the deconstruction of positive theology. The God of negative theology is transcendent in that He transcends being, all conceptions of being as presence, as well as the categories of gender." Hart, *TS,* 202.

[92] Derrida, *HAS,* 79–81.

[93] Derrida, *HAS,* 99, 81.

garding the cause and end of negative theology, it would seem to me that this only becomes limiting where it becomes a question of proof rather than one of faith, since faith itself only emerges out of *différance*. God may not be *différance*, but perhaps the experience of God is given according to *différance*.

"Sauf le nom" begins with a recognition that the apophatic voice is plural, and in fact Derrida constructs the essay as if it were a dialogue (or the minutes of a discussion group), so that there is an ambiguity in the way it unfolds.[94] Negative theology is being considered by negative theology. While not wishing to overlook the effects of this complex device, I shall continue to refer to the authorial voice as if it were singular.

Derrida once again explores the parameters of negative theology. He acknowledges that negative theology is *like* the experience of deconstruction.[95] It is a language, yet it exceeds language. He tells us that "the proposition ('What is called "negative theology" . . . is a language') has no rigorously determinable reference: neither in its subject nor in its attribute, we just said, but not even in its copula."[96] It is as though we have a preunderstanding of negative theology, but once we begin to articulate it, we are already too late, and its possibilities have already been exhausted.[97] Negative theology is the kenosis of discourse, a formalization without content.[98] What is most striking about these descriptions is a sense that they are driven by immemoriality. Negative theology always comes after the event, although it has a future dimension as well in that it always will have been.[99] We discern that negative theology makes no reference to a presence,

---

[94] Regarding plurality, see Derrida, *SLN*, 35, 66.

[95] Derrida, *SLN*, 43: "This thought seems vaguely familiar to the experience of deconstruction. Far from being a methodical technique, a possible or necessary procedure, unrolling the law of a program and applying rules, that is unfolding possibilities, deconstruction has often been defined as the very experience of the (impossible) possibility of the impossible, of the most impossible, a condition that deconstruction shares with the gift, the 'yes,' the 'come,' decision, testimony, the secret etc. And perhaps death."

[96] Derrida, *SLN*, 48.

[97] Derrida, *SLN*, 49.

[98] "The statement of negative theology empties itself by definition, by vocation, of all intuitive plenitude." Derrida, *SLN*, 50, 51.

[99] Derrida, *SLN*, 60, 58.

not even—in that sense—an absent presence.[100] So we find a series of passages that emphasize the way in which negative theology refers only through its bearing of a trace.[101] It refers us to the impossible possible, or as we read in "Foi et Savoir," "l'incalculable au coeur du calculable," the incalculable in the heart of the calculable.[102]

Negative theology is like a memory, testifying to a yet immemorial event that leaves a mark on language.[103] Derrida describes it as a "passion that leaves the mark of a scar in that place where the impossible takes place."[104] It carries a wound, just legible.[105] It bears witness to an unknowable God who has nothing save a name:

> Save the name that names nothing that might hold, not even a divinity (*Gottheit*), nothing whose withdrawal does not carry away every phrase that tries to measure itself against him. "God" "is" the name of this bottomless collapse, of this endless desertification of language. But the trace of this negative operation is inscribed *in* and *on* and *as* the *event* (what *comes,* what there is and which is always singular, what finds in this kenosis the most decisive condition of its coming or its upsurging). *There is* this event, which remains, even if this remnance is not more substantial, more essential than this God, more ontologically determinable than this name of God of whom it is said that he names nothing that is, neither this nor that. It is even said of him that he is not what is *given there* in the sense of *es gibt:* He is not what gives, his is beyond all gifts.[106]

---

[100] On this question of presence, I would refer back to Hart's introduction: "The theologian should remember that Derrida nowhere rejects the notion of presence. He argues that presence cannot present itself; the possibility of inscription is a necessary one, and one that ensures the possibility of division. There may be a God, and this God may be pure self-presence, but He cannot be intuited or revealed in the present." Hart, *IHAS,* 164–65.

[101] Commenting on Angelus Silesius, Derrida remarks: "This 'more,' this beyond, this *hyper* (*über*) obviously introduces an absolute heterogeneity in the order and in the modality of the possible. The possibility of the impossible, of the 'more possible' that as such is also possible ('more impossible than the impossible'), marks an absolute interruption in the regime of the possible that nonetheless remains, if this can be said, in place." Derrida, *SLN,* 43.

[102] Derrida, *FS,* 85; *FK,* 65.

[103] Derrida, *SLN,* 54.

[104] Derrida, *SLN,* 59–60.

[105] Derrida, *SLN,* 60.

[106] Derrida, *SLN,* 55–56.

The name is that of the unnameable nameable, the nameable beyond the name.[107] Here Derrida goes out of his way to tell us that it is not God who is given, or God who gives in the name. But I do not think that he thereby completely dismisses the possibility of the gift or the self-giving of God. What he dismisses is the demand for any more than the event, any more than the "collapse" or the "remnance." He dismisses the association of God with Heidegger's given or with a place of givenness. God is not "what gives"; God is "beyond all gifts," in the sense that God cannot be identified as giver save by a trace that is read in faith. All we are left with is the name that constantly escapes us, a "desertification" reminiscent of *khôra.*

Whereas in "How to Avoid Speaking" we gain a sense of the failure of negative theology owing to its inability to desist from speaking of the unspeakable, in "Sauf le nom" we get a sense that negative theology nevertheless functions as a supplementary discourse of rupture. In general terms, how does negative theology work? Most significantly, negative theology works aporetically. The event to which it bears witness (is) impossible, unknowable, an aporia. Negative theology opens onto the aporia of the secret.[108] We are reminded that the only way through an aporia is via decision, a decision that passes through madness.[109] This does not force us to the decision of religious faith, but it opens up its possibility, as much negatively as positively. The mystic can never prove that God has passed in his or her "experience." Nevertheless, that aporetic experience is possible means that we cannot exclude the possibility that God may so pass.[110]

Negative theology works as hyperbole. "This hyperbole *announces.* It announces in a double sense: it *signals* an open possibility, but it also *provokes* thereby the opening of the possibility. Its event is at once revealing and producing, *post-scriptum* and prole-

---

[107] Derrida, *SLN,* 58.

[108] Derrida, *SLN,* 60.

[109] "But isn't the uncleared way also the condition of *decision* or *event,* which consists in opening the way, in *(sur)passing,* thus in going *beyond?* In (sur)passing the aporia?" Derrida, *SLN,* 54. "The sole decision possible passes through the madness of the undecidable and the impossible: to go where (*wo, Ort, Wort*) it is impossible to go." *SLN,* 59.

[110] With regard to aporetic experience, see Derrida, *Ap,* for example at 15, 19, 32.

gomenon, inaugural writing."[111] Then it works in conversion, arising out of the conversion of the one who writes, but also involving a conversion from God to others. At the very start of this section, it was observed that the context of negative theology was prayer and the address to the other. There is a movement that occurs where prayer, the address to God, becomes confession, a testimony.[112] In the end, negative theology involves surrender.[113] It is desire that lets go of its object.[114] Emerging from the address to God, it becomes an address to no matter whom.[115]

Finally, negative theology works through plurality: the plurality of voices (the voice of radical critique and the voice of dogmatic assurance) that contradict one another; the plurality of places (the place of revelation and the place of *khôra*) that exclude one another; the plurality of paths (Greek philosophy and Christian mysticism) that cross one another.[116] Negative theology produces fissures: it fractures the cogito, divides being from knowing, undermines every thesis, and drives a wedge into the analogy between creator and creature.[117] The fissure is the madness through which we can only pass by decision.

Having considered briefly the first two of the three texts that have a bearing on Derrida's speaking of God, I turn now to the third, "Foi et Savoir," which has a completely different style and focus. "Foi et Savoir" is a meditation on the very possibility of religion. Derrida notes that religion often concerns itself with "the name," with speaking "in the name of" something or someone, with naming, speaking in its own name. Additionally, reli-

---

[111] Derrida, *SLN,* 62. Are we able to link the "hyper" of hyperbole with the "hyper" of hyperessentiality? Since Derrida here translates "hyper" as "*ultra, au-delà, beyond, über,*" are we finally able to redeem hyperessentiality from the clutches of ontology? If it is hyperbole that "names the movement of transcendence that carries or transports beyond being or beingness," surely hyperessentiality cannot name what does not utterly transcend, or transgress?

[112] Derrida, *SLN,* 39, 40: "This moment of writing is done for 'afterwards.' But it also follows the conversion. It remains the trace of a present moment of the confession that would have no sense without such a conversion, without this address to the brother readers."

[113] Derrida, *SLN,* 74.

[114] Derrida, *SLN,* 37.

[115] Derrida, *SLN,* 74.

[116] Derrida, *SLN,* 66–67, 75–76, 62.

[117] Derrida, *SLN,* 66, 65, 67, 66.

gion is often about light. It sheds light, brings to light, and approaches the luminous. Phenomenology is also about bringing to light, or learning to see.[118] Yet religion has to do with empty places, what Derrida will call places of the aporia. He names three: the island, the promised land, and the desert, although it will be on the desert that he focuses by and large. While these places form the horizon of thought, they also indicate the need for a certain suspension or interruption of any horizon. "Paradoxically, the absence of horizon conditions the future itself. The springing up of the event should breach any horizon of expectation. From where the apprehension of an abyss in these places, for example a desert in the desert, there where the one neither can nor should see coming that which would have to or would be able to—*perhaps*—come."[119]

There is a distinction to be made between faith and religion, and also between faith and theology.[120] Derrida then discusses the historical nature of revelation, which leads him to develop the notion of "revealability," which would be the possibility of any revelation at all. Perhaps, he wonders, revealability is that which is revealed in revelation; revealability is the origin of light. And yet Derrida has in mind a more "nocturnal" light, a more "anarchic" and "anarchival" origin, "*more than* the arch-original": "a certain desert *in* the desert, the one that would make possible, open, hollow out or infinitize the other."[121] This origin would be heterogeneous (and so non-original), bearing two names, the "messianic" and "*khôra*."[122] It is this double experience of the desert, prior to revelation, that Derrida wants to think.

Derrida speaks elsewhere of a messianism without a messiah, where the messiah would always be coming but would never be

---

[118] Derrida, *FS*, 14–15; *FK*, 6. Hence the contrast with Marion, who can seem also to be making religion a question of the light.

[119] Derrida, *FS*, 15: "Paradoxalement, l'absence d'horizon conditionne l'avenir même. Le surgissement de l'événement doit trouer tout horizon d'attente. D'où l'appréhension d'un abîme en ces lieux, par example un désert dans le désert, là où l'on ne peut ni doit voir venir ce qui devrait ou pourrait—*peut-être*—venir." *FK*, 7.

[120] Derrida, *FS*, 17; *FK*, 10.

[121] Derrida, *FS*, 26: "*plus que* l'archi-originaire"; "un certain désert *dans* le désert, celui qui rend possible, ouvre, creuse ou infinitise l'autre." *FK*, 16.

[122] Derrida, *FS*, 27; *FK*, 17.

present, never arrive. Here he speaks of "the opening to the future or to the coming of the other *as* the advent of justice, but without horizon of expectation and without prophetic foreshadowing."[123] The messianic would expose us to surprise. Experience (*l'expérience*) would be structured by a waiting without expectation, by the sheer desire for or hope in justice. There would here be faith without dogma.[124]

The other aspect of the desert experience, or of the experience of desertification, would take the name of *khôra*. The word is taken from Plato's *Timaeus*, and Derrida uses it frequently because it suggests for him a place of absolute exteriority that is no place at all, but more of a "spacing."

> *Khôra* . . . would be the place-name, *a* place-name, and very singular, for *this* spacing which, not letting itself be dominated by any theological, ontological or anthropological instance, without age, without history and "older" than all oppositions, . . . would not even show itself as "beyond Being," according to a negative way. As a result, *khôra* remains absolutely impassible and heterogeneous to all processes of historical revelation or anthropo-theological experience, which nonetheless presuppose its abstraction. It will never have entered into religion and it will never let itself be sacralized, sanctified, humanized, theologized, cultivated, historicized. Radically heterogeneous to the healthy and to the safe, to the holy and to the sacred, it never lets itself be *indemnified*. Even this cannot be said in the present, because *khôra* never presents itself as such. It is neither Being, nor the Good, nor God, nor Man, nor History. It will always resist them, it will always have been (and no future anterior, even, will have been able to reappropriate . . .) the very *place* of an infinite resistance, of an infinitely impassible remaining: a completely other without face.[125]

---

[123] Derrida, *FS*, 27: "l'ouverture à l'avenir ou à la venue de l'autre *comme* avènement de la justice, mais sans horizon d'attente et sans préfiguration prophétique." *FK*, 17.

[124] Derrida, *FS*, 28; *FK*, 18. Of course, faith without dogma would mean that the object of faith could never be identified. But this is not so unusual in one sense. Rahner's God, too, is unthematized, at least insofar as being the goal of self-transcending desire.

[125] Derrida, *FS*, 31: "*Khôra* . . . serait . . . le nom de lieu, *un* nom de lieu, et fort singulier, pour *cet* espacement qui, ne se laissant dominer par aucune instance théologique, ontologique ou anthropologique, sans âge, sans histoire et plus 'ancien' que toutes les oppositions . . . ne s'annonce même pas comme 'au-delà de l'être,' selon une voie négative. Du coup, *khôra* reste absolument impassible

Derrida is quick to add that while *khôra* is not anything ("not a being or of the present"), it is also not the Heideggerian Nothing. He maintains that this desert would be "prior to" (if the language of priority can maintain any sense here) the desert of "revelations and withdrawals, lives and deaths of God, all figures of kenosis or of transcendence," and so forth.[126] But it would also be subsequent to it, Derrida noting the oscillation between revelation and revealability that cannot be ultimately decided.[127] The experience of "the desert in the desert" would lead, Derrida says, to a new tolerance for alterity, to a respect for the "distance of infinite alterity as singularity."[128]

In a "post-scriptum" that is longer than that which precedes it, Derrida talks about religion as response and responsibility.[129] The passage is reminiscent of Levinas, for whom religion is relationship with the Other.[130] Religion is response and it is testimony, with or without God as a witness.[131] Religion involves faith, but faith suffers the constant temptation to try to convert itself into knowledge.[132] Faith is not about seeing, not about knowing, not about conceiving anything.[133] Here Derrida seems to align himself

---

et hétérogène à tous les processus de révélation historique ou d'expérience anthropo-théologique, qui en supposent néanmoins l'abstraction. Elle ne sera jamais entrée en religion et ne se laissera jamais sacraliser, sanctifier, humaniser, théologiser, cultiver, historialiser. Radicalement hétérogène au sain et au sauf, au saint et au sacré, elle ne se laisse jamais *indemniser.* Cela même ne peut se dire au présent, car *khôra* ne se présente jamais comme telle. Elle n'est ni l'Être, ni le Bien, ni Dieu, ni l'Homme, ni l'Histoire. Elle leur résistera toujours, elle aura toujours été (et aucun futur antérieur, même, n'aura pu réapproprier . . .) le *lieu* même d'une résistance infinie, d'une restance infiniment impassible: un tout autre sans visage." *FK,* 20–21.

[126] Derrida, *FS,* 31–32; *FK,* 21. What kind of priority is Derrida talking about? It would be unlike him to refer to a priority in time. It seems he speaks once again of a quasi-transcendental priority, since it enables (and presumably disables) revelation.

[127] Derrida, *FS,* 32; *FK,* 21.

[128] Derrida, *FS,* 33; *FK,* 22.

[129] Derrida, *FS,* 39; *FK,* 26.

[130] Levinas, *TI,* 40.

[131] Derrida, *FS,* 39–41; *FK,* 26–29. Note Caputo's gloss: "For this desert, khôral religion does not necessarily involve God, and while it certainly involves faith, faith is not necessarily faith in the God of the great monotheisms." Caputo, *PTJD,* 157.

[132] Derrida, *FS,* 43–45; *FK,* 30–32.

[133] Derrida, *FS,* 56; *FK,* 41. See also the discussion of photology in Derrida, *GD,* 98ff.

with Levinas. And once again, we are reminded of Marion's difficulty, where in setting himself within the theological orientation of "seeing" (Balthasar) and within the phenomenological tradition of "presenting" (Husserl), he leaves himself little room to move where agnosticism is required. Yet religion is more than faith. Derrida in fact observes two experiences of religion: the experience of belief (in which category he includes faith, rather than the inverse), and the experience of "*l'indemne*" (which could be translated as the "not lost"), which includes the experiences of sacredness or holiness.[134] While the two approaches cannot be reduced to one, they do come together in the experience of testimony, or as Derrida seems to suggest at another point, in the oscillation between possibility and determined necessity.[135] Attestation is what incarnates possibility, as it were. And attestation is always before another, if not also before God. The faith that makes attestation possible is what enables a relationship with the other, a relationship that is, nevertheless, without relation. Faith, response, responsibility, testimony, the possible, the embodied—these are the words Derrida uses to think religion, and to think it from a *khôral* place (with a twist of the messianic). But while *khôra* "gives a place (perhaps)," it does so without any semblance of generosity.[136] Any *khôral* gift would be forever undecidable.

I have sought in three places something of Derrida's response to the question of God, and have found instead only what it means to fail in speaking and to speak with a kind of failure. In looking for God as a question I have encountered only secrecy: Derrida never gives a direct answer.[137] Yet the secret has its own

[134] Derrida, *FS,* 46; *FK,* 33. "*L'indemne*" is a juridical term meaning "without loss." In its usage here it almost suggests "the indemnified." Caputo translates "not being damned or damaged." Caputo, *PTJD,* 157. The division between belief and sacrality is an interesting move for Derrida to make, and it may represent two styles of religiosity, the one desirous of the invisible, and the other comforted by the visible, the ritual, the tangible signs that apparently point to the holy. It is not a distinction I would have drawn naturally, but it does have a certain logic to it.

[135] With regard to the experience of testimony, see Derrida, *FS,* 83; *FK,* 63. With regard to the "irreducible gap" between possibility and determined necessity (or history), see *FS,* 76; *FK,* 58.

[136] Derrida, *FS,* 84–86; *FK,* 64–66.

[137] And I do not believe we are any closer with the following profession: ". . . but she must have known that the constancy of God in my life is called by other

call, and as we have seen, a call is a call for a response. It could perhaps safely be said that if there is a question of God for Derrida, then it would be found in that place where faith responds to the other. And there it would be impossible to say, impossible to know (since secret), whether or not God had called, much less whether or not God gave or was given or was gift. All horizons of expectation would need to have been suspended. Yet the admission of such nescience is not so strange. It is not foreign to faith but necessarily at its heart, making choice possible, and obedient to the exigency of the gift.[138] If God were (to be) the one who gives, if God were given, if God made a gift of Godself, then I could not know it, but only believe it, and believe it only in responding to *every* other who is (every bit) *other. The Gift of Death*

---

names, so that I quite rightly pass for an atheist, the omnipresence to me of what I call God in my absolved, absolutely private language being neither that of an eyewitness nor that of a voice doing anything other than talking to me without saying anything, nor a transcendent law or an immanent *schechina,* that feminine figure of Yahweh who remains so strange and so familiar to me, but the secret I am excluded from, when the secret consists in the fact that you are held to a secrecy by those who know your secret, how many are there, and do not dare admit to you that this is no longer a secret for them, that they share with you the open secret, letting you reckon that they know without saying, and, from that point on, what you have neither the right nor the strength to confess, it is just as useless to make it known, to hand it over to this public notoriety you are the first and the only one to be excluded from, properly theological hypothesis of a blank sacrifice sending the bidding up to infinity, God coming to circulate among the unavowables, unavowable as he remains himself, like a son not bearing my name, like a son not bearing his name, like a son not bearing a name, and if, to give rise to this beyond of the name, in view and by reason of this unacceptable appellation of self for my mother has become silenced without dying, I write that there is *too much* love in my life, emphasizing *too much,* the better and the worse, that would be true, love will have got the better of me, my faithfulness stands any test, I am faithful even to the test that does harm, to my euthanasias." Jacques Derrida, "Circumfession," in Bennington and Derrida, *Jacques Derrida,* 155–57.

[138] Hart concludes *IHAS* with a "quick sketch" of the believer who would be prepared to take Derrida's conclusions on board: "He or she would trust in God's presence while not expecting to experience it in the present. The life of faith would depend on the interpretation of traces. It would be a negative way, not necessarily by virtue of accepting a 'negative theology' but by dint of experiencing an aporia, an inexorable demand to choose between legitimate alternatives. One would look to the God rendered possible by exegesis and philosophy, while at the same time answering to the God who upsets the realm of the possible, who arrives in a singular manner outside the known and the expected" (165). In discussion of this passage, Hart adds that "the traces are not thematised at first but become thematised in the exercise of faith."

offers, I believe, Derrida's most sustained thinking on this secret gift:

> On what condition is responsibility possible? On the condition that the Good no longer be a transcendental objective, a relation between objective things, but the relation to the other, a response to the other; an experience of personal goodness and a movement of intention. . . . On what condition does goodness exist beyond all calculation? On the condition that goodness forget itself, that the movement be a movement of the gift that renounces itself, hence a movement of infinite love. Only infinite love can renounce itself and, in order to *become finite,* become incarnated in order to love the other, to love the other as a finite other. This gift of infinite love comes from somewhere and is addressed to someone; responsibility demands irreplaceable singularity. Yet only death or the apprehension of a death can give this irreplaceability.[139]

---

[139] Derrida, *GT1,* 50–51.

EPILOGUE: NAMING THE GIFT, GIVING A NAME, RETHINKING GOD AS GIFT

THE QUESTION with which I have been occupied throughout this study is a theological one: how is it possible to speak of God as gift? And the path that has been traveled in response to that question perhaps seems to have had little to do with theology as such. Yet if Anselm's famous definition of theology as "faith seeking understanding" is in any way valid, then this book has not been far from theology at all, at least in the sense that it is an attempt to understand what it might mean for God to give Godself. That the resources on which I have drawn are not from theological tradition, but from contemporary thought, does not exclude my reflection on this question at its most preliminary level of possibility. At the same time, those resources do not lead to specifically Christian answers, or at least they serve to illustrate that any specification of religious "experience" will have to rely on a risk of faith. To say as much seems like a commonplace, but it also seems that the radical nature of this position is rarely taken on board in its entirety. No serious theologian suggests that God can be known *as such* (where knowing has the sense of comprehending, or bringing to presence). But if it is the case that any "experience" of God must therefore overwhelm (or, equally, underwhelm) consciousness, it must also be confessed that affirming such an experience *as* one of God involves a hermeneutic from the start. There is no revelation that is not always and already interpreted (as Revelation), that leaves open the possibility of its reinterpretation over and over again.[1] At this point the real difficulty becomes evident. It is one thing to admit that the object of theology cannot be made an object, and that God overwhelms the

[1] I am indebted to Kevin Hart for his discussions with me on this point.

understanding. But it is another to allow—really to allow—that there are no theological givens that are purely given. It is a humbling thing to admit that truth depends on a judgment and not on a "fact." The stakes are high. Suddenly the nature of risking one's life on the Gospel takes on its proper degree of danger.

To say that revelation/Revelation is always and already interpreted is not to underplay the role of religious communities in passing on a tradition or traditions of interpretation, but only to point out that it is *interpretations* that are passed on. The desire, on the one hand, to harden those interpretations into static doctrines is perhaps understandable. But to do that is like trying to seize the gift, and having it turn to dust before our eyes. To speak, on the other hand, of God as gift is to assent both to God and to gift as the impossible. It is not, as Milbank perhaps fears, to consign each to simple impossibility, but to recognize the nature of the risk we are taking in desiring their "reality." It is to speak at the point of words' failure, which is why the passage through phenomenology has been instructive. And it is to be overwhelmed by transcendence, yet not a transcendence that exists somewhere "out there," but one that has already interrupted me before I can begin speaking, before I am "here, now."

Throughout this work I have had cause to refer to the debate that took place between Marion and Derrida at Villanova in 1997. We find in the text of this debate not only confrontation over the nature of phenomenology and the question of the gift, but also over the question of negative theology. I noted earlier a point that Caputo brings out very well in his discussion of that debate, which is that for Marion, thought is overwhelmed by excess (the saturated phenomenon), whereas for Derrida, thought is interrupted by the desert (the aporia).[2] Neither of these positions, I observed, is too far from the theological tradition(s) known as mysticism. It is possible that in mystical theology we find the clearest recognition of the gap between thought and referent that must always unsettle theological discourse in the way I have suggested. But to pursue a detailed discussion of mystical theology and its relation to deconstruction is beyond the scope of this book, although of course it is of genuine relevance to Marion's

[2] See Caputo, *AI*, 185–86 and passim.

theological work. It has, in any case, already been explored elsewhere.[3] In closing I simply draw attention to the extraordinary discussion on the name/Name that to some extent seems to align Marion and Derrida, in spite of the many differences between them, especially where this name/Name might be thought in terms of gift.

Marion's opening address at the 1997 conference is titled "In the Name."[4] Here he rearticulates and responds to Derrida's reading of negative theology, and also puts forward his own account of mystical theology and its relationship to the saturated phenomenon. Marion argues that mystical theology is misunderstood if it is merely seen as negation, and instead puts forward the Dionysian "third way," which goes beyond affirmation and negation in favor of "the experience of incomprehension."[5] He maintains that Derrida reads mystical theology only in its negative mode (a reading Derrida vigorously contests), which allows Derrida to suspect "the supposedly ultimate and freestanding negation of implicitly and surreptitiously smuggling in and re-establishing an affirmation."[6] Dionysius, on the contrary,

> denies first that negation itself suffices to define a theology, next that negation opposes affirmation in a simple duel, and finally that negation re-establishes affirmation while pretending to invert it. In short, Dionysius always thinks negation exactly as he thinks affirmation—as one of the two values truths can have, one of the two forms of predication which it is precisely a matter of transgressing completely, as the discourse of metaphysics. With the third way, not only is it no longer a matter of saying (or denying) something about something, it is also no longer a matter of saying or unsaying, but of referring to Him who is no longer touched by nomination. It is solely a matter of de-nominating.[7]

---

[3] On negative theology, mysticism, Derrida, and deconstruction, see, for example, Hart, *TS;* Hart, *IHAS;* and Hart, *JDGE.* There are many other places where this sort of discussion takes place, but few where the knowledge of Derrida is as detailed and the expression as measured. On Marion and negative and mystical theology, see in particular Carlson's *Indiscretion,* as well as Caputo and Scanlon, *GGP.*

[4] Jean-Luc Marion, "In the Name" [hereafter Marion, *IN*], in Caputo and Scanlon, *GGP,* 20–53, including Derrida's response.

[5] These words are quoted by Marion from Nicholas of Cusa, but they illustrate the point to perfection.

[6] Marion, *IN,* 25.

[7] Marion, *IN,* 28.

The reference to de-nomination is an important one because it leads Marion to speak about another of Derrida's objections to "negative theology," that prayer and praise have a destination, and therefore an object in mind. Marion's response on this point is sound (and we later find Derrida in agreement with it):

> [Derrida's objection] presupposes that it is unquestionable that praising, that is attributing a name to an interlocutor, indeed dedicating to him one name in particular, necessarily implies identifying him in and with his essence and thereby submits him to the "metaphysics of presence." Now what is proper to the proper name consists precisely in the fact that it never belongs properly—by and as his essence—to the one who receives it. . . .
>
> Thus, supposing that praise attributes a name to a possible God, one should conclude that it does not name him properly or essentially, nor that it names him in presence, but that it marks his absence, anonymity and withdrawal—exactly as every name dissimulates every individual, whom it merely indicates without ever manifesting. In this sense, praise in mystical theology would in the case of divine proper names only reproduce an aporia.[8]

It is next necessary for Marion to repeat his arguments from elsewhere about the transgression of being, for he needs to inscribe the naming of mystical theology otherwise than according to any ontological horizon. Here, once again, we observe the characteristic of reverse intentionality:

> It's a matter of being exposed in one's intending a non-object, exposed to the point of receiving from this non-object determinations that are so radical and so new that they speak to me and shape me far more than they teach and inform me. Henceforth, the words spoken no longer say or explain anything about some thing kept for and by my gaze. They expose me to what lets itself be said only for the sake of no longer permitting me to say it, but to acknowledge it as goodness, and thus to love it.[9]

Theology is not, Marion claims, "obsessed with presence," but only really theology insofar as it relinquishes the need to have a concept of God fulfilled. "God cannot be seen, not only because nothing finite can bear his glory without perishing, but above all

---

[8] Marion, *IN,* 28–29.

[9] Marion, *IN,* 32.

because a God that could be conceptually comprehended would no longer bear the title 'God.' "[10] Naming God does not result in a theology of presence, but one of absence, a phrase Marion immediately qualifies: "By theology of absence . . . we mean not the non-presence of God, but the fact that the name that God is given, the name which gives God, which is given as God . . . serves *to shield God from presence* . . . and offers him precisely as an exception to presence."[11]

I have quoted Marion at length here because he addresses several important objections to his theological work and because these observations correspond to a number of the points that have already been made with reference to Derrida and "negative theology." But I also include this material because it serves as a prelude to his further explication of the saturated phenomenon. For Marion, proceeding with Dionysius's "third way" means passing from a simple naming to a de-nomination, or better, it means entering into the Name and letting it name us. Preeminently, this entry into the Name takes place in baptism (a point with which Derrida quite understandably has some difficulty). In order to support this very Balthasarian reversal, Marion tries to think the third way as a saturated phenomenon, which he describes following the pattern of *Étant donné.* He then concludes: "The Name—it has to be dwelt in without saying it, but by letting it say, name and call us. The Name is not said, it calls."[12]

Now, it has already been observed that Paul Ricoeur speaks of "the retreat of the Name," and that Derrida refers to the name as that of the unnameable nameable, the nameable beyond the name.[13] And it has been further noted that Derrida is in agreement with Marion on the question of the proper of the name. "The proper name . . . is never proper" are Derrida's words in response to Marion on the same point: "what is proper to the proper name consists precisely in the fact that it never belongs properly . . . to the one who receives it."[14] A name—even a proper Name—is never proper because it never makes present; always

[10] Marion, *IN,* 34.
[11] Marion, *IN,* 37.
[12] Marion, *IN,* 42.
[13] Derrida, *SLN,* 58.
[14] Derrida, in his response to Marion in *IN,* 45.

iterable, its condition of possibility is also its condition of impossibility. The meaning of a name/Name can never be exhausted. Like the gift, a name/Name is no-thing, gives no-thing. If God gives Godself as a name/Name, then we will never know if the name/Name is a gift, and we will never be able to return it.

Do Marion and Derrida speak the same language after all, even if they resist the language of the same? In one sense it seems in the Villanova debate that the protagonists could not be further apart, at least insofar as Marion still argues for the success of phenomenology, and for excessive phenomena, whereas Derrida puts forward the failure of phenomenology and opts for aporetic experience. But in another sense, in this dialogue on the name, they could be quite close. If Janicaud were to interject, nonetheless, he would point out that Marion's "name" is a "Name," which seems to implicate Marion in going beyond a mere "possibility" and making a commitment to the outcome. Yet it could also be argued that here Marion is just another punter. He lays his bets on the Name, but "his" Name gives—from the outside at least—no more than Derrida's. That, it seems to me, is the substance of his argument with regard to mystical theology, and provided he remains within the betting ring, it is quite a convincing one.

It is my argument that the question of God and the question of the gift come from the same aporetic space, that it is not only possible to think God as gift, but highly appropriate to do so. I maintain this on the basis of an approach to the gift by way of and beyond phenomenology. There may well be other and better ways to approach God, but they do not serve to show, as I have hoped to do, the distinctive and problematic character of the gift itself. Instead, many of the theological debates about the nature of grace simply affirm its gift quality, while at the same time struggling with the extent to which it can be received or must be cooperated with, and are less cognizant of the question of how it can be gift at all. A gift is both that which is passed freely from one person to another with generous intent and that which is never present as gift, never identifiable as such. It seems to me that the Christian belief that God gives Godself in relationship with persons, freely and generously, must be characterized by the same condition of impossibility. If God gives Godself without condition, then we will not be able to identify that gift *as such:* it will never be present. The relationship must rest on a freedom that risks the possibility of misunderstanding or rejection, or else it will not be a relationship of love but one opening onto coercion. Further, the gift will never be returned, not only because there could never be sufficient return, but because there will be no return address. Any God-gift will disseminate in desire, as Levinas (in conversation with Derrida) might say, not for God but for the undesirable par excellence, my neighbor. Not every gift (is) God, but it seems that God is only to be thought starting from the gift, which places us in agreement with Marion in orientation if not entirely in terms of method. With a kind of Heideggerian flourish, we could write this "belonging together" as "God: gift." Of course, to observe the common aporetic structure of God and the gift does not solve the aporia. An aporia, by definition, cannot be solved, but only resolved by a decision to act in a particular way, to act *as if* there were a way forward. I can never know whether or not I give or whether or not I receive, but I can believe it or desire it or act as if it were possible. So it is with God. That is not to say that faith is a matter of wishful thinking, but to affirm that faith can only be faith, as much faith in the gift as faith in God.

Much religious mentality is devoted to a calculation of debts. It is a very human thing to keep score, and it is even more human to despair under the weight of the goodness of another, fearing that the debt will be too great ever to be paid in full. The thought of a God to whom we owe our very lives, and in whose sight we are always having to be made right, is often too much to bear.[15] But if there is any good news, then the good news is that we owe God nothing, that God's (is) a gift that is really free, and that in this gift, giving, which is strictly impossible, stirs in us as desire. We will never know whether God gives, or what God gives; we can only believe, struggling with traces and with words half said and needing to be unsaid, that there (is) gift.

---

[15] This theme is beautifully explored in the works of Sebastian Moore, OSB.

SELECT BIBLIOGRAPHY

Selected Books by Jean-Luc Marion

L'idole et la distance. Paris: Grasset, 1977. *ID*

L'être et Dieu. Paris: Cerf, 1986.

Sur le prisme métaphysique de Descartes. Paris: Presses Universitaires de France, 1986.

Dieu sans l'être: Hors-texte. 1982. Paris: Quadrige/Presses Universitaires de France, 1991.

Prolégomènes à la charité. 2nd ed. Paris: Editions de la Différence, 1991. *PC*

Réduction et donation: Recherches sur Husserl, Heidegger, et la phénoménologie. Paris: Presses Universitaires de France, 1989. *RED*

God Without Being. Trans. Thomas A. Carlson. Chicago: University of Chicago Press, 1991. *GWB*

Questions cartésiennes: Méthode et métaphysique. Paris: Presses Universitaires de France, 1991. *QCI*

La croisée du visible. 2nd ed. Paris: Presses Universitaires de France, 1996. *CV*

Questions cartésiennes II: Sur l'ego et sur Dieu. Paris: Presses Universitaires de France, 1996. *QCII*

Étant donné. Paris: Presses Universitaires de France, 1997. *ED*

Reduction and Givenness: Investigations of Husserl, Heidegger, and Phenomenology. Trans. Thomas A. Carlson. Evanston: Northwestern University Press, 1998. *RAG*

Cartesian Questions: Method and Metaphysics. Trans. Jeffrey L. Kosky et al. Chicago: University of Chicago Press, 1999.

On Descartes' Metaphysical Prism. Trans. Jeffrey L. Kosky. Chicago: University of Chicago Press, 1999.

The Idol and Distance: Five Studies. Trans. with an introduction by Thomas A. Carlson. New York: Fordham University Press, 2001.

Selected Essays by Jean-Luc Marion

"La double idolatrie: Remarques sur la différence ontologique et la pensée de Dieu." *Heidegger et la question de Dieu.* Ed. Richard Kearney and Joseph S. O'Leary. Paris: Grasset, 1980. 46–74.

"La vanité de l'être et le nom de Dieu." *Analogie et dialectique: Essais de théologie fondamentale.* Ed. P. Gisel and Ph. Secretan. Geneva: Labor et Fides, 1982. 17–49.

"De la 'mort de dieu' aux noms divins: L'itinéraire théologique de la métaphysique." *Laval théologique et philosophique* 41, no. 1 (1985): 25–41.

"L'Interloqué." *Who Comes After the Subject?* Ed. Eduardo Cadava, Peter Connor, and Jean-Luc Nancy. New York: Routledge, 1991. 236–45.

"Réponses à quelques questions." *Revue de Métaphysique et de Morale* 96, no. 1 (1991): 65–76. *RQQ*

"Le sujet en dernier appel." *Revue de Métaphysique et de Morale* 96, no. 1 (1991): 77–96.

"Heidegger and Descartes." Trans. Christopher Macann. *Martin Heidegger: Critical Assessments.* Ed. Christopher Macann. London: Routledge, 1992. 178–207.

"La phénomène saturé." Jean-François Courtine, Jean-Louis Chrétien, Michel Henry, Jean-Luc Marion, and Paul Ricoeur. *Phénoménologie et théologie.* Paris: Criterion, 1992. 79–128. *PS*

"Métaphysique et phénoménologie: Une rélève pour la théologie," *Bulletin de Littérature Ecclésiastique* 94, no. 3 (1993): 189–206.

"Metaphysics and Phenomenology: A Relief for Theology." Trans. Thomas A. Carlson. *Critical Inquiry* 20 (1993–94): 573–91.

"Esquisse d'un concept phénoménologique du don." *Archivio di Filosofia.* Anno 62, nos. 1–3 (1994): 75–94. *E*

"L'autre philosophie première et la question de la donation." Institut Catholique de Paris. *Philosophie 17: Le statut contemporain de la philosophie première.* Paris: Beauschesne, 1996. 29–50. *LAPP*

"The Saturated Phenomenon." Trans. Thomas A. Carlson. *Philosophy Today* 40 (Spring 1996): 103–24.

"Descartes and Onto-Theology." *Post-Secular Philosophy: Between Philosophy and Theology.* Ed. Phillip Blond. London: Routledge, 1998. 67–106.

"L'évènement, le phénomène et le révélé." *Transversalités: Revue de L'Institut Catholique de Paris* 70 (April–June 1999): 4–25.

"In the Name." *God, the Gift, and Postmodernism.* Ed. John D. Caputo and Michael J. Scanlon. Bloomington: Indiana University Press, 1999. 20–53. *IN*

"Sketch of a Phenomenological Concept of the Gift." Trans. John Conley, S.J., and Danielle Poe. *Postmodern Philosophy and Christian Thought.* Ed. Merold Westphal. Bloomington: Indiana University Press, 1999. 122–43. *SPCG*

Selected Books by Jacques Derrida

La Communication. Montréal: Edition Montmorency, 1973.

Speech and Phenomena and Other Essays on Husserl's Theory of Signs. Trans. David B. Allison and Newton Garver. Evanston: Northwestern University Press, 1973. *SP*

Spurs: Nietzsche's Styles. Trans. Barbara Harlow. Chicago: University of Chicago Press, 1978.

Writing and Difference. Trans. Alan Bass. London: Routledge, 1978. *WD*

Dissemination. Trans. and ed. Barbara Johnson. Chicago: University of Chicago Press, 1981. *D*

Positions. Trans. Alan Bass. Chicago: University of Chicago Press, 1981. *Pos*

Glas. Trans. John P. Leavey, Jr., and Richard Rand. Lincoln: University of Nebraska Press, 1986. *G*

The Post-Card: From Socrates to Freud and Beyond. Trans. Alan Bass. Chicago: University of Chicago Press, 1987.

Psyché: Inventions de l'autre. Paris: Galilée, 1987.

The Truth in Painting. Trans. Geoffrey Bennington and Ian McLeod. Chicago: University of Chicago Press, 1987. *TP*

Edmund Husserl's "Origin of Geometry": An Introduction. Trans. John P. Leavey, Jr. Rev. ed. Lincoln: University of Nebraska Press, 1989.

Of Spirit: Heidegger and the Question. Trans. Geoffrey Bennington and Rachel Bowlby. Chicago: University of Chicago Press, 1989.

Cinders. Trans. Ned Lukacher. Lincoln, Nebraska: University of Nebraska Press, 1991.

Donner le temps: 1. La fausse monnaie. Paris: Galilée, 1991. *DT1*

Given Time: 1. Counterfeit Money. Trans. Peggy Kamuf. Chicago: University of Chicago Press, 1992. *GT1*

The Other Heading. Trans. Pascale-Anne Brault and Michael B. Naas. Bloomington: Indiana University Press, 1992.

Aporias. Trans. Thomas Dutoit. Stanford: Stanford University Press, 1993. *Ap*

Spectres of Marx: The State of the Debt, the Work of Mourning, and the New International. Trans. Peggy Kamuf. New York: Routledge, 1994.

The Gift of Death. Trans. David Wills. Chicago: University of Chicago Press, 1995. *GD*

Points: Interviews, 1974–1994. Ed. Elisabeth Weber. Trans. Peggy Kamuf et al. Stanford: Stanford University Press, 1995. *Po*

Adieu: à Emmanuel Levinas. Paris: Galilée, 1997. *Ad*

Politics of Friendship. Trans. George Collins. London: Verso, 1997. *PF*

Of Grammatology. Trans. Gayatri Chakravorty Spivak. Rev. ed. Baltimore: Johns Hopkins University Press, 1998.

Adieu: to Emmanuel Levinas. Trans. Pascale-Anne Brault and Michael Naas. Stanford: Stanford University Press, 1999.

Sur parole: Instantanés philosophiques. Paris: Éditions de l'Aube, 1999.

Bennington, Geoffrey, and Jacques Derrida. *Jacques Derrida.* Chicago: University of Chicago Press, 1993.

Dufourmantelle, Anne, and Jacques Derrida. *De L'hospitalité.* Paris: Calmann-Lévy, 1997. *DL'H*

Selected Essays by Jacques Derrida

"At This Very Moment in This Work Here I Am." *Re-reading Levinas.* Ed. Robert Bernasconi and Simon Critchley. Bloomington: Indiana University Press, 1991. 11–48. *ATVM*

"How to Avoid Speaking." Trans. Ken Frieden. *Derrida and Negative Theology.* Ed. Harold Coward and Toby Foshay. Albany: SUNY Press, 1992. 73–142. *HAS*

"On an Apocalyptic Tone Newly Adopted in Philosophy." *Derrida*

and Negative Theology. Ed. Harold Coward and Toby Foshay. Albany: SUNY Press, 1992. 25–72.
"Passions." Trans. David Wood. *On the Name*. Ed. Thomas Dutoit. Stanford: Stanford University Press, 1995. 3–31. *Pass*
"Sauf le nom." Trans. John P. Leavey, Jr. *On the Name*. Ed. Thomas Dutoit. Stanford: Stanford University Press, 1995. 35–85. *SLN*
"Faith and Knowledge." Trans. Samuel Weber. *Religion*. Stanford: Stanford University Press, 1996. 1–78. *FK*
"Foi et Savoir." *La Religion*. Ed. Jacques Derrida and Gianni Vattimo. Paris: Editions du Seuil, 1996. 9–86. *FS*

Selected Books by Emmanuel Levinas

Autrement qu'être ou au-delà de l'essence. 1974. Paris: Livre de Poche, 1990.
Existence and Existents. Trans. Alphonso Lingis. The Hague: Martinus Nijhoff, 1978. *EE*
Totality and Infinity: An Essay on Exteriority. Trans. Alphonso Lingis. The Hague: Martinus Nijhoff, 1979. *TI*
Otherwise Than Being or Beyond Essence. Trans. Alphonso Lingis. The Hague: Martinus Nijhoff, 1981. *OBBE*
De l'évasion. Paris: Fata Morgana, 1982.
Ethique et infini. 1982. Paris: Livre de poche, 1996.
Ethics and Infinity. Trans. Richard A. Cohen. Pittsburgh: Duquesne University Press, 1985.
Autrement que savoir. Paris: Osiris, 1986.
Time and the Other. Trans. Richard A. Cohen. Pittsburgh: Duquesne University Press, 1987.
Totalité et Infini: Essai sur l'extériorité. 1961. Paris: Le Livre de Poche, 1987.
De l'existence à l'existant. 2nd ed. Paris: L'édition du poche, 1990.
Nine Talmudic Readings. Trans. Annette Aronowicz. Bloomington: Indiana University Press, 1990.
Entre nous: Essaies sur le penser-à-l'autre. 1991. Paris: Livre de Poche, 1993.
De Dieu qui vient à l'idée. 2nd ed. Paris: Vrin, 1992.
Dieu, la mort et le temps. Paris: Grasset, 1993.

Outside the Subject. Trans. Michael B. Smith. London: Athlone Press, 1993.

En découvrant l'existence avec Husserl et Heidegger. 5th ed. Paris: Vrin, 1994. *EDEHH*

Liberté et commandement. Paris: Fata Morgana, 1994.

Le temps et l'autre. 5th ed. Paris: Presses Universitaires de France, 1994. *TA*

The Theory of Intuition in Husserl's Phenomenology. Trans. André Orianne. 2nd ed. Evanston: Northwestern University Press, 1995. *TIHP*

Basic Philosophical Writings. Ed. Adriaan Peperzak, Simon Critchley, and Robert Bernasconi. Bloomington: Indiana University Press, 1996.

Proper Names. Trans. Michael B. Smith. London: Athlone Press, 1996. *PN*

Transcendence and Intelligibilité. Geneva: Labor et Fides, 1996.

Discovering Existence with Husserl. Trans. Richard A. Cohen and Michael B. Smith. Evanston: Northwestern University Press, 1998.

Entre Nous: On Thinking-of-the-Other. Trans. Michael B. Smith and Barbara Harshav. New York: Columbia University Press, 1998.

Selected Essays by Emmanuel Levinas

"Jacques Derrida: Tout Autrement." *Noms Propres.* Paris: Fata Morgana, 1976. 65–72.

"Beyond Intentionality." *Philosophy in France Today.* Ed. A. Montefiore. Cambridge: Cambridge University Press, 1983. 100–115.

"Bad Conscience and the Inexorable." *Face to Face with Levinas.* Ed. Richard A. Cohen. Albany: SUNY Press, 1986. 35–40.

"The Trace of the Other" *Deconstruction in Context.* Ed. Mark C. Taylor. Chicago: University of Chicago Press, 1986. 345–59. *TO*

"God and Philosophy." Trans. Richard A. Cohen and Alphonso Lingis. *The Levinas Reader.* Ed. Seán Hand. Oxford: Blackwell, 1989. 166–89. *GP*

"1933–1934: Thoughts on National Socialism: Reflections on the Philosophy of Hitlerism." Trans. Seán Hand. *Critical Inquiry* 17 (1990–91): 62–71.

"Philosophy and Awakening." *Who Comes After the Subject?* Ed. Eduardo Cadava, Peter Connor, and Jean-Luc Nancy. New York: Routledge, 1991. 206–16.

"Ethics As First Philosophy." *The Continental Philosophy Reader.* Ed. Richard Kearney and Mara Rainwater. London: Routledge, 1995. 124–35.

Other Works

Adorno, Theodor W. *Aesthetic Theory.* Trans. Robert Hullot-Kentor. London: Athlone Press, 1997.

Alliez, Eric. *De l'impossibilité de la phénoménologie: Sur la philosophie française contemporaine.* Paris: Vrin, 1995.

Balthasar, Hans Urs von. *The Glory of the Lord: A Theological Aesthetics.* Vol. 1, *Seeing the Form.* Trans. Erasmo Leiva-Merikakis. 2nd ed. San Francisco: Ignatius Press, 1982. *GL1*

———. *The Glory of the Lord: A Theological Aesthetics.* Vol. 2, *Studies in Theological Style: Clerical Style.* Trans. Andrew Louth, Francis McDonagh, and Brian McNeil, C.R.V. San Francisco: Ignatius Press, 1984.

———. *The Glory of the Lord: A Theological Aesthetics.* Vol. 3, *Studies in Theological Style: Lay Styles.* Trans. Andrew Louth, John Saward, Martin Simon and Rowan Williams. San Francisco: Ignatius Press, 1984.

———. *The Glory of the Lord: A Theological Aesthetics.* Vol. 4, *The Realm of Metaphysics in Antiquity.* Trans. Brian McNeil, C.R.V., Andrew Louth, John Saward, Rowan Williams, and Oliver Davies. San Francisco: Ignatius Press, 1989.

———. *The Glory of the Lord: A Theological Aesthetics.* Vol. 5, *The Realm of Metaphysics in the Modern Age.* Trans. Oliver Davies, Andrew Louth, Brian McNeil, C.R.V., John Saward, and Rowan Williams. San Francisco: Ignatius Press, 1991.

———. *The Glory of the Lord: A Theological Aesthetics.* Vol. 6, *Theology: The Old Covenant.* Trans. Brian McNeil, C.R.V., and Erasmo Leiva-Merikakis. San Francisco: Ignatius Press, 1991.

———. *The Glory of the Lord: A Theological Aesthetics.* Vol. 7, *Theology: The New Covenant.* Trans. Brian McNeil, C.R.V. San Francisco: Ignatius Press, 1990. *GL7*

———. *New Elucidations.* Trans. Mary Theresilde Skerry. San Francisco: Ignatius Press, 1986.

———. *Mysterium Paschale.* Trans. Aidan Nichols, O.P. Grand Rapids, Mich.: Eerdmans, 1990. *MP*

———. *Theodrama: IV: The Action.* Trans. Graham Harrison. San Francisco: Ignatius Press, 1992.

———. *The Theology of Karl Barth: Exposition and Interpretation.* Trans. Edward T. Oakes, S.J. San Francisco: Communio Books–Ignatius Press, 1992.

———. *My Work in Retrospect.* Trans. Brian McNeil, C.R.V., et al. San Francisco: Ignatius Press, 1993.

Bataille, Georges. *The Accursed Share: An Essay on General Economy.* Trans. Robert Hurley. Vol. 1, *Consumption.* New York: Zone Books, 1988.

Beardsworth, Richard. *Derrida and the Political.* London: Routledge, 1996.

Belk, Russell W. "The Perfect Gift." *Gift-Giving: A Research Anthology.* Ed. Cele Otnes and Richard F. Beltramini. Bowling Green, Ohio: Bowling Green State University Popular Press, 1996. 58–94. *PG*

Benveniste, Émile. *Problèmes de linguistique générale.* Paris: Gallimard, 1966. *PLG*

Bernasconi, Robert. "Levinas: Philosophy and Beyond." *Philosophy and Non-Philosophy since Merleau-Ponty.* Ed. Hugh J. Silverman. New York: Routledge, 1988. 232–58.

Bernasconi, Robert, and Simon Critchley, eds. *Re-reading Levinas.* Bloomington: Indiana University Press, 1991.

Blanchot, Maurice. *Thomas l'Obscur.* New ed. Paris: Gallimard, 1950.

———. *The Space of Literature.* Trans. Ann Smock. Lincoln: University of Nebraska Press, 1982. *SL*

———. *Thomas the Obscure.* Trans. Robert Lamberton. New York: Station Hill Press, 1988.

———. *The Infinite Conversation.* Trans. Susan Hanson. Minneapolis: University of Minnesota Press, 1993. *IC*

———. *The Writing of the Disaster.* Trans. Ann Smock. Lincoln: University of Nebraska Press, 1995. *WOD*

Blond, Phillip, ed. *Post-Secular Philosophy: Between Philosophy and Theology.* London: Routledge, 1998. *PSP*

Bourdieu, Pierre. *The Field of Cultural Production: Essays on Art and Literature.* Oxford: Polity-Blackwell, 1993.

Cadava, Eduardo, Peter Connor, and Jean-Luc Nancy, eds. *Who Comes After the Subject?* London: Routledge, 1991. *WCAS*

Caputo, John D. *Heidegger and Aquinas: An Essay on Overcoming Metaphysics.* New York: Fordham University Press, 1982.

———. *The Mystical Element in Heidegger's Thought.* New York: Fordham University Press, 1986.

———. *Radical Hermeneutics.* Bloomington: Indiana University Press, 1987. *RH*

———. *Against Ethics.* Bloomington: Indiana University Press, 1993.

———. *Demythologizing Heidegger.* Bloomington: Indiana University Press, 1993. *DH*

———, ed. *Deconstruction in a Nutshell: A Conversation with Jacques Derrida.* New York: Fordham University Press, 1997. *DN*

———. *The Prayers and Tears of Jacques Derrida: Religion without Religion.* Bloomington: Indiana University Press, 1997. *PTJD*

Caputo, John D., and Michael J. Scanlon, eds. *God, the Gift, and Postmodernism.* Bloomington: Indiana University Press, 1999. *GGP*

Carlson, Thomas A. *Indiscretion: Finitude and the Naming of God.* Chicago: University of Chicago Press, 1999.

Chalier, Catherine, and Miguel Abensour, eds. *Emmanuel Levinas.* Cahier de L'Herne. Paris: L'Herne, 1991.

Cohen, Richard A., ed. *Face to Face with Levinas.* Albany: SUNY Press, 1986.

Colette, Jacques. "Phénoménologie et métaphysique." *Critique* 548–49 (January–February 1993): 56–73.

Comay, Rebecca. "Gifts without Presents: Economies of 'Experience' in Bataille and Heidegger." *Yale French Studies* 78 (1990): 66–89. *GWP*

Critchley, Simon. *The Ethics of Deconstruction: Derrida and Levinas.* Oxford: Blackwell, 1992. *EDDL*

———. "Derrida: Private Ironist or Public Liberal?" *Deconstruction and Pragmatism.* Ed. Chantal Mouffe. London: Routledge, 1996. 19–40.

Critchley, Simon, and Peter Dews, eds. *Deconstructing Subjectivities.* Albany: SUNY Press, 1996. *DS*

Davis, Colin. *Levinas: An Introduction.* Cambridge: Polity Press, 1996. *LAI*

Dilthey, Wilhelm. "The Understanding of Other Persons and Their Expressions of Life" (1910). *Descriptive Psychology and Historical Understanding.* Trans. Kenneth L. Heiges. The Hague: Martinus Nijhoff, 1977. 121–44.

Gasché, Rodolphe. *The Tain of the Mirror: Derrida and the Philosophy of Reflection.* Cambridge: Harvard University Press, 1986.

———. *Inventions of Difference: On Jacques Derrida.* Cambridge: Harvard University Press, 1994. *IDJD*

Greisch, Jean. "L'herméneutique dans la 'phénoménologie comme telle.' " *Revue de Métaphysique et de Morale* 96, no. 1 (1991): 43–63. *HPT*

———. "Index sui et non dati." *Transversalités: Revue de L'Institut Catholique de Paris* 70 (April–June 1999): 27–54.

Hand, Seán, ed. *The Levinas Reader.* Oxford: Blackwell, 1989.

Hart, Kevin. *The Trespass of the Sign.* Cambridge: Cambridge University Press, 1989. *TS*

———. Rev. of *The Gift of Death,* by Jacques Derrida. *Modern Theology* 12, no. 4 (1996): 495–96.

———. Introduction to "How to Avoid Speaking." *The Postmodern God: A Theological Reader.* Ed. Graham Ward. Oxford: Blackwell, 1997. 159–67. *IHAS*

———. "The Experience of Poetry." *Boxkite: A Journal of Poetry and Poetics* 2 (1998): 285–304. *EP*

———. "Jacques Derrida: The God Effect." *Post-Secular Philosophy: Between Philosophy and Theology.* Ed. Phillip Blond. London: Routledge, 1998. 259–80. *JDGE*

———. "Shared Silence." Rev. of *Friendship,* by Maurice Blanchot, and *Politics of Friendship,* by Jacques Derrida. *Australian's Review of Books* 3, no. 2 (1998): 8–9.

———. *The Dark Gaze: Maurice Blanchot and Friends.* [forthcoming]

Heidegger, Martin. *Existence and Being.* Trans. R. F. C. Hull and Alan Crick. 2nd ed. London: Vision, 1956.

———. *Being and Time.* Trans. John Macquarrie and Edward Robinson. Oxford; Blackwell, 1962. *BT*

———. *What Is Called Thinking?* Trans. J. Glenn Gray. New York: Harper and Row, 1968. *WCT*

———. *The Essence of Reasons.* Trans. Terence Malick. Evanston: Northwestern University Press, 1969.
———. *Identity and Difference.* Trans. Joan Stambaugh. New York: Harper and Row, 1969.
———. *Poetry, Language, Thought.* Trans. Albert Hofstadter. New York: Harper and Row, 1971.
———. "Time and Being." *On Time and Being.* Trans. Joan Stambaugh. New York: Harper and Row, 1972. *TB*
———. *The Piety of Thinking.* Trans. and ed. James G. Hart and John C. Maraldo. Bloomington: Indiana University Press, 1976.
———. *The Question Concerning Technology and Other Essays.* Trans. William Lovett. New York: Garland, 1977.
———. *Basic Problems of Phenomenology.* Trans. Albert Hofstadter. Rev. ed. Bloomington: Indiana University Press, 1982. *BPP*
———. *History of the Concept of Time.* Bloomington: Indiana University Press, 1985.
———. *The Principle of Reason.* Trans. Reginald Lilly. Bloomington: Indiana University Press, 1991. *PR*
———. "Letter on Humanism." *Basic Writings: Martin Heidegger.* Rev. ed. by David Farrell Krell. London: Routledge, 1993. 217–65. *LH*
———. "What Is Metaphysics?" *Basic Writings: Martin Heidegger.* Rev. ed. by David Farrell Krell. London: Routledge, 1993. 93–110.
———. *The Fundamental Concepts of Metaphysics.* Trans. William McNeill and Nicholas Walker. Bloomington: Indiana University Press, 1995.
———. *Being and Time.* Trans. Joan Stambaugh. Albany: SUNY Press, 1996.
Henry, Michel. *L'essence de la manifestation.* Paris: Presses Universitaires de France, 1963.
———. *Phénoménologie matérielle.* Paris: Presses Universitaires de France, 1990.
———. "Quatre principes de la phénoménologie." *Revue de Métaphysique et de Morale* 96, no. 1 (1991): 3–26. *QPP*
Holzer, Vincent. "Phénoménologie radicale et phénomène de révélation. Jean-Luc Marion, *Étant donné.* Essai d'une phénoménologie de la donation." *Transversalités: Revue de L'Institut Catholique de Paris* 70 (April–June 1999): 55–68. *PRPR*

Husserl, Edmund. *The Idea of Phenomenology*. Trans. William P. Alston and George Nakhnikian. The Hague: Martinus Nijhoff, 1964. *IP*

———. "Philosophy As a Rigorous Science." *Phenomenology and the Crisis of Philosophy*. Trans. Quentin Lauer. New York: Harper and Row, 1965.

———. *Cartesian Meditations*. Trans. Dorion Cairns. The Hague: Martinus Nijhoff, 1970. *CM*

———. *Ideas: General Introduction to Pure Phenomenology*. Vol. 1. Trans. W. R. Boyce Gibson. London: Allen and Unwin, 1972. *I1*

Hyde, W. Lewis. *The Gift: Imagination and the Erotic Life of Property*. New York: Random House, 1983. *GIELP*

Ingraffia, Brian D. *Postmodern Theory and Biblical Theology*. Cambridge: Cambridge University Press, 1995.

Janicaud, Dominique. *Le tournant théologique de la phénoménologie française*. Combas: Éditions de l'éclat, 1991. *TTPF*

———. *La phénoménologie éclatée*. Combas: Éditions de l'éclat, 1998.

Janicaud, Dominique, Jean-François Courtine, Jean-Louis Chrétien, Michel Henry, Jean-Luc Marion, and Paul Ricoeur. *Phenemenology and the "Theological Turn": The French Debate*. New York: Fordham University Press, 2000.

Kant, Immanuel. *Religion within the Limits of Reason Alone*. Trans. Greene and Hudson. New York: Harper, 1960.

———. *The Conflict of the Faculties*. New York: Abaris, 1979.

Kearney, Richard. *Dialogues with Contemporary Continental Thinkers*. Manchester: Manchester University Press, 1984. *DCCT*

———. "Derrida's Ethical Return." *Working Through Derrida*. Ed. Gary B. Madison. Evanston: Northwestern University Press, 1993. 28–50.

Kohák, Erazim. *Idea and Experience*. Chicago: University of Chicago Press, 1978.

Komter, Aafke E., ed. *The Gift: An Interdisciplinary Perspective*. Amsterdam: Amsterdam University Press, 1996.

Kovacs, George. *The Question of God in Heidegger's Phenomenology*. Evanston: Northwestern University Press, 1990.

Krell, David Farrell. "General Introduction: The Question of Being." *Basic Writings: Martin Heidegger*. Rev. ed. by David Farrell Krell. London: Routledge, 1993. 3–35.

Lacoue-Labarthe, Philippe. *L'imitation des modernes.* Paris: Galilée, 1986.

Laruelle, François. "L'Appel et le Phénomène." *Revue de Métaphysique et de Morale* 96, no. 1 (1991): 27–41. *AP*

Lescourret, Marie-Anne. *Emmanuel Levinas.* Paris: Flammarion, 1994.

Llewelyn, John. *Emmanuel Levinas: The Genealogy of Ethics.* London: Routledge, 1995. *ELGE*

Lukacher, Ned. *Primal Scenes.* Ithaca: Cornell University Press, 1986.

Lyotard, Jean François. *The Postmodern Explained to Children.* Trans. Don Barry et al. Sydney: Power Publications, 1992.

Macquarrie, John. *Heidegger and Christianity.* London: SCM Press, 1994. *HC*

Madder, Clive. "Blanchot's Neutral Space: A Negative Theology." *Pacifica* 9, no. 2 (June 1996): 175–84.

Martis, John. "The Debate between Levinas in 'God and Philosophy' and Derrida in 'Violence and Metaphysics' Investigated through Levinas' Concept of the Immemorial Past." Unpublished essay, 1994.

———. "Postmodernism and God As Giver." *The Way* 36 (July 1996): 236–43.

Mauss, Marcel. *The Gift: The Form and Reason for Exchange in Archaic Societies.* Trans. W. D. Halls. London: Routledge, 1990. *GFREAS*

McKenna, William R., and J. Claude Evans, eds. *Derrida and Phenomenology.* Dordrecht: Kluwer Academic, 1995.

Merleau-Ponty, Maurice. "The Primacy of Perception and Its Philosophical Consequences." *Readings in Existential Phenomenology.* Ed. N. M. Lawrence et al. Englewood Cliffs, N.J.: Prentice Hall, 1967. 31–54.

Milbank, John. *Theology and Social Theory.* Oxford: Blackwell, 1990.

———. "Can a Gift Be Given?" *Rethinking Metaphysics.* Ed. L. Gregory Jones and Stephen E. Fowl. Oxford: Blackwell, 1995. 119–61. *CGG*

———. "Stories of Sacrifice: From Wellhausen to Girard." *Theory, Culture, and Society* 12, no. 4 (November 1995): 15–46.

———. "Socialism of the Gift, Socialism by Grace." *New Blackfriars* 77.910 (1996): 532–48.

———. *The Word Made Strange.* Oxford: Blackwell, 1997.

Miller, Jerome A. *In the Throe of Wonder: Intimations of the Sacred in a Post-Modern World.* Albany: SUNY Press, 1992.

Nancy, Jean-Luc. *The Sense of the World.* Trans. Jeffrey S. Librett. Minneapolis: University of Minnesota Press, 1997.

O'Donnell, John., S.J. *Hans Urs von Balthasar.* London: Geoffrey Chapman, 1992.

O'Leary, Joseph S. *Questioning Back: The Overcoming of Metaphysics in the Christian Tradition.* Minneapolis: Seabury, 1985.

———. "Theological Resonances of *Der Satz vom Grund.*" *Martin Heidegger: Critical Assessments.* Ed. Christopher Macann. London: Routledge, 1992. 214–56. *TRSG*

———. *La vérité chrétienne à l'age du pluralisme religieux.* Paris; Les Editions du Cerf, 1994.

———. *Religious Pluralism and Christian Truth.* Rev. ed. Edinburgh: Edinburgh University Press, 1996. *RPCT*

Otnes, Cele, and Richard F. Beltramini, eds. *Gift-Giving: A Research Anthology.* Bowling Green, Ohio: Bowling Green State University Popular Press, 1996.

Ott, Hugo. *Martin Heidegger: A Political Life.* Trans. Allan Blunden. London: Fontana, 1994.

Peperzak, Adriaan T. *To the Other: An Introduction to the Philosophy of Emmanuel Levinas.* West Lafayette, Ind.: Purdue University Press, 1993. *TTO*

———, ed. *Ethics As First Philosophy.* New York: Routledge, 1995.

———. *Beyond: The Philosophy of Emmanuel Levinas.* Evanston: Northwestern University Press, 1997. *B*

Poirié, François. *Emmanuel Levinas: Qui êtes-vous?* Lyon: La Manafacture, 1987.

Rabate, Jean-Michel, and Michael Wetzel, eds. *L'éthique du don: Jacques Derrida et la pensée du don. Colloque de Royaumont décembre 1990.* Paris: Transition, 1992.

Raheja, Gloria Goodwin. *The Poison in the Gift: Ritual, Prestation, and the Dominant Caste in a North Indian Village.* Chicago: University of Chicago Press, 1988. *PG*

Rahner, Karl. *Foundations of Christian Faith.* Trans. William V. Dych. 1976. New York: Crossroad, 1992.

Richardson, William J., S.J. *Heidegger: Through Phenomenology to Thought.* The Hague: Martinus Nijhoff, 1963. *HTPT*

Richir, Marc. "Phénomène et Infini." *Emmanuel Levinas.* Ed.

Catherine Chalier and Miguel Abensour. Cahier de L'Herne. Paris: L'Herne, 1991. 241–61.

Ricoeur, Paul. *Husserl: An Analysis of His Phenomenology*. Trans. Edward G. Ballard and Lester E. Embree. Evanston: Northwestern University Press, 1967. *HAP*

———. *Freud and Philosophy: An Essay on Interpretation*. Trans. Denis Savage. New Haven: Yale University Press, 1970.

———. *The Conflict of Interpretations*. Evanston: Northwestern University Press, 1974.

———. *Hermeneutics and the Human Sciences*. Trans. John B. Thompson. Cambridge: Cambridge University Press, 1981.

———. "Expérience et langage dans le discours religieux." Jean-François Courtine, Jean-Louis Chrétien, Michel Henry, Jean-Luc Marion, and Paul Ricoeur. *Phénoménologie et théologie*. Paris: Criterion, 1992. 15–38. *ELDR*

———. *Oneself As Another*. Trans. Kathleen Blamey. Chicago: University of Chicago Press, 1992.

———. *Figuring the Sacred*. Trans. David Pellauer. Minneapolis: Fortress Press, 1995.

Sahlins, Marshall. *Stone Age Economics*. Chicago: Aldine Atherton, 1972.

Schrift, Alan D., ed. *The Logic of the Gift: Toward an Ethic of Generosity*. New York: Routledge, 1997.

Scola, Angelo. *Hans Urs von Balthasar: A Theological Style*. Grand Rapids, Mich.: Eerdmans, 1995.

Seyhan, Azade. *Representation and Its Discontents*. Berkeley: University of California Press, 1992.

Silverman, Hugh J., ed. *Derrida and Deconstruction*. New York: Routledge, 1989.

Steiner, George. *Heidegger*. 2nd ed. London: Fontana, 1992.

Taylor, Mark C. *Erring: A Postmodern A/Theology*. Chicago: University of Chicago Press, 1984.

———. *Altarity*. Chicago: University of Chicago Press, 1987.

Tracy, David. *Plurality and Ambiguity: Hermeneutics, Religion, Hope*. London: SCM Press, 1987.

———. *On Naming the Present: God, Hermeneutics, and Church*. Maryknoll, N.Y.: Orbis, 1994.

Ward, Graham. "Why Is Derrida Important for Theology?" *Theology* 95.766 (1992): 263–69.

———. *Barth, Derrida, and the Language of Theology*. Cambridge: Cambridge University Press, 1995.

———, ed. Special issue on Jean-Luc Marion's *God Without Being*. *New Blackfriars* 76.895 (1995).

———. *Theology and Contemporary Critical Theory*. London: Macmillan, 1996.

———, ed. *The Postmodern God: A Theological Reader*. Oxford: Blackwell, 1997.

———. "The Theological Project of Jean-Luc Marion." *Post-Secular Philosophy: Between Philosophy and Theology*. Ed. Phillip Blond. London: Routledge, 1998. 229–39.

Yan, Yunxiang. *The Flow of Gifts: Reciprocity and Social Networks in a Chinese Village*. Stanford: Stanford University Press, 1996. *FG*

INDEX OF NAMES

INDEX OF SUBJECTS